AF553804

HTML
4U

HTML
4U

Editor

ROHIT KHURANA

A.P.H. PUBLISHING CORPORATION
5, ANSARI ROAD, DARYA GANJ
NEW DELHI - 110 002

Published by
Kul Bhushan Nangia
A P H Publishing Corporation
4435-36/7, Ansari Road, Daryaganj
New Delhi 110002
Ph.: 23274050
E-mail : aphbooks@gmail.com

2025

Printed at
Balaji Offset
Navin Shahdara, Delhi 110032

Editor's Note

Dear Students,

It is often said that success in life can be attributed to goal setting. Setting and reaching apparently unreachable targets or goals has been a part of **ITLESL's (ITL Education Solutions Ltd.)** philosophy from day one. **ITLESL is a dream of people who have dedicated themselves to the ever-changing world of IT.**

Most of the students today have a dream of becoming an IT professional. We are committed to turn that dream into a reality. With **eAcademy**, we take another step to improve the quality of IT education in India. **eAcademy** is increasing its network of centres and is established as a premium IT education solutions provider.

We understand people's growing appetite for newer technologies. Considering such preferences, we make sure that only the latest technologies are chosen. To add to that, we're working with highly qualified professionals and content developers for quality course materials, which is used in all our centres.

As an organisation we have started to build many new relationships, which will help us in business generation, customer contact, new technology absorption and will also help expose our technologies, work processes and services to the market place.

I would like to thank all my team members without whom a mission like this would have been almost impossible to achieve.

All the very best to all our readers.

Company Profile

eAcademy is a division of ITL Education Solutions Ltd, which is a quality IT career education solutions provider managed by top-notch professionals with vast experience in the IT education industry.

ITL Education Solutions Ltd, is a part of the Rs. 200 crore ITL Group. The group has operations in software development and ERP unit for the domestic SME segment and a state of the art set up for Medical Transcription in association with C Bay of California. ITL Group has keen interest in the education field. We have two-Senior Secondary Schools in Delhi, providing the best of education to the students.

eAcademy has been a pioneer in introducing new Concepts and Methodologies for imparting IT education. The implementation of these concepts has led to the success of the most comprehensive IT career course, the market has to offer to the industry today. At **eAcademy** we believe in providing Quality Education to our students. This quality reflects both in our courseware as well as in the people who develop it. The course is designed after taking a feedback from the user industry on their requirement of skills in the next few months and also technical gurus of the IT industry have been consulted for the designing of the courseware.

At **eAcademy,** our mission is to deliver to the Global market, the best and highly skilled trained e-commerce professionals who can develop software applications and set new trends in this ever-changing world of IT.

Preface

The frantic pace of progress on the internet has made it a more mature medium now. Once the exclusive realm of academia and big institutions the medium has wormed its way into everyday activities and culture. Email and web URL's are becoming as common as business cards these.days.

As a part of the Internet, the World Wide Web is the predominant force in the growth of a computer network that is global in reach and access. It's language much richer that what was a few years ago is still quite simple.

HyperText Markup Language (HTML) is the language that puts a face on the web. It consists of a variety of elements called tags, which are used for everything from defining a title to outlining a frame, from creating headings to inserting line breaks, from inserting an image to including a custom java applet.

This book gives an in-depth knowledge of HTML, imparting presentation features of a web page with a Cascading Style Sheet and dynamicity to a page with DHTML technologies.

We hope you enjoy reading this and please feel free to send in your suggestions and queries to the **Research and Development** team in the feedback form.

e academy Research and Development Wing

TRADEMARKS

All the brand and product names referred to in this course material are hereby acknowledged to be the trademarks or registered trademarks of their respective organizations.

DISCLAIMER

We have made a sincere effort to ensure the accuracy of the contents described in the book, however ITL EDUCATION SOLUTIONS LTD. gives no warranty, expressed or implied with respect to the quality, correctness, accuracy or freedom from error of this document or of the product it describes. ITL EDUCATION SOLUTIONS LTD. makes no representation or warranty with respect to the contents hereof and specially disclaims any implied warranties of fitness for any direct, indirect, incidental, consequential, special or exemplary damages resulting from the use of the information in this document or from the use of any products described in this document. Mention of any product does not constitute an endorsement or recommendation of that product by ITL Education. Data used in examples and sample data files are intended to be fictional. Any resemblance to any person or company/ies is purely coincidental.

COPYRIGHT NOTICE

Designed, developed and Published by the Research & Development Wing, ITL EDUCATION SOLUTIONS LTD., C-88, South Extension - II, New Delhi - 110 049, India.

Part No.: HTML04002

Product Line: e Academy

Contents

Chapter 3: Cascading Style Sheets 133

Chapter 4: Dynamic HTML 191

Appendix - A 219

HTML: An Introduction

Objectives

- Introduction
- About the World Wide Web Consortium
- Client/Server Architecture
- Components of World Wide Web
- An Introduction to SGML
- An Introduction to XML
- A Brief History of HTML
- Types of HTML documents
- Getting Started

Introduction

Interest in and use of the World Wide Web has been expanding at a phenomenal rate. As the Web grows, so must its vehicle of communication, **HTML**. World Wide Web is the most exciting and useful aspect of Internet. World Wide Web is a way to share resources with many people at the same time, even if some of those resources are located at opposite ends of the world.

Generally, Web and Internet are mistaken with each other, to explain the misconception - the **Internet** simply provides the medium for the Web to run on, just as a telephone line provides the medium for telephone conversations, whereas the **Web** provides the technology for publishing, sending and obtaining information over the Internet.

The World Wide Web is a collection of linked documents or pages on millions of computers spread over the entire internet. The pages are written in HTML - **H**ypertext **M**arkup **L**anguage which defines their appearance and layout and more importantly creates the links to other documents.

Hypertext Markup Language (HTML) is a major language of the Internet's World Wide Web. Web Sites and Web Pages are written in HTML. HTML and WWW services, together provide the ability to bring together text, pictures, sounds, and links... all at one click. HTML files are plain-text files so they can be edited on any type of computer i.e., IBM, Mac, UNIX, Intel etc.

About the World Wide Web Consortium (W3C)

The World Wide Web Consortium was created in October 1994 to lead the World Wide Web to its full potential by developing common protocols that promote its evolution and ensure its interoperability. W3C has more than 400 Member organizations from around the world and has earned international recognition for its contributions to the growth of the Web. W3C is financed primarily by its members and to a lesser extent by public funds. By promoting interoperability and encouraging an open forum for discussion, W3C commits to leading the technical evolution of the Web. In just over five years, W3C has developed more than 20 technical specifications for the Web's infrastructure. However, the Web is still young and there is still a lot of work to do especially as computers, telecommunications, and multimedia technologies converge. To meet the growing expectations of users and the increasing power of machines, W3C is already laying the foundations for the next generation of the Web. W3C's technologies will help make the Web a robust, scalable and adaptive infrastructure for a world of information.

W3C Mission

In October 1994, Tim Berners-Lee inventor of the Web founded the World Wide Web Consortium (W3C) at the Massachusetts Institute of Technology, Laboratory for Computer Science [MIT/LCS] in collaboration with CERN, where the Web originated with support from DARPA and the European Commission.

W3C's mission is to lead the evolution of the Web - the universe of information accessible through networked machines. W3C's long term goals for the Web are:

- **Universal Access:** To make the Web accessible to all by promoting technologies that take into account the vast differences in culture, education, ability, material resources, and physical limitations of users on all continents.
- **Semantic Web:** To develop a software environment that permits each user to make the best use of the resources available on the Web.
- **Web of Trust:** To guide the Web's development with careful consideration for the novel, legal, commercial and social issues raised by this technology.

Client/Server Architecture

A client server model for a networked computer system involves three components: the client, the server and the network.

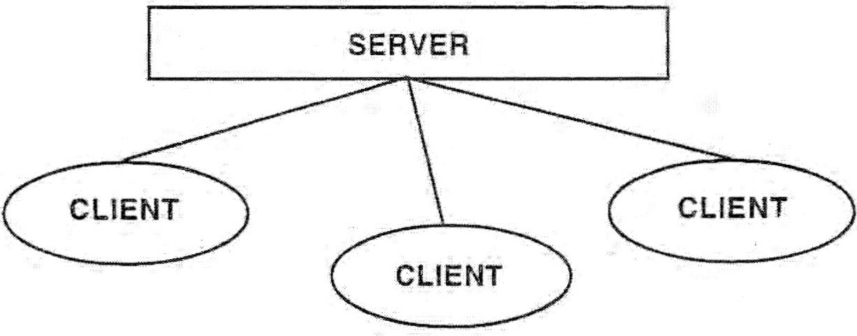

Figure 1.1: Client/Server Architecture

A client is a software application that most often runs on the end user's computer host. A server is a software application that most often runs on the information provider's computer hosts.

- The user can initiate a request for information or action through the client software.
- This request travels over the network to the server which interprets the request and takes some desired action. This action might include a database lookup or a change in recorded database information.
- The results of the requested transaction (if any) are sent back to the client for display to the user.

All client/server communications follow a set of rules or protocols, that are defined for the client/server system.

The distributed form of request and serve activities of the client/server model allows for many efficiencies. Because the client software interacts with the server according to a predefined protocol, the client software can be customized for the user's particular computer host.

Components of World Wide Web

The *World Wide Web* (Web) is a network of information resources. The Web relies on following mechanisms to make these resources readily available to the widest possible audience:

- **Web Server**
- **Web Browser**
- **Uniform Resource Locator**
- **Hypertext and Hypermedia**
- **HTML**
- **Hyperlink**
- **Hypertext Transfer Protocol**
- **Search Engines**
- **Common Gateway Interface**

Web Servers

Any computer can be turned into a Web server by installing server software and connecting the machine to the Internet. There are many Web server software applications including public domain software from NCSA and Apache and commercial packages from Microsoft, Netscape and others. A server is a member of a class of programs in a modern software architecture paradigm called client/server software architecture, in which all applications have two components: the client component and the server component. The server component typically has the following characteristics:

- A server is most often centralized, usually on a large computer (a client usually runs in multiple instances on desktops or other small stations throughout a network).
- A server is passive; it does little or nothing until it receives an explicit request from a client to do something. (A client is active since it's a tool in the hands of a human).
- A server usually runs continuously waiting for requests while a client runs only on-demand (when invoked by a human).
- It usually runs in the background and interfaces only with other software (clients) and rarely interfaces directly with humans (whereas a client is usually invoked by a human and takes commands from a human).
- It must handle multiple tasks concurrently since many clients may be requesting its services simultaneously. A client usually works for one person and does one thing after another in sequence, as the user commands it.

Web Browsers

Web browser also known as **web clients** is a software application used to locate and display Web pages. The two most popular browsers are Netscape Navigator and Microsoft Internet Explorer. Both of these are graphical browsers, which means that they can display graphics as well as text. In addition most modern browsers can present multimedia information including sound and video, though they require plug-ins for some formats. What began as a research tool has blossomed into something unexpected and much more fun. With the introduction of Mosaic and other graphical web browsers, the web has become a communications tool for a much wider audience.

Web is also known as a client server based system, browsing software is the client and the remote computer where data is stored is server. The final appearance of a document is dependent on the program used to view it, the browser. Depending on the Web browser used, the final appearance of a document may vary significantly.

What to look for in a Web Browser ?

With so many browsers available it's really difficult to select the browser. Some of the features and functions that should be looked for before selecting a browser are:

- Should display the latest HTML tags included in HTML 4.0 specification
- Should support multiple sessions.
- Should be empowered with easy Web Navigation tools such as - history, search, home, bookmark, backward and forward buttons.
- Should provide with E-mail facilities i.e., ability to send and receive mails. Netscape has a full featured e-mail program that also lets the user to receive, sort and organize e-mail messages and any file attachments.
- Should provide browser Newsgroup Access i.e., option that will open newsgroups and allow to post messages to specific newsgroups.

Uniform Resource Locator (URL)

The URL an acronym for Uniform Resource Locator gives a WWW browser the location and the means to get a resource on the Internet. A uniform naming scheme for locating resources on the Web.

Syntax of a URL is:

protocol/data source://domain name:port number/ <directory path>/<object name>#<spot>

Example:

http://www.itleducation.com/education/eacademy/home.html

- The first portion of the URL address on the left side of the colon refers to the method of access or the protocol used to retrieve a resource such as – HTTP, FTP, Gopher etc.
- "//" indicates that a valid internet address follows
- The information between the first set of double forward slashes (//) and next single forward slash (/) in the address refers to the specific computer host on which the information resides and to which port on the server the connection has to be made.
- The remaining portion of the address details the path on the computer to the specific resource that is required by the client.

Hypertext and Hypermedia

The glue that holds the web together is hypertext and hyperlinks. Links are the foundation of the Web; they tie the world's content together letting us surf from page to page.

The term *hypertext* is used to describe text that contains links to other text. *Hypermedia* is an extension to hypertext that supports linking graphics, sound, and video elements in addition to text elements. The World Wide Web is a partial hypermedia system since it supports graphical hyperlinks and links to sound and video files. New hypermedia systems under development will allow objects in computer videos to be hyperlinked.

HTML

HTML is a descriptive markup language that describes the structure and behavior of a Web document. HTML files usually end with the suffix ".html" or ".htm" and are in ASCII (plain text) format and can be created in any text editor.

HTML is just a series of tags that are integrated into a text document. They are a lot like stage directions - silently telling the browser what to do and what props to use. HTML document is formatted by enclosing sections of a plain text file between opening and closing tags. This is an example of a tag: <TAG>. Most tags come in pairs with the closing tag preceded by a forward slash "/", like this: </TAG>.

Tags define how the section of text they enclose will be displayed, create connections to other documents and files such as multimedia documents like video clips and sound files and cause images to be displayed within a document. These codes, or "tags" instruct the viewing program (most likely a Web browser) to format sections of text, display images, and create hotlinks (connections) to other documents and files. Some tags dictate how the page will be formatted (for instance, <p> begins a new paragraph) and others dictate how the words appear (<b> makes text bold). Still others provide information - such as the title - that doesn't appear on the page itself. No programming is involved at any point.

Hyperlinks

Hyperlink is an element in an electronic document that links to another place in the same document or to an entirely different document. Links can be simply referred to as references to other documents. Hyperlinks are the most essential ingredient of all hypertext systems including the World Wide Web.

Whenever a hyperlink is held, clicking on it makes the browser connect to the linked page. The complete process can be explained as - a hyperlinked phrase or image has attached to it the URL- the Internet address of another page, clicking on the phrase or image makes the web browser pick up this URL and send it down the line to the remote computer. The links are processed and the documents are transferred using HTTP, the Hypertext Transfer Protocol. That is why the URL's of web pages always start with '**http://**'.

Hypertext Transfer Protocol (HTTP)

A protocol is a set of rules defining a standard of communication. Some popular protocols used for communication between computers are HTTP, FTP, Gopher, SMTP and NNTP.

The HTTP has been designed especially for the WWW at CERN. It is very fast and is used to serve most documents found on the Web. As HTTP is an Internet protocol for a specific application, the World Wide Web, therefore it rides at the top of the stack of protocols that make up the Internet. When HTTP link is traversed, the browser will connect to the appropriate machine, retrieve the document and close the connection. The HTTP server will tell the browser about the type of document it is sending so that the browser at the client side can display it correctly.

HTTP provides a way for Web clients and servers to communicate with one another, primarily through the exchange of messages from clients and servers. The message types for HTTP are classified in four parts:

- **Connection:** This type of message occurs when a client tries to connect to a specific Web server and displays a "Connecting to HTTP server" message. If the client can't make the connection, the attempt will usually time out and the browser displays a "Connection timed out" message.
- **Request:** This is where the client asks for the Web resource it's looking for. This includes the protocol to be used, the name of the object to be provided and information about how the server should respond to the client.
- **Response:** If the server can deliver the requested object, it responds in the manner requested by the client to deliver the necessary data. If it can't deliver, it sends an error message explaining why not.
- **Close:** After the information has been transferred in response to the request, the connection between client and server will be closed.

Search Engines

A *search engine* or search tool is a computer program that will search its database to find items whose text contains all or at least one of the words given to search. The home page for each search tool contains a dialog box or frame where you type in a keyword or phrase. Click on a button labeled Search or Submit and the search begins. The search engine then examines a database for items that contains the keyword(s). The database consists of a large collection of information the search program has gathered from the WWW. The search engine then brings back the search results - a list of hyperlinks and in some cases, a summary of the information found by clicking on each hyperlink. The search results are used in the same way as any other web page.

Web Search engines provide many valuable services such as:

- Automated search of Web pages for new sites.
- Indexing of available sites by URL
- Indexing of site by page titles, text content, freshness of contents.

Some of the popular search engines are Lycos, Infoseek, Altavista, Rediff, Goto etc.

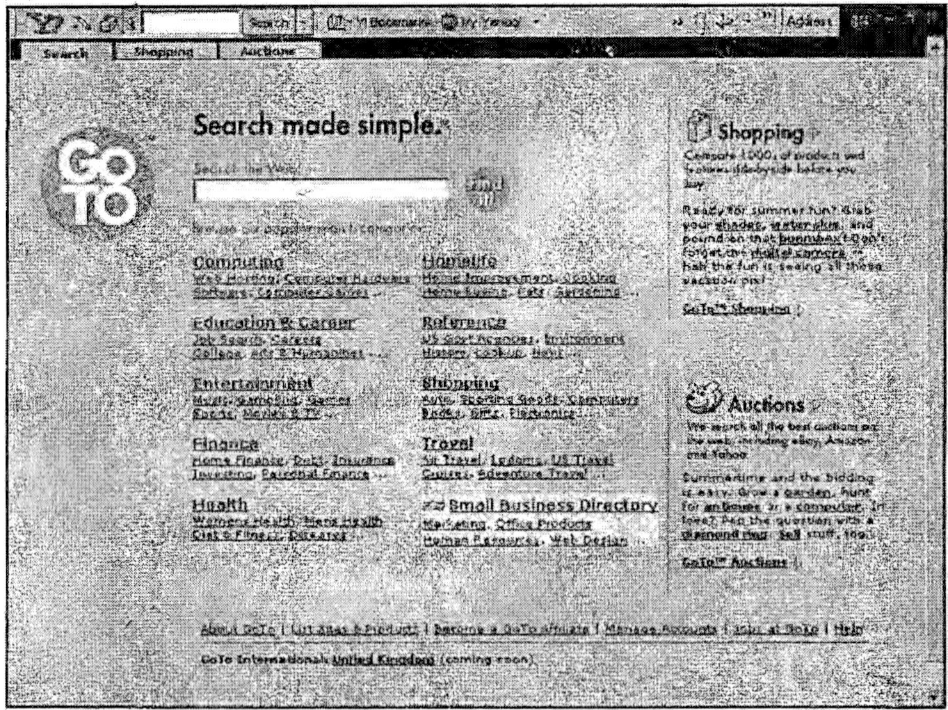

Figure 1.2: GOTO Search Engine

Common Gateway Interface

Common Gateway Interface (CGI) - a set of standards by which servers communicate with external programs. It's a method for sending information back and forth between server and client simultaneously using information on either side. It is not a programming language. Most CGI programs are written in Perl or in C although Visual Basic, C++, Java and many programming languages available and usable by the server can be used. CGI programs are run on the Web Servers. Other similar server side includes are Active Server Pages (ASP), Java Server Pages (JSP), Cold Fusion etc.

How the Web works?

The chain of processes involved in processing a request on Web:

1. The client or Web browser submits a request to the Web Server.

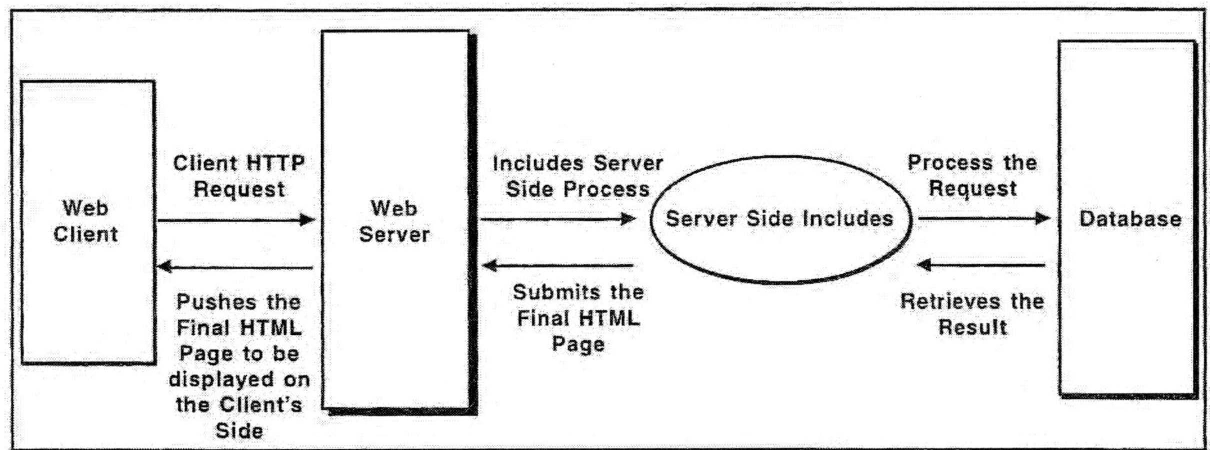

Figure 1.3: Working of Web

2. The Web Server invokes the Server Side Include (e.g. CGI program) which will process the request.

3. The CGI program processes the request i.e., the program might consult a database, perform calculations on the data, use the data to add the user to a mailing list, etc., i.e., whatever the programmer wants it to do.

4. The CGI program then generates HTML page with the result of the client request and submits to the Web Server.

5. The Web Server then pushes and displays the final HTML page at the client side browser.

An Introduction to SGML

Standard Generalized Markup Language (SGML) is an international standard for the definition of device-independent, system-independent methods of representing texts in electronic form. SGML is a *metalanguage* i.e., a means of formally describing a language, in this case a *markup language*. Historically, the word *markup* has been used to describe annotation or other marks within a text intended to instruct a compositor or typist how a particular passage should be printed or laid out. By *markup language* we mean a set of markup conventions used together for encoding texts. A markup language must specify what markup is allowed, what markup is required, how markup is to be distinguished from text, and what the markup means. SGML is a system for defining markup languages. Authors *mark up* their documents by representing structural, presentational, and semantic information alongside content. HTML is one example of a markup language.

There are three characteristics of SGML which distinguish it from other markup languages: its emphasis on descriptive rather than procedural markup; its *document type* concept; and its independence of any one system for representing the script in which a text is written.

Introduction to XML

XML is a set of rules, guidelines, conventions, for designing text formats for data such as spreadsheets, address books, configuration parameters, financial transactions, technical drawings, etc. in a way that produces files that are easy to generate and read.

Like HTML, XML makes use of *tags* (words bracketed by '<' and '>') and *attributes* (of the form name = "value"), but while HTML specifies what each tag

& attribute means (and often how the text between them will look in a browser), XML uses the tags only to delimit pieces of data and leaves the interpretation of the data completely to the application that reads it. In other words, if you see "<p>" in an XML file don't assume it is a paragraph. Depending on the context it may be a price, a parameter or a person.

Development of XML started in 1996 and it is a W3C standard since February 1998, which may make you suspect that this is rather immature technology. But in fact the technology isn't very new. Before XML there was SGML, developed in the early '80s, an ISO standard since 1986 and widely used for large documentation projects. And of course HTML, whose development started in 1990. The designers of XML simply took the best parts of SGML guided by the experience with HTML and produced something that is no less powerful than SGML but vastly more regular and simpler to use. And it must be said that while SGML is mostly used for technical documentation and much less for other kinds of data, with XML it is exactly the opposite.

XML files are text files because it allows experts (such as programmers) to more easily *debug* applications and in emergencies, they can use a simple text editor to fix a broken XML file. But the rules for XML files are much stricter than for HTML. A forgotten tag or an attribute without quotes makes the file unusable, while in HTML such practice is often explicitly allowed or at least tolerated. It is written in the official XML specification: applications are not *allowed* to try to second-guess the creator of a broken XML file; if the file is broken, an application has to stop right there and issue an error. And since XML as a W3C technology is license-free, you can build your own software around it without paying anybody anything. The large and growing support means that you are also not tied to a single vendor.

A Brief History of HTML

In addition to this official work on HTML, the browsers have been making their own additions to HTML. Some changes were eventually adopted into W3C HTML Recommendations; others remain proprietary coding aspects that only the individual browsers recognize. The browsers' versions of HTML changed too, in a game of marketing and programming one-upmanship hoping to lock Web developers into using one browser or the other exclusively. The latest HTML version is HTML 4.0. Earlier versions were - Level 0 HTML, Level 1 HTML, HTML + and the Advent of graphics, HTML 2.0, HTML 3.0, HTML 3.2 and HTML 4.0.

Some major capabilities that HTML 4.0 adds to previous versions of HTML includes the following:

- **Various new elements or tags introduced:** such as ABBR, ACRONYM, BUTTON, COL, COLGROUP, FIELDSET, LEGEND, LABEL.

- **Enhanced Table Support:** There have been significant changes to the table model for HTML 4.0 including the capability for incremental rendering, enhanced accessibility and fixed header and footers. In a table, the new <COL>element allows you to group together attributes for table columns (this grouping is for attributes only, it does not allow to group items together structurally). COLGROUP element allows you to create a specific column group. Other new table elements THEAD, TBODY and TFOOT allow you to specify table header, body and footer.

- **Enhanced Support for Forms:** Forms support several new attributes allowing the author to specify direct keyboard access to form controls, disabled forms, read-only forms. Support for in-line frames by <IFRAME> tag which allows you to insert a frame within a text block and NOFRAMES which allows you to specify content that should be displayed in browsers which does not support frames. In addition, authors can take advantage of the LABEL element to associate a label with a form control and the FIELDSET and LEGEND elements to field groups together and provide captions.

- **Script and Object support:** HTML 4.0 provides a standard mechanism for using the <OBJECT> tag to embed media objects such as video, images and sounds in html documents.

- **Internationalization Support:** HTML 4.0 supports the ISO/IEC:10646 standard as the document character set for HTML. This standard deals with key internationalization issues such as representation of international characters, text direction and punctuation.

- **Elements that have been depreciated:** A deprecated element or attribute is one that is superseded by newer constructs and may become obsolete in future versions of HTML. Elements that have been deprecated are: BASEFONT, CENTER (use the DIV element with align attribute set to "center" instead), DIR (use UL instead), ISINDEX (use the INPUT element instead), MENU (use UL instead), S, STRIKE, U, APPLET (use OBJECT instead), <XMP>, <PLAINTEXT> and <LISTING>. In all cases replace these tags with <PRE>.

Types of HTML documents

HTML pages are of three types:

- **Static**
- **Dynamic**
- **Directory Listing**

Static Pages

Static pages are static HTML pages that are prepared in advance of the request. The Web server returns the HTML pages to the user, but takes no special action. The user requests a static page by typing in an URL (in the following illustration, http://www.company.com /home.htm) or by clicking a link pointing to an URL. The URL request is sent to the server. The server responds by returning the static HTML page.

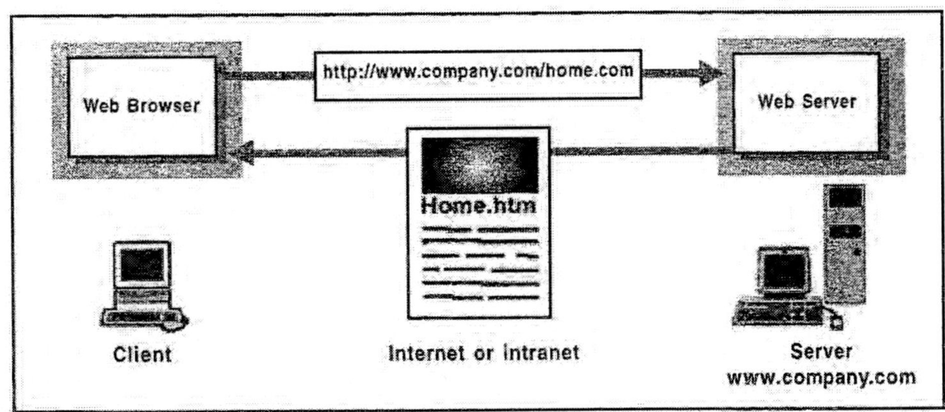

Figure 1.4: Static Pages Requires No Action at the Server

Dynamic Pages

Dynamic pages are created in response to a user's request. A Web browser collects information by presenting a page with text boxes, menus and check boxes that the user fills in or selects. When the user clicks on a button on a form, the data from the form is sent to the Web server. The server either passes the data to a script or application to be processed or it queries or posts data to a database. The server then returns the results to the user in HTML page.

The following illustration shows how a user can send a query to a server application that adds two numbers. The user types the two numbers to be added, then clicks a button, which in turn sends the two numbers to the Web server. The Web server calls the application to add the numbers, then returns the results to the user in HTML page.

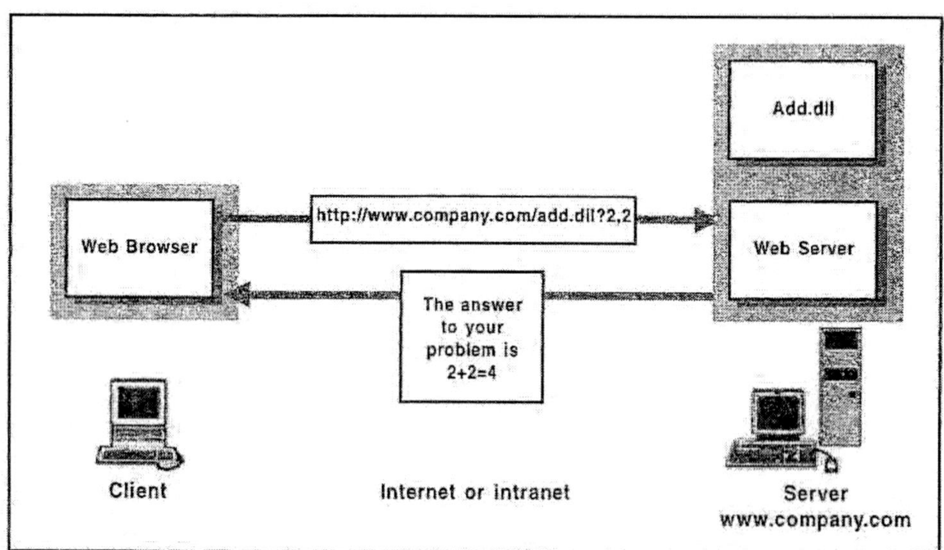

Figure 1.5: Dynamic Pages need an Application at the Server

The following illustration shows a user posting an order to a database using the Internet Database Connector. The user completes a form, then clicks a button, which in turn sends the data in the form to the server. The server posts the data to a database then confirms the order by sending HTML page.

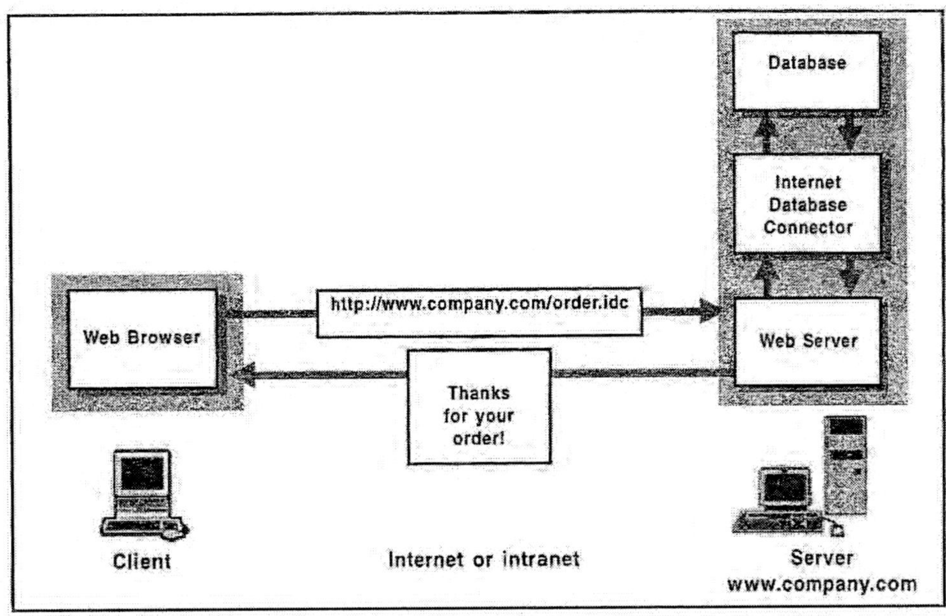

Figure 1.6: A Dynamic Page using Databases kept at the Server

Directory Listing

If users send queries without specifying a particular file, you can either create a default document for a Web site or for a particular directory or you can configure your server for directory browsing. If no default document is created for a directory and directory browsing is configured, a directory listing (a hypertext version of a Windows Explorer or File Manager listing) is returned to the user in the form of HTML page. The user can then jump to the appropriate file by clicking it in the directory listing.

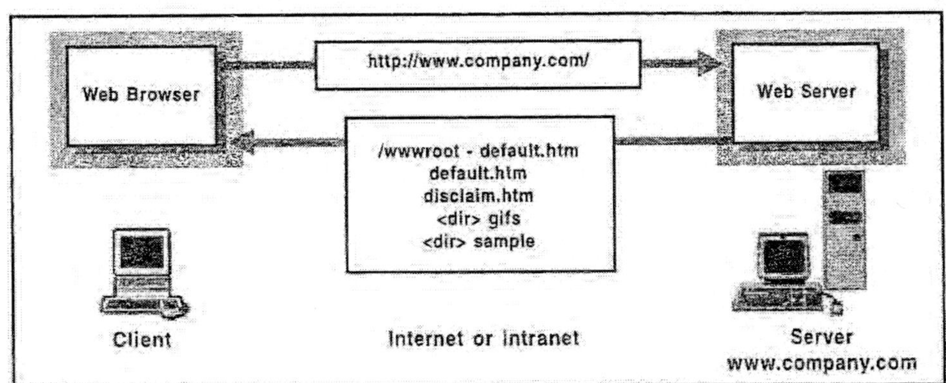

Figure 1.7: Web Servers also allow listing of directories

Getting Started

Here are certain things you'll need to get started. These are:

- **Text Editor:** Any text editor. If it can save in plain (ASCII) text will do. This means that anything from Microsoft Word 6.0, Notepad, UNIX vi will work. All it has to do is save the documents in plain, flat, ASCII-style text. Some of the popular HTML editors are MS FrontPage, Netscape Composer, HotDog Pro.

- **Web Browser:** Netscape Navigator, NCSA Mosaic, Microsoft Internet Explorer, Lynx, Cello, Chimera, Web Explorer, Net Cruiser, etc.

- **Graphics Tool:** Though you can draw pictures with no problem in Paint brush or MS Power Point, but to get them into the right format (Graphic Interchange Format (GIF) you need a graphic tool such as Adobe PhotoShop. There are a number of format converters in the market.

- **Web Server:** Strictly speaking this is optional. You can write Web pages in a text editor, save them to your machine's hard drive and load the pages into your Web browser in order to see how they look. You don't even need a network connection to do this. The option to load pages from your hard drive is typically called something like "Open Local" (Mosaic) or simply "Open File" (Netscape). However, if you plan to publish your documents so the rest of the world can benefit from them, you'll need to put them on a Web server. As long as you're using a Windows-based PC, a Macintosh or a UNIX box and is connected to the Internet you can set your machine up as a Web server.

Document Structure Elements

All HTML documents are composed of four parts:

- A HTML document begins with a line declaring which version of HTML is being used to create the document. The tag used is <!DOCTYPE>. (Though this tag is not mandatory).

- A HTML element that describes the document as a HTML document.
- A declarative header section which is enclosed in the <HEAD> element.
- The main body of the document which contains the actual document content. The body can be contained within either the <BODY> or <FRAMESET>elements.

The "head" contains information about the document such as the title, indexing information, and ownership. The "body" consists of images, text and hotlinks to other documents and files displayed by the Web browser.

These elements are required within HTML document for it to conform to HTML standards. Apart from the prologue document identifier, they represent the only HTML elements which are explicitly required for a document to conform to the standard.

The essential document structure elements are:

```
<HTML> ... ...........</HTML>
<HEAD> ... ..........</HEAD>
<BODY> ............ </BODY>
```

Model HTML document:

```
< !DOCTYPE  HTML PUBLIC "html version">

<HTML>
      <HEAD><TITLE> Sample HTML Document </TITLE></HEAD>
      <BODY>........................................</BODY>
</HTML>
```

Document Type Declaration

HTML follows the SGML notation for defining structured documents. To be valid, HTML document must declare which version of HTML was used to compose it. This statement is the document-type declaration for the document. It names the document type definition (DTD) that's being used for the document. The DTD is the document in which all the <HTML> tags details are documented.

Some of the DTD used in HTML 4.0 specification are:

- **HTML 4.0 Strict:** Includes all elements that have not been deprecated or are not used in framesets, i.e., no presentational elements are defined in this.

  <!DOCTYPE HTML PUBLIC "-//W3C//DTD HTML 4.0/EN" "http://www.w3c.org/TR/REC-html40/strict.dtd">

- **HTML 4.0 Transitional:** Includes everything in the Strict DTD but adds deprecated elements and attributes that deal with presentation. It does not include frameset elements.

  <!DOCTYPE HTML PUBLIC "-//W3C//DTD HTML 4.0 Transitional//EN" "http://www.w3c.org/TR/REC-html40/loose.dtd">

- **HTML 4.0 Frameset:** Includes everything in transitional DTD and adds in the elements necessary for framesets.

  <!DOCTYPE HTML PUBLIC "-//W3C//DTD HTML 4.0 Frameset//EN" "http://www.w3c.org/TR/REC-html40/frameset.dtd">

To explain the above statements, PUBLIC defines the DTD as being generally available, the next string enclosed within the quotation marks is known as public identifier for this particular DTD. The first segment //W3C indicates that W3C is the author of this DTD. The second segment, say DTD HTML 4.0 Transitional // is the common name for the DTD. //EN indicates the U.S. English version. In the last URL provided, specifies the address where the public copy of this DTD is available on the Web.

Head Section

The head section is opened and closed by the <HEAD> and </HEAD> tags. Information belonging in the head section should be placed between these two tags. The tags in the example above form a minimal head section and should be included at the beginning of every HTML document. The head of HTML document is an unordered collection of information about the document. A number of tags can be placed between the <HEAD> and </HEAD> tags including <BASE>, <ISINDEX>, <LINK>, <META>, <SCRIPT>, <STYLE> and <TITLE>.

These tags will be discussed in detail later in this book.

It requires the Title element between <HEAD> and </HEAD> elements:

Example:
```
<html>
<HEAD><TITLE> Introduction to HTML </TITLE> </HEAD>
<body>.............................</body>
</html>
```

The <HEAD> and </HEAD> elements do not directly affect the look of the document when rendered.

Body Section

The body section is opened and closed by the <BODY> and </BODY> tags. The text and images of the document itself to be displayed by the Web browser, should be placed within these two tags. The opening tag should be placed immediately after the closing head tag (</HEAD>) and before any images or text included in the document itself as in the example above. A matching </BODY> must be placed at the foot of the page. This tag ends the body section and should be placed at the end of the document after any images or text included in it.

Syntax: `<html> <head>........</head><body>..........................</body></html>`

Example:
```
<html> <head>.....</head><body> Welcome!!!!!!!!!! </body></html>
</HEAD>
<BODY>
<H1>Introduction</H1>
```

Tags Ending a Page

```
</BODY>
</HTML>
```

</BODY> ends the portion of the page containing the document itself and should be placed after any text or images that will be displayed by the Web browser. </HTML> ends the page itself. The head and body sections are enclosed within the opening <HTML> and closing </HTML> tags. The body of HTML

document contains all the text and images that make up the page together with all the HTML elements that provide the control/formatting of the page (unless the document uses a style sheet to control presentation). The format is:

```
<BODY>
The document included here
</BODY>
```

It is possible to control the document color scheme and background by specifying certain attributes in the <BODY ...> declaration. However, it should be noted that most browsers provide the user with a means to over-ride color schemes and prevent images from loading.

The **BACKGROUND** attribute can be used to point to an image file that will be tiled across the browser window to provide a background for the document.

Specifying:

```
<BODY BACKGROUND="URL or path/filename.gif">
Document here
</BODY>
```

Would cause whatever text, images, etc. appeared in that document to be placed on a background consisting of the (filename.gif) graphics file being tiled to cover the viewing area.

The **BGCOLOR** attribute allows setting of the background color for the document.

```
<BODY BGCOLOR="#rrggbb">
Document here
</BODY>
```

Where "#rrggbb" is a hexadecimal red-green-blue triplet used to specify the background color. If a background image or color is used it will probably be necessary to alter the foreground colors in order to establish a sensible contrast for the document.

TEXT

This attribute is used to control the color of all the normal text in the document. This basically consists of all text that is not specially colored to indicate a link. The format of TEXT is the same as that of BGCOLOR.

```
<BODY TEXT="#rrggbb">
Document here
</BODY>
```

LEFTMARGIN attribute

This Internet Explorer attribute allows the left-hand margin of the document to be set.

For example:

```
<BODY LEFTMARGIN="60">This document is indented 60 pixels from the left hand side of the page</BODY>
```

TOPMARGIN attribute

This Internet Explorer specific attribute allows the top margin of the document to be set.

For example:

```
<BODY TOPMARGIN="60">This document is indented 60 pixels from the top of the page </BODY>
```

☞ *Note: Both of the above attributes can be set to 0, making the page start at the very top and very left hand side of the page.*

Information Type and Character Formatting Elements

Different information type elements may be rendered in the same way. The following are what are sometimes called logical formatting elements. They suggest to the browser that the enclosed text should be rendered in a way according to the browser rather than fixing the display type. Elements that do this are character formatting elements (also known as Physical Elements) that produce strict rendering of the text.

Information Type Elements

- **CITE:** The Citation element specifies a citation typically rendered as Italics. Used to highlight external resource in a page to which the page is referring to. It has no attribute. <CITE> ... </CITE>

- **CODE:** The Code element indicates an example of code; typically rendered as monospaced. Do not confuse with the Preformatted Text element. <CODE> ... </CODE>

- **EMPHASIS:** The Emphasis element indicates typographic emphasis typically rendered as Italics. <EM> ... </EM>

- **Keyboard Input:** The Keyboard element indicates text typed by a user; typically rendered as monospaced. It might commonly be used in an instruction manual. <KBD> ... </KBD>

- **SAMPLE:** The Sample element indicates a sequence of literal characters; typically rendered as monospaced. <SAMP> ... </SAMP>

- **STRONG:** The Strong element indicates strong typographic emphasis typically rendered in bold. <STRONG> ... </STRONG>

- **VARIABLE:** The Variable element indicates a variable name; typically rendered as italic. <VAR> ... </VAR>

- **COMMENT:** To include comments in HTML document that will be ignored by the HTML user agent, surround them with <! — and —>. After the comment delimiter, all text up to the next occurrence of —> is ignored. Hence comments cannot be nested. White space is allowed between the closing — and > but not between the opening <! and —>.

For example:

```
<HEAD>
<TITLE>The HTML know-how</TITLE>
<! — Prepared by ITL R&D Wing  —>
</HEAD>
```

Example:

```
<html>
    <head>
        <title>information type elements</title>
<! —This is an example of information type elements, 2000—>
</head>

<body>
    <CITE>This sentence, containing a citation reference</CITE><br>
    <CODE>This sentence contains an example of code</CODE>. <br>
    <EM>Emphasis element typically renders as Italics. </EM><br>
    <KBD>The text inside the KBD element would typically render as monospaced font.
    </KBD><br>
    <SAMP>A sequence of literal characters commonly renders as monospaced font.
    </SAMP><br>
    <STRONG>the instructions must be read before continuing. </STRONG><br>
    <VAR>When coding, LeftIndent () must be a variable<VAR><br>
</body>
</html>
```

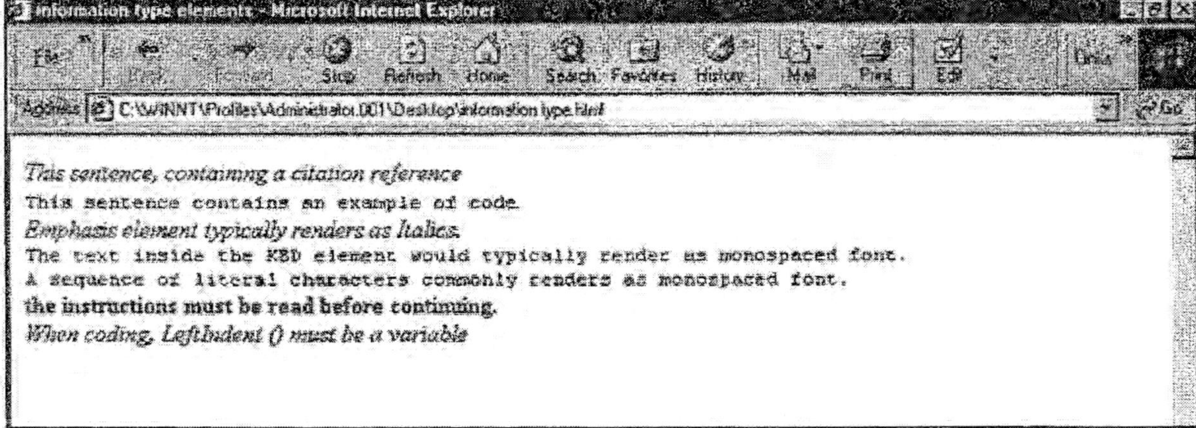

Figure 1.8: Information Type Elements

Character Formatting Elements

- **Bold:** The Bold element specifies that the text should be rendered in boldface where available. Otherwise, alternative mapping is allowed. <B> ... </B>.

- **BIG:** The <BIG> element specifies that the enclosed text should be displayed if practical using a big font (compared with the current font).

- **BLINK:** Surrounding any text with this element will cause the selected text to blink on the viewing page. This can serve to add extra emphasis to selected text.

☞ *Note: The <BLINK> ... </BLINK> element is currently only supported by Netscape.*

- **ITALIC:** The Italic element specifies that the text should be rendered in italic font where available. Otherwise alternative mapping is allowed. <I> ... </I>.

- **SMALL:** The <SMALL> element specifies that the enclosed text should be displayed if practical using a small font (compared with the current font).

- **STRIKE:** The <STRIKE> ... </STRIKE> element states that the enclosed text should be displayed with a horizontal line striking through the text. Alternative mappings are allowed if this is not practical.

- **SUBSCRIPT:** The <SUB> element specifies that the enclosed text should be displayed as a subscript and if practical using a smaller font (compared with normal text).

- **SUPERSCRIPT:** The <SUP> element specifies that the enclosed text should be displayed as a superscript and if practical using a smaller font (compared with normal text).

- **TYPEWRITER:** The Teletype element specifies that the text should be rendered in fixed-width typewriter font. <TT> ... </TT>.

- **UNDERLINE:** The <U> ... </U> Elements state that the enclosed text should be rendered as underlined text.

Example:

```
<html>
      <head>
            <title>character formatting elements</title>
      </head>
<body>
      <B>The instructions must be read before continuing. </B><br>
      <BIG>this is normal text, with this bit being big text. </BIG><br>
      <SMALL>this is normal text, with this bit being small text. </SMALL><br>
      <BLINK>This text would blink on the page in Netscape only</BLINK><br>
      <I>Anything between these elements should be Italics. </I><br>
      <STRIKE>This text would be struck through</STRIKE><br>
      This is the main text, with <SUB>this bit</SUB> being subscript. <br>
      This is the main text, with <SUP>this bit</SUP> being superscript<br>
      <TT>Text between the typetype elements should be rendered in fixed width typewriter
      font. </TT><br>
      The <U>main point</U> of the exercise. <br>
</body>
</html>
```

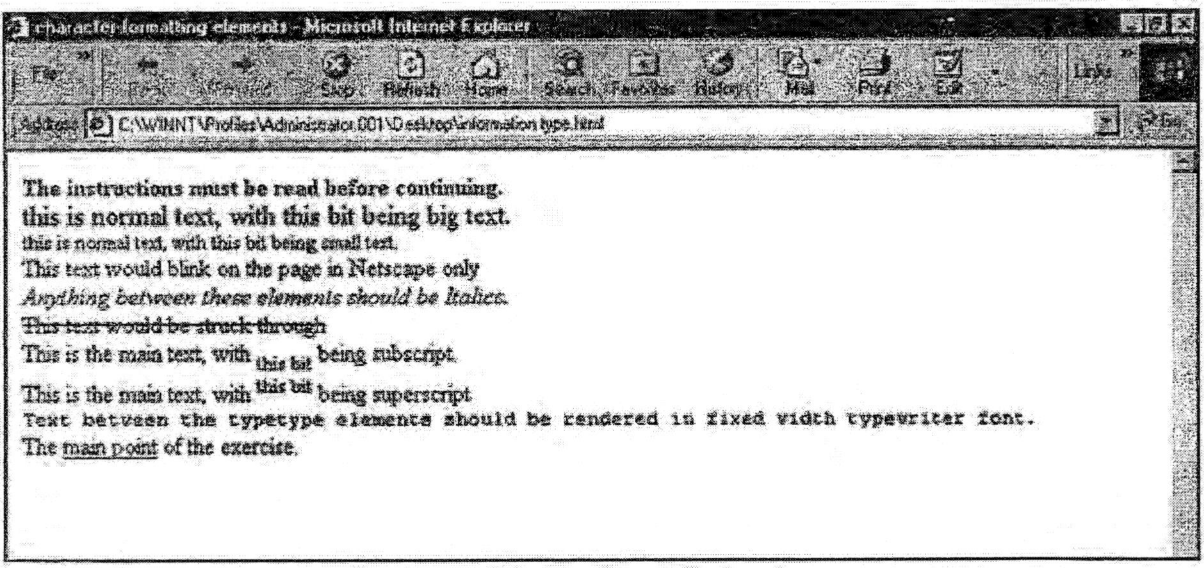

Figure 1.9: Character Formatting Elements

Block Formatting Elements

- **Preformatted text:** The Preformatted Text element presents blocks of text in fixed-width font and so is suitable for text that has been formatted on screen.

  The <PRE> element may be used with the optional WIDTH attribute The WIDTH attribute specifies the maximum number of characters for a line and allows the HTML user agent to select a suitable font and indentation. If the WIDTH attribute is not present a width of 80 characters is assumed. Where the WIDTH attribute is supported, widths of 40, 80 and 132 characters should be presented optimally with other widths being rounded up.

  Within preformatted text:
  - Line breaks within the text are rendered as a move to the beginning of the next line.
  - The <P> element should not be used. If found, it should be rendered as a move to the beginning of the next line.
  - Anchor elements and character highlighting elements may be used.
  - Elements that define paragraph formatting (headings, address, etc.) must not be used.

Example:

```
<HTML>
    <HEAD>
        <TITLE>Pre-formatted Paragraphs</TITLE>
    </HEAD>
    <BODY>
        <PRE>

    Department          Number of Employees          Department Code
   ------------------------------------------------------------------
    Finance                     25                         234
    Marketing                   27                         235
    Production                  35                         236
    Operations                  32                         275
    HRD                         24                         278

        </PRE>
    </BODY>
</HTML>
```

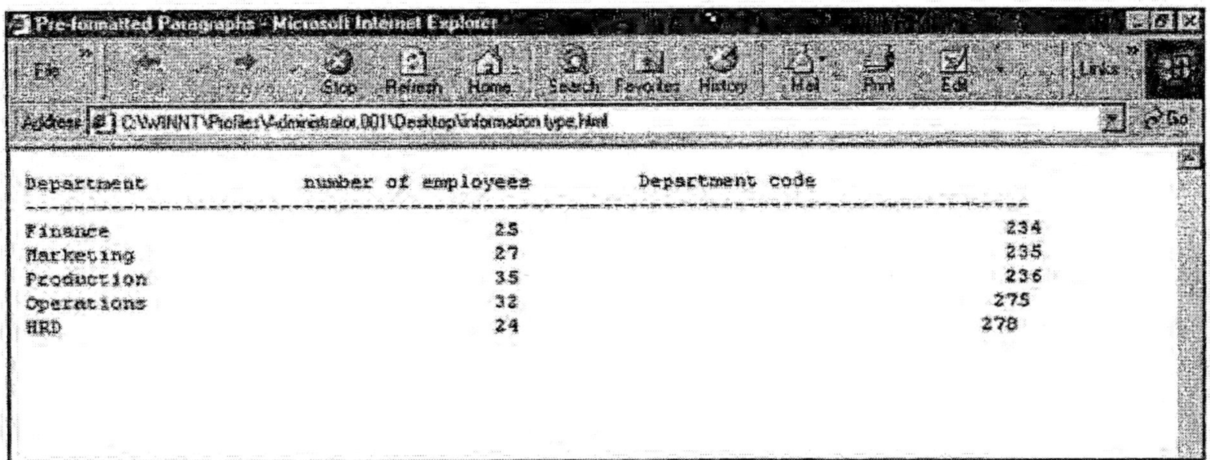

Figure 1.10: Preformatted Text

- **CENTER:** All lines of text between the beginning and end <CENTER> elements are centered between the current left and right margins.

- **FONT:** The element is <FONT SIZE=value>. Valid value range from 1-7 and the default font size is 3. The value given to size can optionally have a '+' or '-' character in front of it to specify that it is relative to the document basefont (if the size specified takes the font size above 7 or below 1 then values of 7 and 1 would be used).

  <FONT SIZE=4> changes the font size to 4 </FONT>
  <FONT SIZE=+2> changes the font size to <BASEFONT SIZE ...> + 2 </FONT>, or to 5 if no <BASEFONT SIZE ...> has been set.
  COLOR = #rrggbb or color name

  The color attribute sets the color of text that will appear on the screen. RRGGBB is a hexadecimal color denoting a color value. Alternately the color can be set to one of the named colors supported by the browsers

  Example:

  <FONT COLOR=#ff0000>This text is red. </FONT>
  OR
  <FONT COLOR=Red>This text is also red. </FONT>

  FACE=name [, name] [, name]

The FACE attribute sets the typeface that will be used to display the text on the screen. The typeface displayed must already be installed on the user computer. Substitute typefaces can be specified in case the chosen typeface is not installed on the customer's computer. If no match is found, the text will be displayed in the default type according to the browser preference settings.

Example:

```
<HTML>
      <HEAD><TITLE>Various Font Sizes</TITLE></HEAD>
      <BODY>
            <P><FONT size=1>Font Size 1</FONT></P>
            <P><FONT size=2>Font Size 2</FONT></P>
            <P><FONT size=3>Font Size 3</FONT></P>
            <P><FONT size=4>Font Size 4</FONT></P>
            <P><FONT size=5>Font Size 5</FONT></P>
            <P><FONT size=6>Font Size 6</FONT></P>
            <P><FONT size=7>Font Size 7</FONT></P>
      </BODY
</HTML>
```

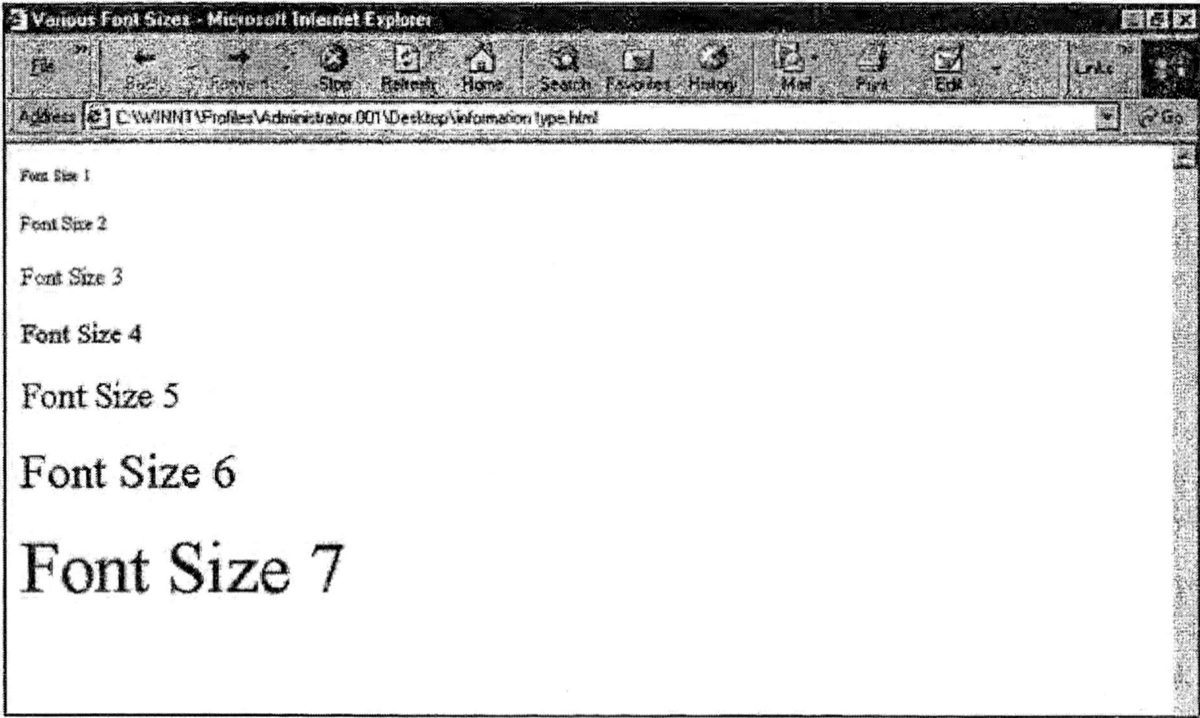

Figure 1.11: Various Font Sizes

- **BASEFONT:** This changes the size of the BASEFONT that all relative <FONT SIZE ...> changes are based on. It defaults to 3 and has a valid range of 1-7. <BASEFONT SIZE=5>.

  - **FACE:** This attribute allows changing of the face of the HTML document BASEFONT exactly as for <FONT FACE= ...>.

  - **COLOR:** This allows the BASEFONT color for the HTML document to be set. Colors can either be set by using one of the color names or as a hex rrggbb triplet value.

☞ *Note: The <BASEFONT...> element, using SIZE and FACE attributes is supported only by Netscape and the Internet Explorer, with the...COLOR attribute being Internet Explorer specific.*

- **ADDRESS:** The Address element specifies such information as address, signature and authorship, often at the top or bottom of a document. Typically, an Address is rendered in an italic typeface and may be indented. It carries an implied paragraph break before and after the text enclosed.

- **BLOCKQUOTE:** The BLOCKQUOTE element is used to contain text quoted from another source. A typical rendering would be a slight extra left and right indent and/or italic font. The BLOCKQUOTE element causes a paragraph break and typically provides space above and below the quote.

- **MARQUEE:** The new <MARQUEE> element allows the author to create a scrolling text marquee (as the name suggests a scrolling text region much like the Windows Marquee screen saver).

  Marquees can be left or right aligned like images and have a variety of attributes to control them.

  - **ALIGN:** This attribute can be set to TOP, MIDDLE or BOTTOM and specifies that the text around the marquee should align with the top, middle or bottom of the marquee.

- **BEHAVIOR:** This can be set to SCROLL, SLIDE or ALTERNATE. It specifies how the text should behave. SCROLL (the default) means start completely off one side, scroll all the way across and completely off then start again. SLIDE means start completely off one side, scroll in and stops as soon as the text touches the other margin. ALTERNATE means bounce back and forth within the marquee.

- **BGCOLOR:** This specifies a background color for the marquee either as a rrggbb hex triplet or as one of the Internet Explorer prename colors.

- **DIRECTION:** This specifies in which direction the text should scroll. The default is LEFT which means scrolling to the left from the right. This attribute can also be set to RIGHT which would cause the marquee to scroll from the left to the right.

- **HEIGHT:** This specifies the height of the marquee either in pixels (HEIGHT=n) or as a percentage of the screen height (HEIGHT=n%).

- **WIDTH:** This specifies the width of the marquee either in pixels (WIDTH=n) or as a percentage of the screen height (WIDTH=n%).

- **HSPACE:** This specifies left and right margins for the outside of the marquee in pixels.

- **LOOP:** LOOP specifies how many times a marquee will loop when activated. If n=-1 or LOOP=INFINITE is specified the marquee will loop indefinitely.

- **SCROLLAMOUNT:** Specifies the number of pixels between each successive draw of the marquee text. That is the amount for the text to move between each draw.

- **SCROLLDELAY:** SCROLLDELAY specifies the number of milliseconds between each successive draw of the marquee text. That is it controls the speed at which text draw takes place.

- **VSPACE:** VSPACE specifies the top and bottom margins for the outside of the marquee in pixels.

Examples:

<MARQUEE>This text will scroll from left to right slowly</MARQUEE>

<MARQUEE BEHAVIOR=SLIDE>This marquee will scroll in and "stick."</MARQUEE>

<MARQUEE HEIGHT=50% WIDTH=80%>This marquee, is half the height of the screen and 80% of the screen width. </MARQUEE>

<MARQUEE SCROLLDELAY=5 SCROLLAMOUNT=50>This is a very fast marquee. </MARQUEE>

- **COMMENT:** Any text placed between the <COMMENT> and </COMMENT> elements will not render on the screen allowing comments to be placed in HTML documents.

☞ *Note: the Internet Explorer and Mosaic only support this element.*

- **PARAGRAPH:** The Paragraph element indicates a paragraph. Typically, paragraphs are surrounded by a vertical space of one line or half a line. With some browsers the first line in a paragraph is indented.

  ALIGN=left|center|right attributes have been added to the <P> element.

  Example: <P ALIGN=left> ... </P>

  All text within the paragraph will be aligned to the left side of the page layout. This setting is equal to the default <P> element.

- **SPACER:** This Netscape specific attribute can be used to include hard coded white space in a document. It accepts the following attributes:

  - **TYPE:** The TYPE of <SPACER> can be horizontal, vertical or block. A horizontal <SPACER> inserts horizontal white space in between words. A vertical <SPACER> inserts vertical space between lines and the block <SPACER> behaves like an image (except doesn't display an image). It essentially reserves a block of space within the document.

- **SIZE:** When a <SPACER TYPE="horizontal"> or <SPACER TYPE="vertical"> is used the SIZE attribute specifies its size in pixels. Any setting of this attribute is ignored if a <SPACER TYPE="block"> is used.

- **WIDTH:** When a <SPACER TYPE="block"> is used the WIDTH attribute specifies the WIDTH of the block to be reserved as white space.

- **HEIGHT:** When a <SPACER TYPE="block"> is used the HEIGHT attribute specifies the HEIGHT of the block to be reserved as white space.

- **ALIGN:** When a <SPACER="block"> is used the ALIGN attribute specifies the alignment of the white space block and can accept any alignments as used by the <IMG> element for embedding images.

  Example:

  ```
  <P>
  This is an example.
  </P>
  ```

  The <P> tag starts a paragraph and the </P> tag ends it. These tags create a space between any images or text preceding the enclosed text (some browsers also create a space after the closing paragraph tag).

- **LINE BREAK TAG:** The line break tag causes any text following it to begin on the following line.

  Example: `This is <BR> an example.`

- **NO BREAK:** The <NOBR> element stands for NO Break. This means all the text between the start and end of the <NOBR> elements cannot have line breaks inserted. While <NOBR> is useful for character sequences that don't want to be broken, care should be taken as long text strings inside of <NOBR> elements can appear strange especially if during viewing the user adjust the page size by altering the window size.

☞ *Note: Netscape and the Internet Explorer support The <NOBR> Element.*

- **WORD BREAK:** The <WBR> element stands for Word Break. This is for the very rare case when a <NOBR> section requires an exact break. Also, it can be used any time the browser can be helped by telling it where a word is allowed to be broken. The <WBR> element does not force a line break (
 does that) it simply lets the browser know where a line break is allowed to be inserted if needed.

☞ *Note: Netscape and the Internet Explorer support The <WBR> Element.*

- **DEFINING INSTANCE: Use of the <DFN> element is currently supported only by the Internet Explorer.**

  The <DFN> element can be used to mark the Defining Instance of a term. For example, the first time some text is mentioned in a paragraph.

  Typically, it will render italicised.

  Example: The <DFN> Internet Explorer </DFN> is Microsoft's Web browser.

  Would render as:

  The *Internet Explorer* is Microsoft's Web browser

- **HORIZONTAL RULE:** A Horizontal Rule element is a divider between sections of text such as a full width horizontal rule or equivalent graphic.

  Example:

```
<HR>
<ADDRESS> February 8, 1995, CERN</ADDRESS>
</BODY>
```

  The <HR> element specifies that a horizontal rule of some sort (The default being a shaded engraved line) be drawn across the page. To this element recent browsers have added support for 4 new attributes which allow the document author to describe how the horizontal rule should look.

- **<HR SIZE=number>:** The SIZE attribute lets the author give an indication of how thick they wish the horizontal rule to be. A pixel value should be given.

- **<HR WIDTH=number I percent>:** The default horizontal rule is always as wide as the page. With the WIDTH attribute the author can specify an exact width in pixels or a relative width measured in percent of document width.

- **<HR ALIGN=left I right I center>:** Now that horizontal rules do not have to be the width of the page, it is possible to specify the horizontal alignment of the rule.

- **<HR NOSHADE>:** For those times when a solid bar is required the NOSHADE attribute specifies that the horizontal rule should not be shaded at all.

- **<HR COLOR=name I #rrggbb>:** Internet Explorer allows the specifying of the hard rule color. Accepted values are any of the Explorer supported color names or any acceptable rrggbb hex triplet.

Example:

```
<HTML>
    <HEAD><TITLE>horizontal rule demo</TITLE></HEAD>
    <BODY>
        <HR align=center SIZE=4 width=200>
        <HR align=center SIZE=4 width=300>
        <HR align=center SIZE=4 width=400>
        <H1 align=center>e-academy</H1>
        <HR align=center SIZE=4 width=400>
        <HR align=center SIZE=4 width=300>
        <HR align=center SIZE=4 width=200>
        <H2 align=center>Presents</H2>
    </BODY>
</HTML>
```

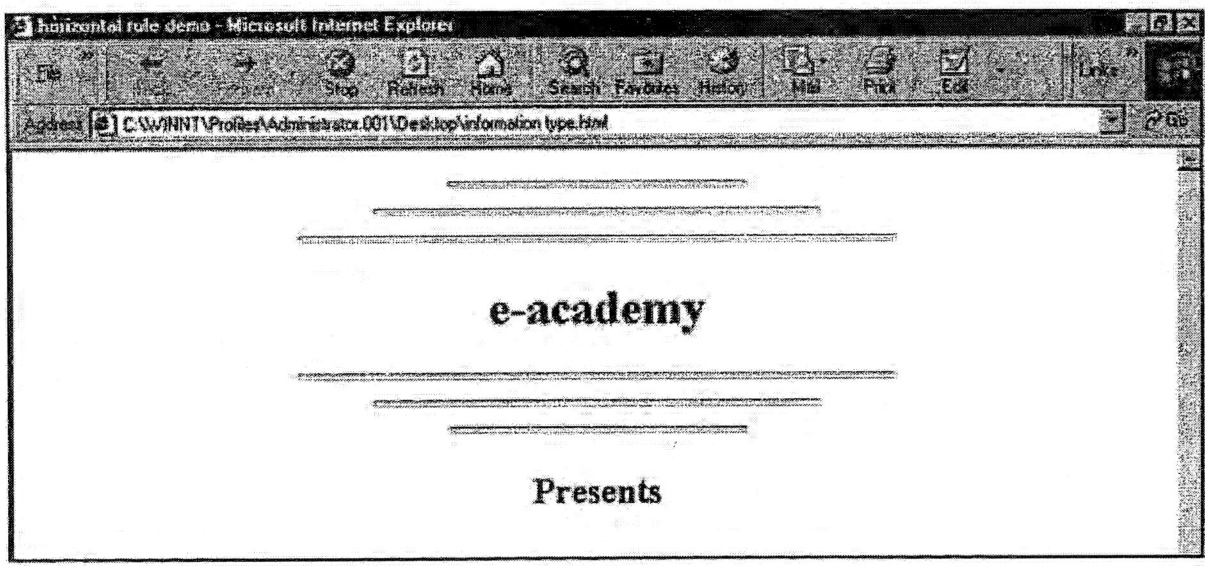

Figure 1.12: Horizontal Rule

Headings

This section demonstrates the use of the heading tag in HTML document. There are six levels of headings. The bigger the number, smaller the size of the resulting text. Examples of all six levels are provided below followed by the tags that produce them. Headings are used to logically organize a page into separate sections for easier comprehension. Lower level headings in turn subdivide each section. Headings automatically create space between them and any text preceding or following them. Therefore, text blocks immediately following them such as this one do not need to have paragraph <P></P> tags around them.

Example:

```
<HTML>
    <HEAD><TITLE>Headings Demo</TITLE></HEAD>
        <BODY>
        <H1>I am doing html</H1>
        <H2>I am doing html</H2>
        <H3>I am doing html</H3>
        <H4>I am doing html</H4>
        <H5>I am doing html</H5>
        <H6> I am doing html</H6>
    </BODY>
</HTML>
```

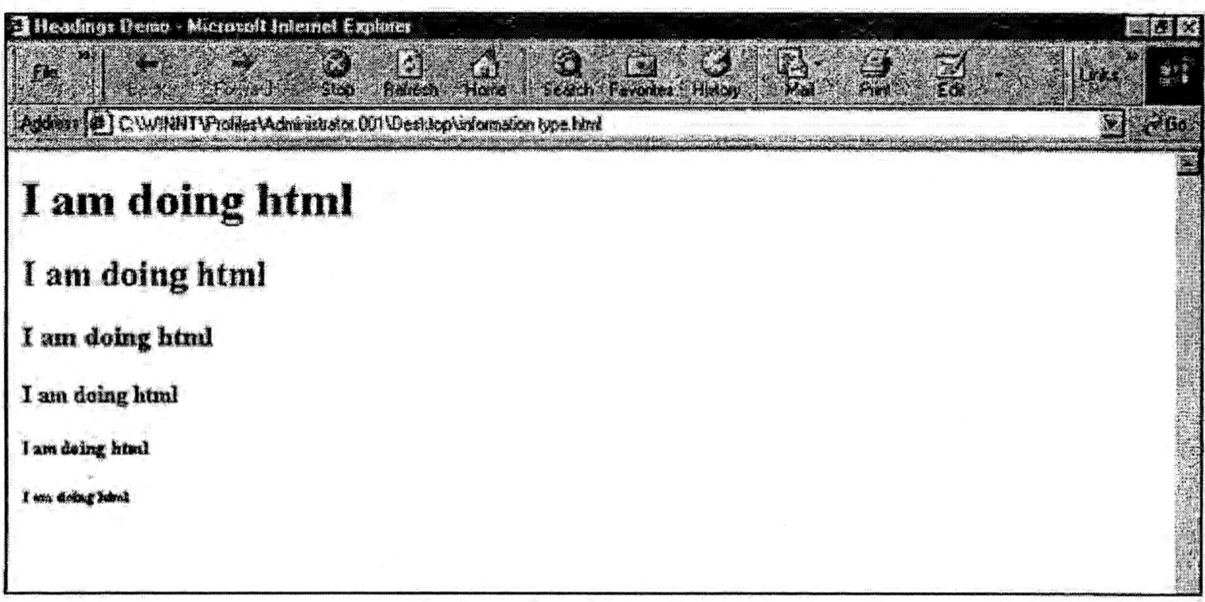

Figure 1.13: Headings

Example:

```
<html>
        <head><title>block formating elements</title></head>
        <body>
        <ADDRESS>
                Mr. dalbir singh<BR>
                new delhi<BR>
                        india
                </ADDRESS><br>
        <BLOCKQUOTE>
        I think the poem ends but i am not sure.
        </BLOCKQUOTE>
                <CENTER> All this text would be centred in the page</CENTER><br>
        <COMMENT>
                This text won't render.  I can say what I like here, it wont appear</COMMENT><br>
                <DFN>The Internet Explorer is Microsoft's Web browser.</DFN><br>
                <H1>This is a heading</H1><BR><H2>Second level heading</H2><br>
        <XMP>The Netscape Navigator doesn't support coloured tables.
        </XMP>
                <HR SIZE=5 WIDTH=200 ALIGN=Left><br>
                <pre> i             am          going  to            bombay </pre><br>
        </body>
</html>
```

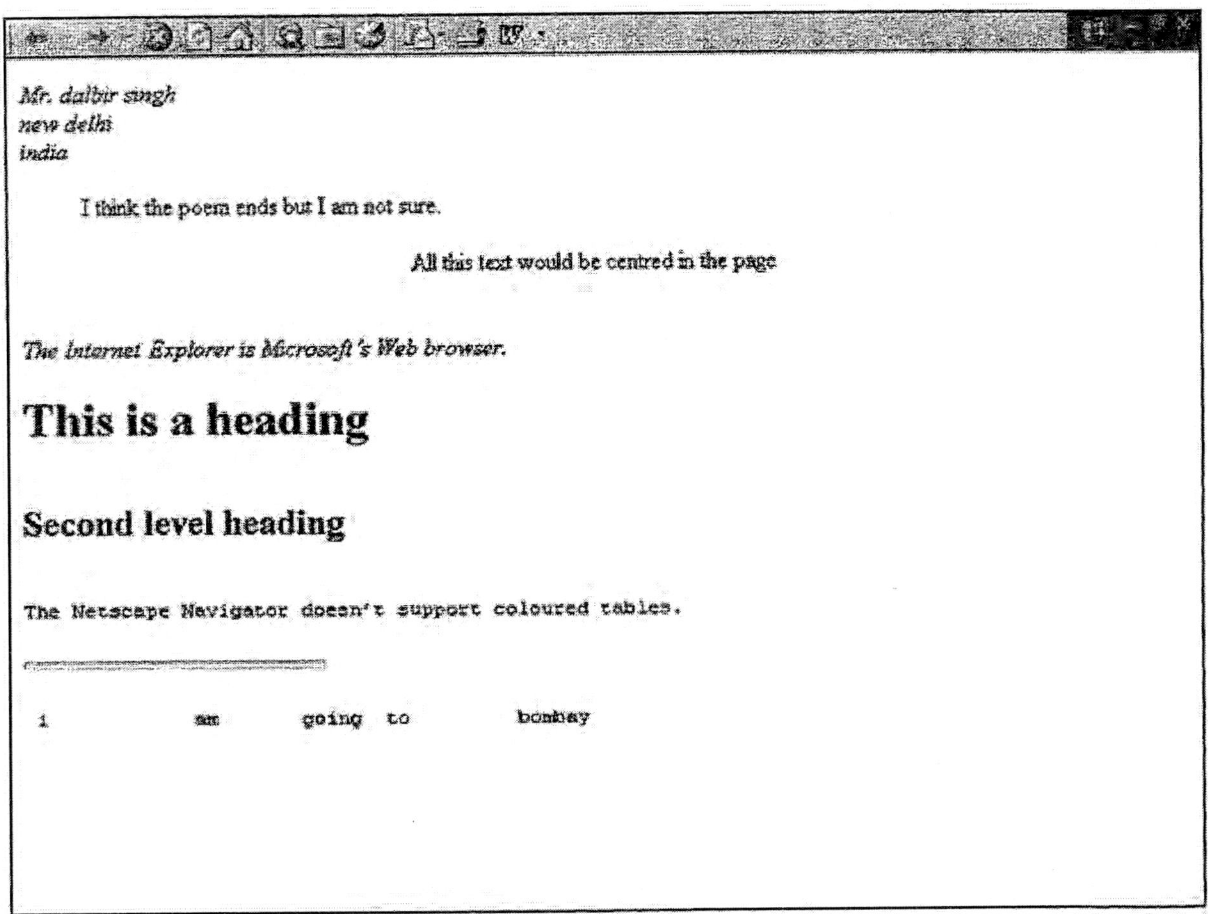

Figure 1.14: Block Formatting Element

SPECIAL CHARACTERS

The following entity names are used in HTML, standard charset always prefixed by ampersand (&) and followed by a semicolon. This list, sorted numerically, is derived from ISO-8859-1 8-bit single-byte coded graphic character set:

Reference	Description	Description
�-	Unused	Unused
	Horizontal tab	Horizontal tab
Line feed	Line feed
-	Unused	Unused
	Space	Space
!	!	Exclamation mark
"	“	Quotation mark
#	Number sign	Number sign
$	$	Dollar sign
%	%	Percent sign
&	&	Ampersand
'	‘	Apostrophe
(	(	Left parenthesis
)	)	Right parenthesis
*	*	Asterisk
+	+	Plus sign
,	,	Comma
-	-	Hyphen
.	.	Period (fullstop)
/	/	Solidus (slash)
0- 9	Digits 0-9	Digits 0-9
:	:	Colon
;	;	Semi-colon
<	<	Less than

Table 1.1: Special Characters

Lists

List tags cause standard items (such as bullets or numbers) to be inserted before the listed text. They can be "nested" within one another to create sub-lists (the effect of this on the appearance of a document differs with the browser used). The text of a list entry uses the same style and fonts as normal text.

The types of lists supported by HTML are:

- **Unordered list**
- **Ordered or Numbered list**
- **Definition List**
- **Directory List**
- **Menu List**

But before discussing the different List tags here is a brief discussion on List Item (LI) tag.

The <LI> denotes an item in a list. It is only used as a sub-element of a list type. <DIR>, <OL>, <UL> and <MENU> all use it to mark a component of their structure.

The <LI> tag can take four attributes:

- **START:** (Ordered lists only) You can change the starting value of the numbering sequence from the default of 1 to any other value you choose.

- **TYPE:** (Ordered and Unordered lists) You can modify the numbering scheme in an ordered list or the bullet character in an unordered list by setting TYPE to one of the list types available. Ordered list types include Arabic numerals (1,2,....), Uppercase alphabets (A,B,...), Lowercase alphabets(a,b,....), Uppercase Roman numerals(I, II, ...) and Lowercase Roman numerals (i, ii, ...). The unordered list types include DISC (solid circular bullet), SQUARE (solid square bullet) and CIRCLE (open circular bullet).

- **Value:** Sets the numbering value of the list item.

- **COMPACT:** Instructs the browser to render the list item in as small a space as possible.

Syntax:

```
<LI  TYPE = "list_type" START = "start_value">......list item goes here...........</LI>
```

Example:

```
<LI TYPE= "a" START = "2">
```

produces an ordered list beginning with the lowercase letter b.

Unordered List

Using an unordered list tag causes bullets to be placed before the listed text. An "unordered list" is opened by <UL> and closed by </UL>. <LI> precedes listed items between them. The basic bulleted list has a default progression of bullet types that change according to the level of the list item from a solid disc to a circle to a square. Netscape allows the TYPE attribute to be used within the <UL> element so that irrespective of the the indent level, the bullet type can be specified. To give even more flexibility to lists, Netscape allows the TYPE attribute to be used within the <LI> element as well. It takes the same values as <UL> and it changes the list type for that item and all subsequent items.

☞ *Note : The TYPE attribute when used in the <UL> and <LI> Elements is Netscape specific.*

The three types which can be specified in a <ul> list tag are:

- **TYPE = disc**
- **TYPE = circle**
- **TYPE = square**

Example:

```
<HTML>
    <HEAD><TITLE>Bulleted Lists Demo</TITLE></HEAD>
    <BODY>
        <P>I am going to learn following packages: </P>
            <UL>
```

```
                    <LI>Dreamweaver </LI>
                    <LI> Adobe photoshop </LI>
                    <LI>Adobe Illustrator</LI>
                    <LI>Macromedia Director </LI>
                    <LI>Macromedia Flash</LI>
               </UL>
     </BODY>
</HTML>
```

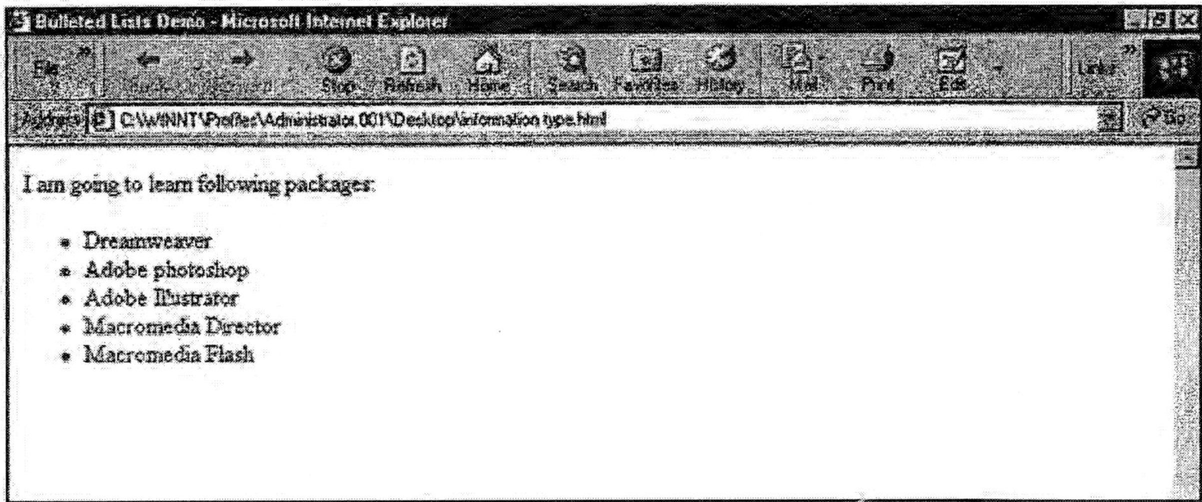

Figure 1.15: Bulleted List

Numbered Ordered List

Using a numerically ordered list tag causes numbers (starting from one) to be placed before the listed text. An "ordered list" is opened by <OL> and closed by </OL>. <LI> precedes listed items between them. The average ordered list counts 1, 2, 3, ... etc.

The TYPE allows different count mark types:

- **(TYPE=A) - capital letters. e.g. A, B, C ...**
- **(TYPE=a) - small letters. e.g. a, b, c ...**
- **(TYPE=I) - large roman numerals. e.g. I, II, III ...**
- **(TYPE=i) - small roman numerals. e.g. i, ii, iii ...**
- **(TYPE=1) - or the default numbers. e.g. 1, 2, 3 ...**

For lists that need to start at values other than 1 the **START** attribute can be used.

START is always specified in the default numbers and converted based on the TYPE attribute before display.

Thus START=5 would display either an 'E', 'e', 'V', 'v' or '5' based on the TYPE attribute.

Example:

This is a list header!

1. One
2. Two
3. Three

Tags used to create this list:

```
<OL>
    <LH>This is a list header!
    <LI>One
    <LI>Two
    <LI>Three
</OL>
```

Definition List

Definition lists place nothing before entries preceded by <DT> and indent entries following <DD>.

A "definition list" is opened by <DL> and closed by </DL>. Listed items between them are preceded by <DT> (Definition Term) and then <DD> (Definition Definition). Use of <DT> without <DD> or vice-versa is non-standard.

Example:

```
<HTML>
      <HEAD><TITLE> Definition Lists</TITLE></HEAD>
      <BODY>
            <DL>
            <DT>Java</DT>
                  <DD>This is a programming language based on OOPS</DD>
                  <DT>JavaScript</DT>
                  <DD>This is scripting language used for designing web
                  pages</DD>
                  <DT>sql server </DT>
                  <DD>it is an RDBMS by microsoft </DD>
            </DL>
      </BODY>
</HTML>
```

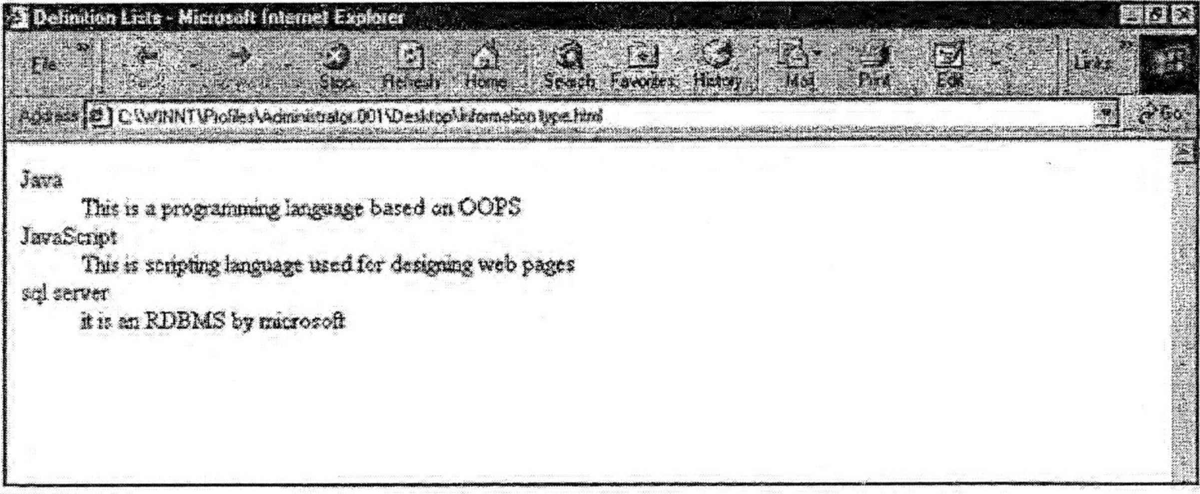

Figure 1.16: Definition List

Directory Lists

The DIR element represents a list of short items typically up to 20 characters each such as file names. Most browsers implement this element exactly the same as an unordered list while a few others arrange the data in columns across the screen. The only content of this list structure is the <li> (list item) element. As with other list elements the closing </li> tag is optional as it is implied by the subsequent <li> or end </dir> tags. The attributes of <DIR> tag are:

1. **Compact:** This is a stand alone attribute flag that indicates a compact rendering be used if possible because the list items are small or the entire list is large.

2. **Type:** The TYPE attribute indicates different marker schemes to be used instead of the default. The values of this attribute are:

   - A [capital letters]
   - a [lower-case letters]
   - I [large roman numerals]
   - i [small roman numerals]
   - 1 [integer numbering]
   - disc [default solid bullet]
   - [solid square]
   - circle [hollow bullet]

Example:

```
<DIR>
      <LI>alpha.html
      <LI>beta.html
      <LI>theta.html
      <LI>zeta.html
</DIR>
```

MENU List

A menu list is a list of items with typically one line per item. The menu list style is more compact than the style of an unordered list.

A menu list must begin with a <MENU> element which is immediately followed by a <LI> (list item) element:

```
<MENU>
	<LI>First item
	<LI>Second item
	<LI>Third item
</MENU>
```

Nested Lists

Lists can be "nested" within each other. The effect of this on the appearance of a document varies with the browser used to view it. Different types of lists can be "nested" within each other. For example, a catalog might list various products with an unordered list and then list each version of the product numerically using an ordered list.

This is a nested list using the unordered (or bullet) list tag as the top-level list and the ordered (or numerical) list tag as the nested list tag.

- Top Level List Entry
  1. Nested
  2. Lists
  3. Entries

- Top Level List Entry
  1. Nested
  2. Lists
  3. Entries

- Top Level List Entry

Tags used to create this list:

```
<UL>
<LI>Top Level List Entry
<OL>
<LI>Nested
<LI>Lists
<LI>Entries
</OL>
<LI>Top Level List Entry
<OL>
<LI>Nested
```

```
<LI>Lists
<LI>Entries
</OL>
<LI>Top Level List Entry
</UL>
```

Example:

```
<HTML><HEAD><TITLE>Starting a List with a Different Number</TITLE>
</HEAD>
<BODY>
<P>The five hot topics today are:</P>
<OL start=7 type=I>
<LI>Java
<LI>Applets
        <LI>Servlets
        <LI>asp
        <LI>corba
        <LI>RMI </LI></OL></BODY></HTML>
```

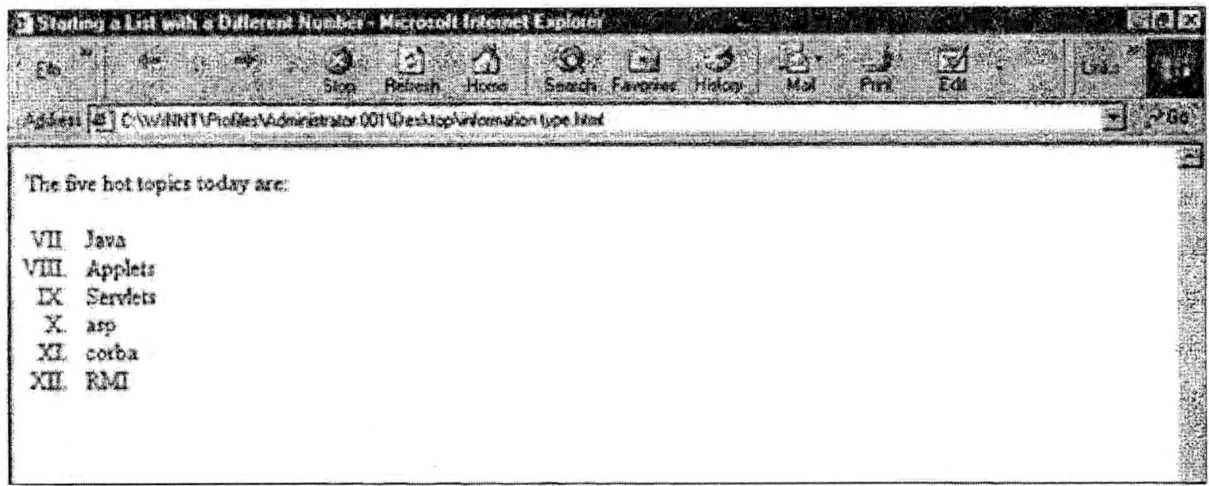

Figure 1.17: Starting with Different Number

Anchor

The Anchor element is the essence of HTML. It is marked text that is the start and/or destination of a hypertext link. Anchor elements are defined by the <A> element. The <A> element accepts several attributes but either the NAME or HREF attribute is required.

Attributes of the <A> element:

HREF

If the HREF attribute is present the text between the opening and closing anchor elements becomes hypertext. If this hypertext is selected by readers they are moved to the document specified by the value of the attribute.

Example:

See <A HREF="http://www.yahoo.com/fashion.html/">The yahoo site</A>for updated info on the fashions.

In this example, selecting "the yahoo site" takes the reader to a document located at http://www.yahoo.com/fashion.html (which is the yahoo web site).

Example:

The <A HREF="document.html#glossary">glossary</A> defines terms used in the document.

In this example, selecting "glossary" takes the reader to another anchor (i.e. <A NAME="glossary">Glossary</A>) in the document document.html.

<A HREF="mailto:"> Activating such a link would bring up the browsers mailing dialog (or registered mail program) allowing the user to send mail messages to the author of the document or whoever's address follows the mailto attribute.

Linking using Anchor Tag

The Anchor element is the essence of HTML. It is marked text that is the start and/or destination of a hypertext link. Anchor elements are defined by the <A> element. Links can be used to move to a named position with your page to open a page in a particular frame within a frameset, to open a page in a new browser window or just to change pages.

The <A> tag can be used for one of the two things: *External navigation* and *Internal navigation* depending on which attribute is used. The attributes associated with the anchor tag are:

- **ACCESSKEY:** An access key is a shortcut key a reader can use to activate the hyperlink. If you set the access key to the letter "C" for example, windows user can press ALT+C on their keyboards to activate the link.
- **CHARSET:** Denotes what character encoding to use for the linked document.
- **HREF:** Gives the URL of the Web resource to which the hyperlink should point.
- **HREFLANG:** Denotes the language context of the linked resource.
- **NAME:** Specifies the name of the anchor being set up.
- **REL:** Describes the nature of the forward link.
- **REV:** Describes the nature of the reverse link.
- **TABINDEX:** Specifies the link's position in the document's tabbing order.
- **TARGET:** Tells the browser into which frame the linked document should be loaded.
- **TYPE:** Specifies the MIME type of the linked resource.

Some of the possible values for REL and REV attributes:

Value	Meaning
Copyright	Web site's copyright page
Glossary	Glossary of terms for a site
Help	Site help page
Home	Site home page
Index	Site index page
Next	Page that logically follows the current page
Previous	Page that precedes the current page
Stylesheet	File containing style information for the page
TOC	Site table of contents
Up	Page that is above the current page in a site's hierarchy

Table 1.2: Table showing possible values of REL and REV Attribute in <anchor> tag

Example:

The <A HREF="document.html#glossary">glossary</A> defines terms used in the document.

In this example, selecting "glossary" takes the reader to another anchor (i.e. <A NAME="glossary">Glossary</A>) in the document *document.html.*

<A HREF="mailto:"> Activating such a link would bring up the browsers mailing dialog (or registered mail program) allowing the user to send mail messages to the author of the document or to whoever's address follows the mailto attribute.

External Navigation

The <A> tag used with the HREF attribute sets up the hyperlink from whatever content is found between the <A> and </A> tags and the document at the URL specified by HREF. This tag is the most common tag used on the net. It is used to navigate outside a page to some other web page.

Syntax:

<a href = "URL of the page"> Text or image for the user to click on </a>

The closing tag </a> is very important. If the user forgets to close the tag, anything the user clicks on after the opening tag (a href = "......") takes the user to the targeted page.

Example:

See <A HREF="http://www.yahoo.com/fashion.html/">The yahoo site</A>for updated info on the fashions.

In this example, selecting "the yahoo site" takes the reader to a document located at *http://www.yahoo.com/fashion.html* (which is the yahoo web site).

The HTML rules for creating hyperlinks are generalizations of the example given above.

☞ *Note: If there's an image between the two tags, its border is highlighted.*

Internal Navigation

When the <A> tag is used with the NAME attribute a named anchor is set up within the document that can be targeted by other hyperlinks. This helps navigating a large document easier because you can set up anchors at the start of major sections and then place a set of links at the beginning of each section. You can navigate within a page using links paired with named "anchors" or with named frames within a frameset (will be discussed later).

Named Anchors

Making a link from one part of the document involves link tags and an anchor tag. The anchor marks a spot within the document and the link tags are ties to that specific anchor.

Syntax:

```
<a name = "whatever"> Text or Image </a>
```

This tag is called an "anchor" tag. This tag names a section of the page.

```
<a href = "#whatever"> Text or Image </a>
```

This is the "link" tag. It directs the browser to the named anchor.

It's the # character that identifies the link as going to a portion of a document. The links shown above are within one document or Web page. The same is applicable to set up links to portions of other documents provided the document has anchors defined in it.

Linking Between Sections of Different Documents

Suppose you want to set a link from document A (documentA.html) to a specific section in another document say (documenB.html).

Enter the HTML coding for a link to a named anchor (here in documentA.html):

Example:

In addition to the many state parks, Corbett Park is also home to <a href="documentB.html#WT"> White tiger </a>

Next create the named anchor (in this example "WT") in DocumentB.html.

Example:

<H2><A NAME="WT"> White Tiger </a> </H2>

Thus clicking on the hyperlink in *documentA.html*, it takes the user to the section linked in *DocumentB.html* file.

Linking in Frames

Each frame in a frameset has a unique name and to open a page in a particular frame the target attribute needs to be specified i.e., the frame name in which the document or image linked has to be displayed. If the target frame name is not specified the page will open in the frame where the link is by default.

This topic will be discussed in detail in the next chapter.

Syntax:

<a href = "URL" target = "Name of Target Frame"> Text or Image </a>

Linking to an Email Address

This can be accomplished using the **MAILTO** attribute in hyperlink. It launches the email program with the **To field** filled with the value from e-mail address and **Subject** field with the subject specified.

Example:

<a href="mailto:ecademy4u@mantraonline.com ? subject = feedback"> ecademy4u </a>

BODY Tag Revisited - LINK, VLINK, and ALINK attributes

These attributes allow control over the link text coloring. VLINK stands for visited link and ALINK stands for active link. The default coloring of these is LINK= blue (#0000FF), VLINK= purple (#400040) and ALINK= red (#FF0000). Again, the format for these attributes is the same as that for BGCOLOR and TEXT.

```
<BODY LINK="#rrggbb" VLINK="#rrggbb" ALINK="#rrggbb">
Document here
</BODY>
```

Microsoft's Internet Explorer supports the ability to watermark HTML documents by fixing a background image (if specified) so that it doesn't scroll as a normal background image does. To give a page with a background image a watermark background add BGPROPERTIES=FIXED to the BODY element as follows:

```
<BODY BACKGROUND="filename.gif" BGPROPERTIES="FIXED">
```

☞ *Note: This attribute is Internet Explorer specific.*

In Line Images

The Image element is used to incorporate in-line graphics in HTML document. This element cannot be used for embedding other HTML text.

The Image element which is empty (no closing element) has these attributes:

- **ALIGN:** This attribute is used to align an image on the web page. The possible values of align are: left, right, top, text, op, middle, absmiddle, baseline, bottom, absbottom.

    - **ALIGN=left** image will float the image to the left margin (into the next available space there) and subsequent text will wrap around the right hand side of that image.

    - **ALIGN=right** will align the image aligns with the right margin and the text wraps around the left.

- **ALIGN=top** aligns itself with the top of the tallest item in the line.
- **ALIGN=texttop** aligns itself with the top of the tallest text in the line (this is usually but not always the same as ALIGN=top).
- **ALIGN=middle** aligns the baseline of the current line with the middle of the image.
- **ALIGN=absmiddle** aligns the middle of the current line with the middle of the image.
- **ALIGN=baseline** aligns the bottom of the image with the baseline of the current line.
- **ALIGN=bottom** aligns the bottom of the image with the baseline of the current line.
- **ALIGN=absbottom** aligns the bottom of the image with the bottom of the current line.

- **ALT:** Optional text as an alternative to the graphic for rendering in non-graphical environments. Alternate text should be provided for whenever the graphic is not rendered (i.e. if the user has image loading turned off). Internet Explorer also uses any ALT text set as a ToolTip to be displayed when the users mouse pauses over the image.

  Example: <IMG SRC="triangle.gif" ALT="Warning:"> Be sure to read these instructions.

- **ISMAP:** The ISMAP attribute identifies an image as an image map. Image maps are graphics in which certain regions are mapped to URLs. By clicking on different regions different resources can be accessed from the same graphic.

  Example: <A HREF="http://www.msn.com/sample">

  <IMG SRC="cloud.gif" ISMAP></A>

- **SRC:** The value of the SRC attribute is the URL of the image to be embedded. Its syntax is the same as that of the HREF attribute of the <A> element. SRC is mandatory.

```
<IMG SRC ="fly.gif"> Be sure to read these instructions.
```

- **HEIGHT and WIDTH:** If the WIDTH and HEIGHT attributes are used the viewer of their document will not have to wait for the image to be loaded and its size calculated. The browser can determine the layout of the text around the image and display the text first. Netscape is the only browser that will scale the whole image if either the WIDTH or HEIGHT attributes are specified maintaining the aspect ratio. If both are specified then the image is displayed accordingly.

- **BORDER:** This lets the document author control the thickness of the border around an image displayed. This can be set to 0 so that if the image is surrounded by <A> elements the normal link border will not be shown.

- **VSPACE and HSPACE:** The VSPACE attribute controls the vertical space above and below the image while HSPACE controls the horizontal space to the left and right of the image. They allow setting of a 'margin' around the image which is kept as white space and is useful to prevent text wrapping right up to floating images.

- **LOWSRC:** Using the LOWSRC attribute it is possible to use two images in the same space. The LOWSRC attribute should be set to the URL of an image to load in first before the so-called high source image indicated by the SRC attribute. In this sense the attribute can be said to the address of a low resolution image which can be downloaded first and then followed by a high resolution image. The syntax is:

```
<IMG SRC="hi-res-photo.gif" LOWSRC="low-photo.gif" HEIGHT="100" WIDTH="100"
ALT="Slope of Himalayas">
```

Example: Image Alignment

```
<HTML>
      <HEAD>
      <TITLE>Image Alignment</TITLE>
      </HEAD>
      <BODY bgColor=#ffffff>
      <P><IMG align=right height=202 src="monkey.gif" width=168>
      Use the Dreamweaver Site Map option to provide a high-level visual representation of the
      structure of a local site. You can also use the Site Map view to add new files to the site;
      to add, remove, and change links; and to create a graphic file of the site that you can
      export to and print from an image editing application.
      </P>
      <br>
      <br>
      <P><IMG align=left height=202 src="monkey.gif" width=168>
      Use the Dreamweaver Site Map option to provide a high-level visual representation of the
      structure of a local site. You can also use the Site Map view to add new files to the site;
      to add, remove and change links; and to create a graphic file of the site that you can export
      to and print from an image editing application.
      <P>
      <BODY>
<HTML>
```

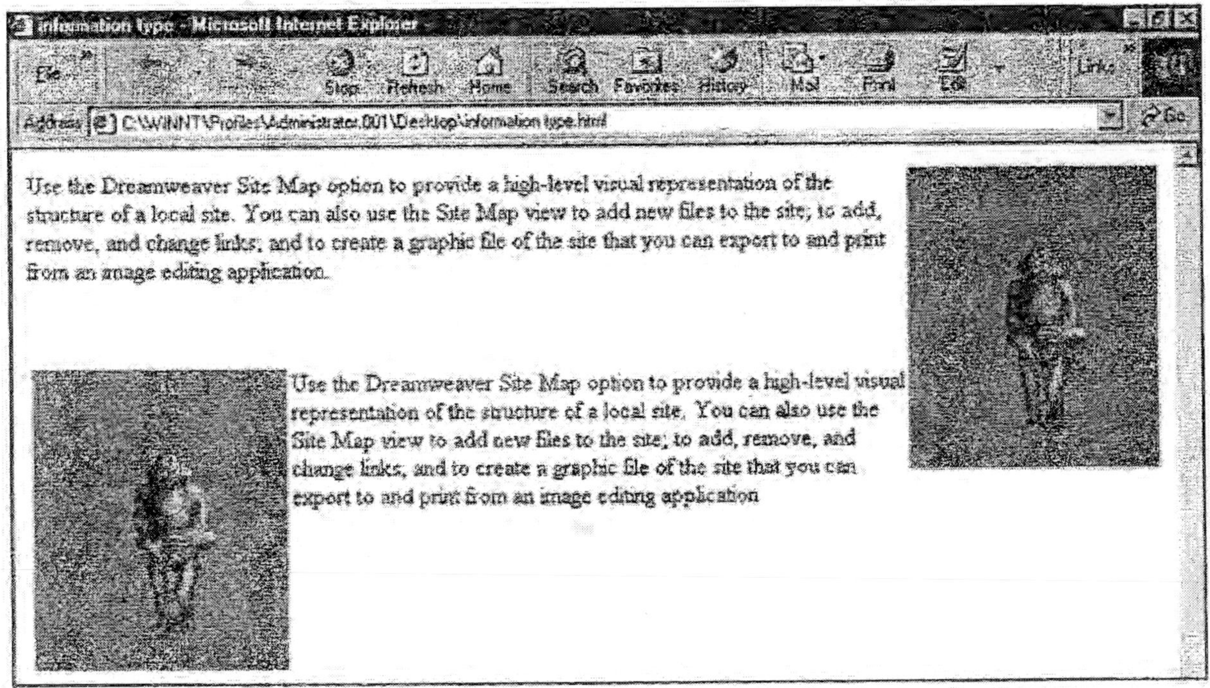

Figure 1.18: Image Alignment

Example: Using Images as Links

```
<HTML>
    <HEAD><TITLE>Using Images as Links</TITLE></HEAD>
    <BODY>
        <P><IMG align=left height=200 hspace=25
        src="chimp23.gif" vspace=25 width=206></P>
        <H1>Multimedia</H1>
        <P>

        Multimedia can be defined as a woven combination of text, sound, video clips,
        images, graphics, animation, quick time movies. Or you can say that the combination
        of two or more media elements bound together to signify a message is known as
        multimedia. When the user has some controls in the movie the presentation is called
        an interactive multimedia.

        </P>
        <P><A href="http://www.macromedia.com"><IMG height=60
        src="monkey.gif" width=60></A>.
        </P>
    </BODY>
</HTML>
```

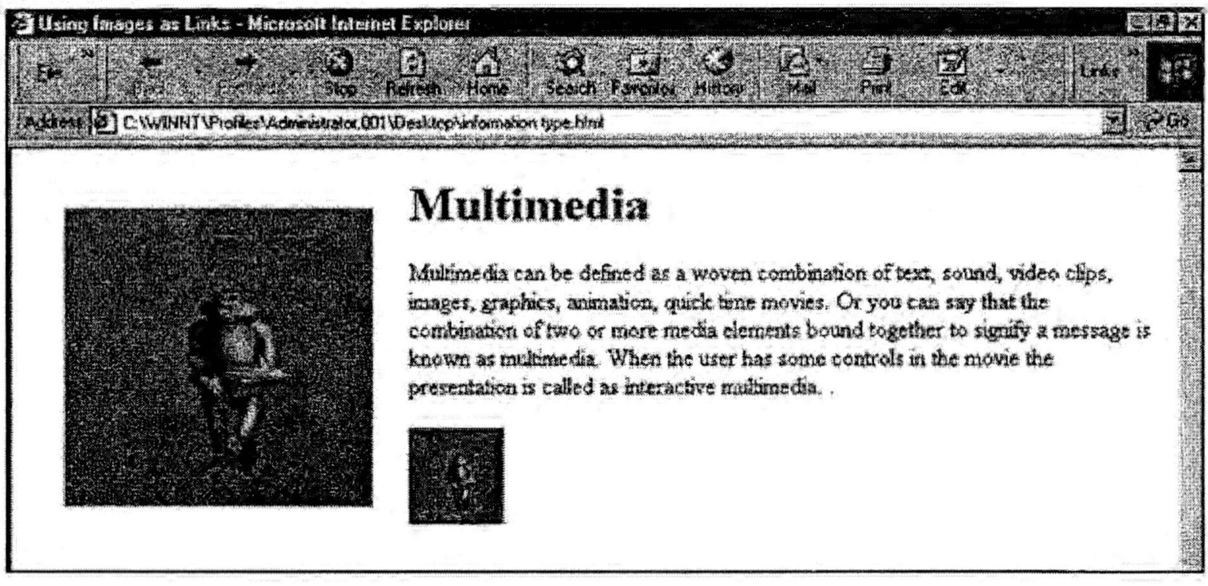

Figure 1.19: Using Images as a Link

In Line Video

Microsoft's Internet Explorer allows the author to embed .avi (Audio Video Interleave) video clips in HTML documents. Adding attributes DYNSRC (Dynamic Source) to the <IMG> element does this. Using the IMG element for this purpose makes it possible to add video clips to pages but also have other browsers display still images in their place.

```
<IMG DYNSRC="video.avi" SRC="TheEarth.gif" WIDTH=50 HEIGHT=50 LOOP=INFINITE ALIGN=RIGHT>
```

- **DYNSRC:** Specifies the address of a video clip to be displayed in the window. It stands for Dynamic Source.

  Example: `<IMG SRC="bird.gif" DYNSRC="game.avi">`

  Internet Explorer will play the movie file "game.avi"; other browsers will display the picture "bird.gif".

- **START:** This attribute specifies when the video file should start playing. This attribute can be set to FILEOPEN or MOUSEOVER. FILEOPEN means that the video will start playing as soon as it has finished opening. This is the default setting. MOUSEOVER means that the video will start playing when the user moves the mouse cursor over the animation. Both can be specified together if necessary.

- **LOOP:** Specifies how many times a video clip will loop when activated. If n=-1, or if LOOP=INFINITE is specified the video will loop indefinitely.

- **LOOPDELAY:** Specifies in milliseconds how long a video clip will wait between play loops.

Embedded Objects

The <EMBED> element allows you to put objects directly into HTML page.

The syntax is:

```
<EMBED SRC= "object_to_embed">
```

The <EMBED> element will allow you to embed documents of any type. User only needs to have an application which can view the data installed correctly on their machine or have a plug-in (for Netscape and Internet Explorer) that can manipulate the embedded file format.

The <EMBED> element can be used more or less the same as the <IMG> element and so accepts typical image embedding attributes such as WIDTH, HEIGHT, BORDER, HSPACE, VSPACE.

Document Sound

The new BGSOUND tag allows you to create pages with background sounds or "soundtracks." Sounds can either be samples (.wav or .au format) or MIDI (.mid format).

The HTML used to insert a background sound into a page is:

```
<BGSOUND SRC="start.wav">
```

The attributes associated with the BGSOUND element are SRC and LOOP.

- **SRC:** This attribute specifies the address of a sound to be played.
- **LOOP:** This attribute specifies how many times a sound will loop when activated. If n=-1 or LOOP=INFINITE is specified the sound will loop indefinitely.

Examples: `<BGSOUND SRC="click.wav">`

This would play the specified WAV file as soon as Internet Explorer has downloaded the file.

```
<BGSOUND SRC="click.wav" LOOP=INFINITE>
```

This would play the specified WAV file as soon as it has finished being loaded and would continuously play the file until another page is loaded.

Meta Tags

A special HTML tag that provides information about a Web page. Unlike normal HTML tags Meta tags do not affect how the page is displayed. Instead they provide information such as who created the page, how often it is updated, what the page is about and which keywords represent the page's content. Many search engines use this information when building their indices. The META element is used within the HEAD element to embed any useful information not defined by other HTML elements. Such information can be extracted by servers/clients for use in identifying indexing and cataloging documents.

Attributes of the META element:

HTTP-EQUIV: This attribute specifies the HTTP response header that the information pertains to. If the semantics of the HTTP response header named by this attribute is known then the contents can be processed based on a well-defined syntactic mapping whether or not the DTD includes anything about it. HTTP header names are not case sensitive. If not present the NAME attribute should be used to identify this meta-information and it should not be used within an HTTP response header.

NAME: Meta-information name. If the name attribute is not present then name can be assumed equal to the value HTTP-EQUIV. Some typical names are: Author, Classification, Copyright, Description, Formatter, Generator, Keywords, Rating, Robots.

```
<META name= "Author" content = "John Grisham">
<META NAME = generator Content = "Microsoft FrontPage">
```

CONTENT: The meta-information content to be associated with the given name and/or HTTP response header.

Typically, the META element would be used to introduce Client Pull into HTML documents or to specify keywords that may be used by search engines to determine a document's relevance to the current search.

Values of HTTP-EQUIV

- **Expires:** This tells the browser the date and time when the document will be considered "expired." If a user is using Netscape Navigator, a request for a document whose time has "expired" will initiate a new network request for the document. An illegal Expiry date such as "0" is interpreted by the browser as "immediately." Dates must be in the format:

  ```
  <META HTTP-EQUIV="expires" CONTENT="Wed, 26 Feb 1997 08:21:57 GMT">
  ```

- **Refresh:** This tag specifies the time in seconds before the Web browser reloads the document automatically. Alternatively it can specify a different URL for the browser to load.

  ```
  <META HTTP-EQUIV="Refresh" CONTENT="0;URL=http://www.newurl.com">
  ```

- **Window-target:** This one specifies the "named window" of the current page and can be used to prevent a page from appearing inside another framed page. Usually this means that the Web browser will force the page to go to the top frameset.

  ```
  <META HTTP-EQUIV="Window-target" CONTENT="_top">
  ```

META Tagging for Search Engines

Keyword and Description Attributes

These allow the search engines to easily index your page using the keywords you specifically tell it along with a description of the site that you yourself get to write.

```
<META NAME ="keywords" CONTENT="fashions, jeans, t-shirts, bermudas, trousers,
suits, shoes, ties, sports, tights">
```

You cannot use the same word repeated over and over in keywords as most search engines have refined their spiders to ignore such activity. Using the META description attribute you add your own description for your page:

<META NAME="description" CONTENT="This page is about the latest fashions trend and sports accessories">.

Another Example can be:

<META NAME = "Keywords" CONTENT = " HTML, CGI, Java, VRML, browsers, plugins, graphics, HTTP servers, JavaScript, Perl, ActiveX, Shockwave">.

<META NAME = "Description" CONTENT=" Locate web authoring & software resources at internet browsing thousands of links about HTML, CGI, Java, VRML, browsers, plugins, graphics, HTTP servers, JavaScript, Perl, ActiveX, Shockwave>.

Dynamic Documents

Client pull

The server sends down a chunk of data including a directive (in the HTTP response or the document header) that says "reload this data in 5 seconds" or "go load this other URL in 10 seconds". After the specified amount of time has elapsed the client loads the given URL.

The main use of client pull is to cause a document to be automatically reloaded on a regular basis such as documents with sports scores or stock quotes. Client Pull can be used to have live video update in a window after a certain amount of time.

For example, consider the following document:

```
<META HTTP-EQUIV="Refresh" CONTENT="x">
<TITLE>Document ONE</TITLE>

<H1>This is a document</H1>

Here's some text. <P>
```

If loaded into a browser supporting Client Pull it would re-load itself every x seconds.

In most cases, Client Pull is used to automatically load another document (automatic re-direction). For this the HTTP response header needs to be:

Refresh: x; URL=http://www.yahoo.com/chat.html

and the corresponding META element syntax is:

```
<META HTTP-EQUIV="Refresh" CONTENT="x;
URL=http:// www.yahoo.com/chat.html">
```

This loads the document referenced by the URL part of the CONTENT attribute after x seconds.

Server Push

Server Push allows for dynamic document updating via a server to client connection that is kept open. This method (as opposed to Client Pull) is totally controlled by the server but the perpetual open connection occupies valuable server resources. It's main advantage over Client Pull though is that using Server Push it is possible to replace single elements within HTML document. It was used mainly for creating animations but nowadays most of the animations are made using GIF animator or JavaScript.

 Hands on Exercise

Write the following code in notepad or any other JavaScript compliant tool and save it with extension *.htm*. Open the file in browser to view the output.

Exercise 1: Different Type of Lists

```
<html>
	<body>
		<a name="top"></a>
		<a href="#example1">Example 1</a><br>
		<a href="#example2">Example 2</a><br>
```

```
            <a href="#example3">Example 3 </a><br>
            <a href="#example4">Nested List Example 4 </a><br>
<br><br>
<a name="example1">Example 1
<P>
Proceed as follows:
</P>
<OL>
            <LI> Try to guess how to use the program.
            <LI> If it fails, send lots of questions to Usenet News.
            <LI> If they flame you, consider contacting local user support.
            <LI> When everything else fails, read the manuals.
</OL></a><br>
<a href="#top"> Top </a><br>
<a name="example2">Example 2
<P>
The declinations of nouns in Latin are best distinguished by the ending of the genitive singular:
</P>
<OL TYPE=I>
            <LI> <I>-ae</I>, eg <I>terra:terrae</I>
            <LI> <I>-i</I>, eg <I>annus:anni</I>
            <LI> <I>-is</I>, eg <I>labor:laboris</I>
            <LI> <I>-us</I>, eg <I>fructus:fructus</I>
            <LI> <I>-ei</I>, eg <I>dies:diei</I>.
</OL>
</a>
<a href="#top"> Top </a>
<br>
<a name="example3"> Example 3
<OL TYPE=a START=3 COMPACT>
            <LI> first item
            <LI> second item
            <LI VALUE=8> item after skipping a few values
            <LI> next item
            <LI TYPE=A> going on with uppercase
            <LI> this is the last item.
</OL>
</a><br>
<a href="#top"> Top </a>

<!— Example 4 Nested List —>
<br>
<a name="example4"> Nested List Example
<!— Begin Main list —>
<ol type =A>
      <li>Body Sustance isolation
      <li>Scene safety
      <li>Initial Size up
```

```
</ol>
<li> Initial patient Assessment
<!— Begin Sub list 2 —>
<ol type=1>
        <li>General Impression
        <li>Unresponsiveness
<!— begin SUB LIST 1 of Sub List 2 —>
<ol type=i>
        <li>Alert to person, place and time
        <li>Verbal response to audible stimuli
        <li>Pain evokes verbal or physical response
        <li> Unresponsiveness to all stimuli
</ol>
</ol>
<li> Patient Critical Needs
<!— Begin Sub list 3 —>
<ol type=1>
        <li>Airway
        <li>Breathing
<!— Begin sub list of sub list 3 —>
<ol type=i>
        <li>Use oxygen if indicated
        <li> Consider use of assisting with bag valve mask
</ol>
<li>Circulation
<li>Bleeding
</ol>
<br>
<a href="#top"> Top </a>
<!— END MAIN LIST —>
</ol>

</body>
</html>
```

Exercise 2: Background Image

```
<HTML>
        <HEAD><TITLE> BackgroundImage</TITLE></HEAD>
                <BODY BGCOLOR="#FFFFFF" BACKGROUND="image.jpg" BGPROPERTIES=FIXED>
                <H1>The computer shop</H1>
                <P>Providing you with the best quality computers for your home or business.latest
                configuration include:</P>
                        <UL>
                <LI>P-III, 550 MHz</LI>
                <LI>17 GB HARD DISK DRIVE</LI>
                <LI>256 MB RAM</LI>
```

```
            <LI>52X CD ROM</LI>
            <LI>15" MONITOR</LI>
                  </UL>
      </BODY>
</HTML>
```

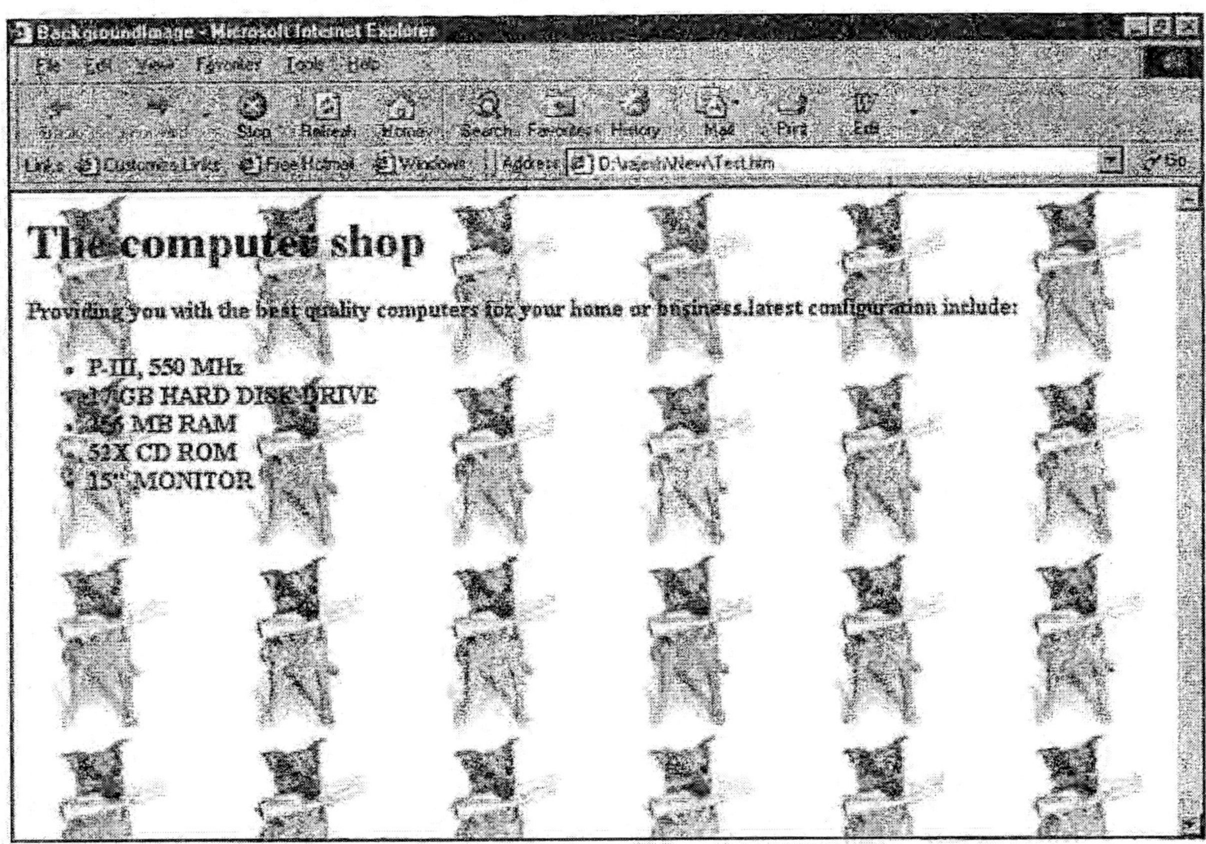

Figure 1.20: Background Image

Exercise 3: Inline Video

```
<HTML>
<HEAD>
<TITLE>moving clock</TITLE>
</HEAD>
<BODY>
<IMG BORDER="0" DYNSRC="clock.avi" START="mouseover"
      LOOP="infinite" WIDTH="150" HEIGHT="200">
<h1>This clock moves on mouseover</h1>
</BODY>
</HTML>
```

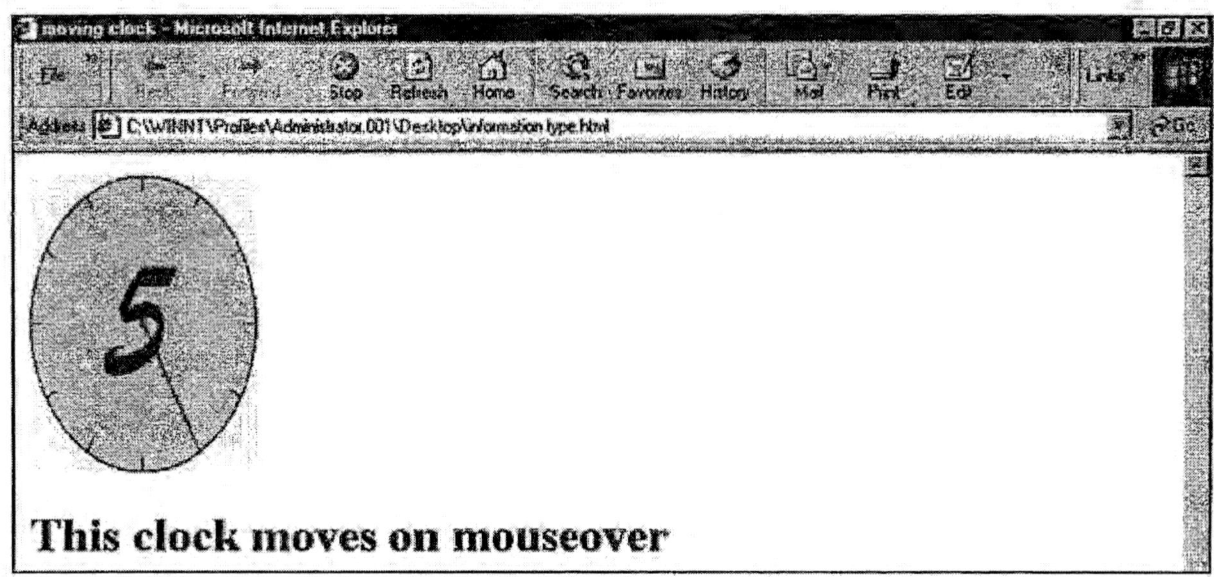

Figure 1.21: Dynamic Source

Exercise 4: Meta tag Attribute

```
<html>
	<head>
		<META HTTP-EQUIV="Refresh" CONTENT="4; URL=http://www.yahoo.com/">
		<title>Meta application</title>
	</head>
<body>
<h1>This is application of meta tag. This page is going to be refreshed after 4 seconds</h1>
</body>
</html>
```

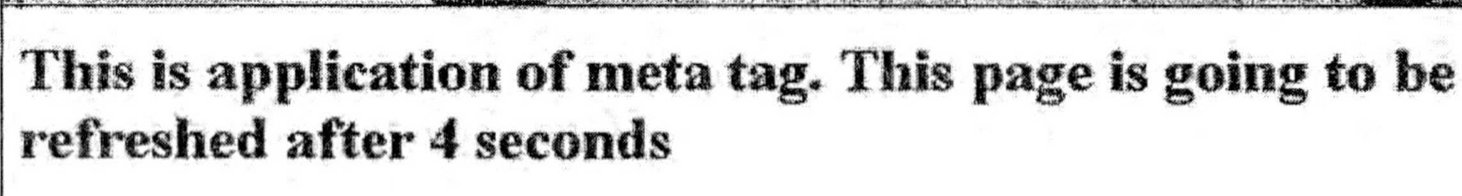

Figure 1.22: Meta Tag

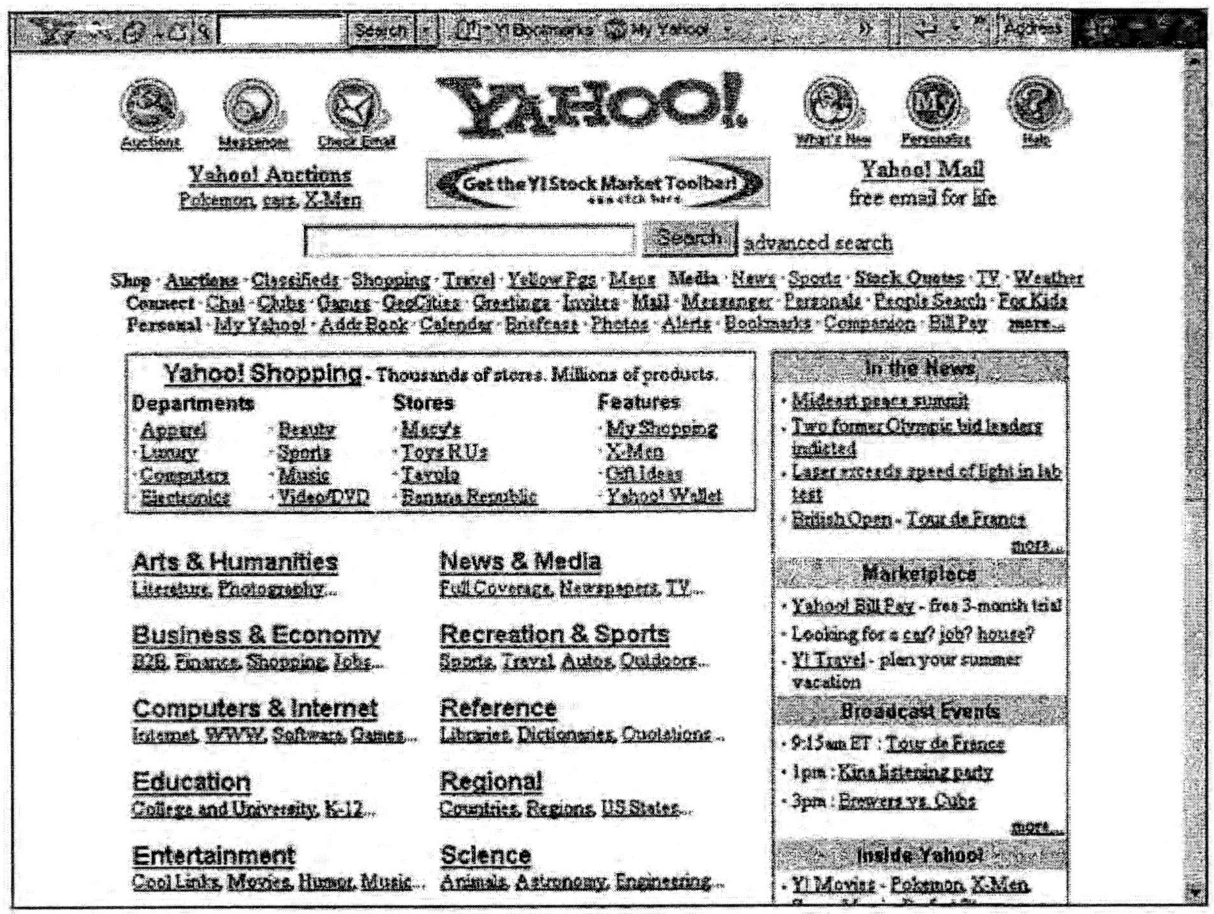

Figure 1.23: Page after 4 seconds

Exercise 5: Embedding Audio-Video Files

```
<HTML>
<HEAD>
<TITLE>New byke</TITLE>
</HEAD>
<BODY>
<EMBED SRC="cycle.avi" BORDER="0"
       AUTOSTART="true" LOOP="true" WIDTH="140" HEIGHT="200">
       <h1>New byke by Yamaha
       </H1>
              <P>Showroom located at rockford club in sydney Australia
</BODY>
</HTML>
```

Figure 1.24: Embedding avi Files

Exercise 6: Marquee Attributes

```
<HTML>
    <HEAD><TITLE>Marquee Attributes</TITLE></HEAD>
        <BODY>
            <H1>
            <MARQUEE bgColor=#ff0000 BORDER="1"direction="right">Add a <FONT
            color=#ffff00>BGCOLOR</FONT>               Attribute</MARQUEE>
            </H1>

<H1>
<MARQUEE bgColor=#0000ff height="20%" BORDER="1">Add a <FONT Color=#ffff00>HEIGHT=20%</
FONT> Attribute</MARQUEE></H1>

<H1>
<MARQUEE bgColor=#00ff00 vspace=20 BORDER="1">Add a <FONT Color=#ffff00>VSPACE=20%</
FONT> Attribute</MARQUEE></H1>

<P>
<MARQUEE bgColor=#00ffff height="20%" width="50%" BORDER="1" ALIGN="bottom">Add A
<FONT color=#ff0000>ALIGN=BOTTOM</FONT> Attribute Example</MARQUEE></P></BODY></
HTML>
```

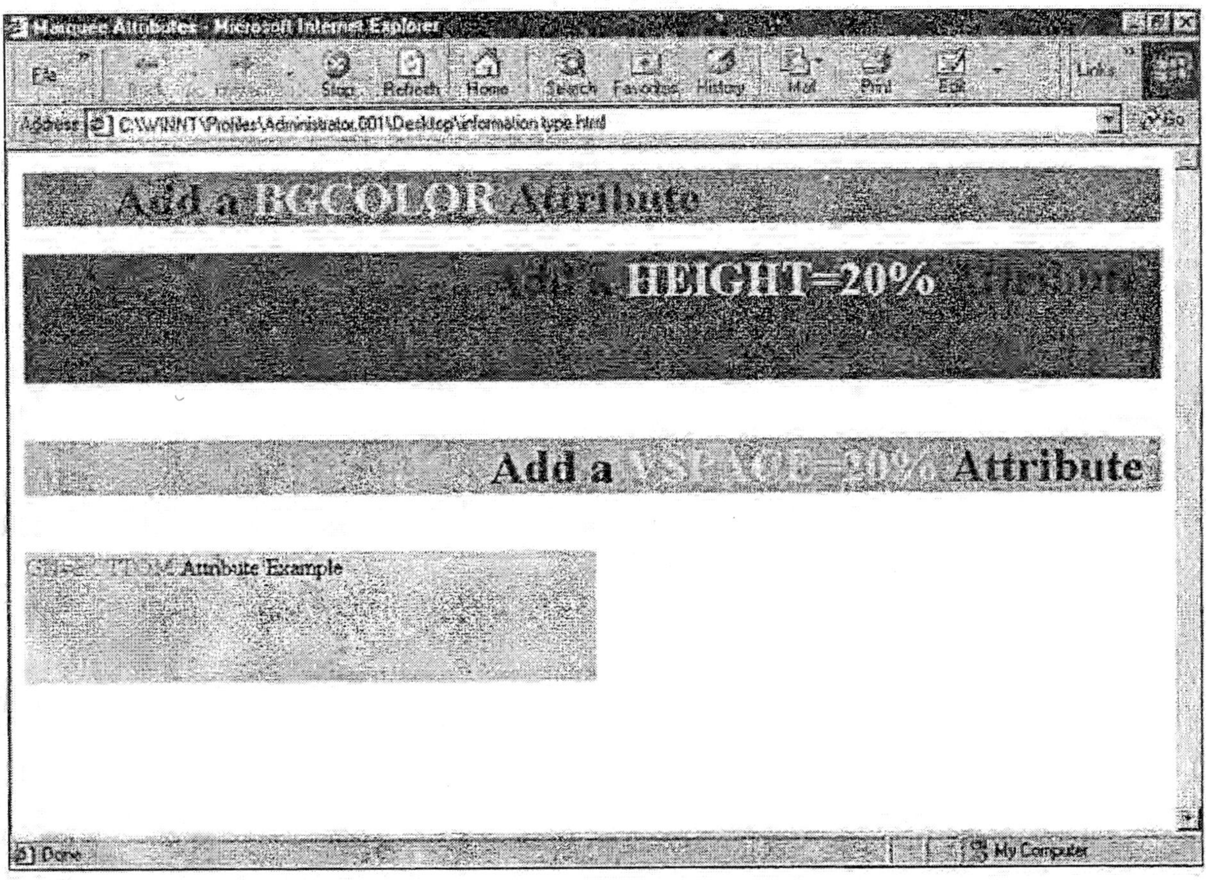

Figure 1.25: Marquee Attribute

 Test Your Knowledge

Students must solve the following assignment and submit to the faculty.

I Fill in the blanks:

1. Web clients are also known as __________.
2. A URL is composed of __________ parts.
3. HTML stands for ______________________________.
4. __________ is used to describe text that contains links to other text.
5. Internet Explorer is a ____________________.
6. The __________ tag is used to mark the beginning of a paragraph.
7. The two tags involved in creating select lists are __________ and __________.
8. The information mentioned in the __________ tag are used by search engines to index the web pages on their servers.
9. <IMAGE> tag __________ attribute is used to link an .avi file in a html page.
10. Blink tag works only in __________ browser.

II State whether True or False:

1. In HTML there are six levels of headings.
2. An image in a web page can't be aligned left or right.
3. A descriptive list starts with the tag <DT>.
4. The <PRE> tag keeps indentation of preformatted lines.
5. To play the background sound infinitely set the LOOP attribute of the <BGSOOUND> tag to –1.
6. Dynamic web pages are created in advance of the user's request.

Advanced HTML

Objectives

- Tables
- Frames
- Forms
- Imagemap
- Advanced HTML

Tables

Tables were officially introduced in HTML 3.2 by Netscape in early 1995 after which they suddenly revolutionized the way web pages were designed and data was represented not just because they could be used for presenting data in a tabular form but also because they gave a web page designer much better control over page layout and placement of various HTML elements on a page.

Basic Table Parts

Before introducing you with the HTML table elements used for creating a table, let's review the common terms frequently used while creating and what do they mean:

- **Caption:** indicates what the table is about
- **Table headings:** label the rows, columns or both. it is optional
- **Table cells:** are the individual squares in the table
- **Table data:** the values in the cells.

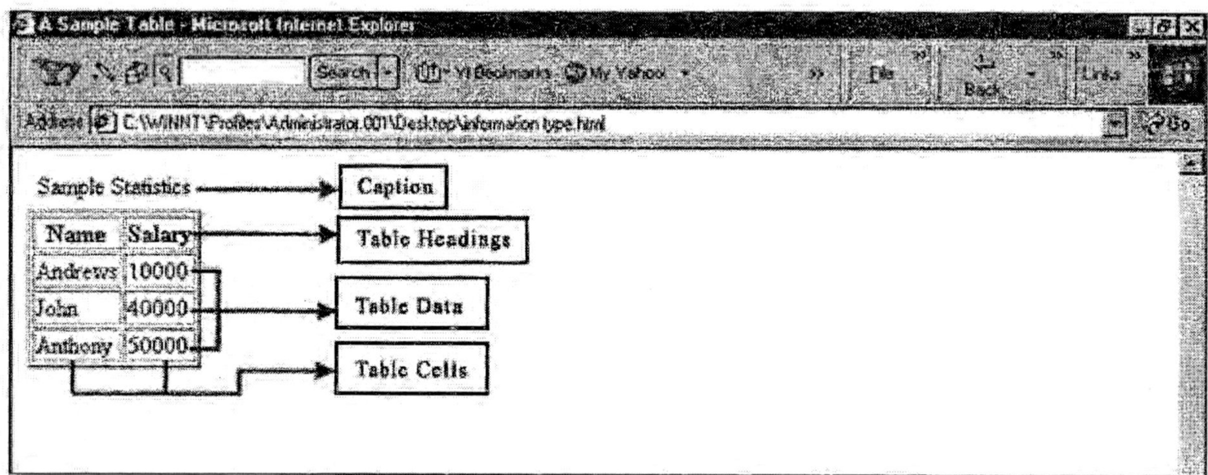

Figure 2.1: The parts of a Table

Now, the HTML tags used to represent the table elements are:

<TABLE> Tag

The <TABLE> tag is used to generate a row/cell matrix within the document. Cells may contain objects such as text, images, anchors and so on. All table-related tags occur between the <TABLE> and </TABLE> container tags. Any table related tags occurring outside of these tags will be ignored. A simple table structure is like:

```
<TABLE>
        <TR> <!- - table row — >
                <TD> Content <! - - table data — >
</TABLE>
```

The <TR> and </TR> tags are used for representing a row which contain the HTML tags that define individual cells. As many <TR> and </TR> tags as required can be placed inside the table.

Table cells can be represented in two ways: header cells for headers that appear over a column of data and data cells for the individual entries in the table.

A table header cell is defined with the <TH>and </TH> tag pair. The contents of the table header cells are automatically centered and appear in boldface.

The data within the cells is defined between <TD> and </TD> tag. Text in data cells is left justified by default. Any special formatting such as boldface or italic has to be done by including the appropriate formatting tags inside the <TD> and </TD> pairs.

To give a caption to the table, <CAPTION> </CAPTION> tag is used. It is an optional tag and is defined within the <TABLE> </TABLE > tag and above the <TR>and </TR> tag.

At present, the table HTML elements are:

<TABLE> ... </TABLE> - The Table delimiter.
<TR ...> ... </TR> - Used to specify number of rows in a table.
<TD ...> ... </TD> - Specifies table data cells.

<TH ...> ... </TH> - Table Header cell.
<CAPTION ...> ... </CAPTION> - Specifies the table Caption.

Internet Explorer has introduced support for various HTML 3.0 table elements. Those introduced are:

<THEAD> ... </THEAD> , <TBODY> ... </TBODY>, <TFOOT> ... </TFOOT>, <COLGROUP> ... </COLGROUP>, <COL> ... </COL> -

Also, some new attributes have been introduced. These are:

<TABLE BACKGROUND="...">, <TH BACKGROUND="...">, <TD BACKGROUND="...">, <TABLE FRAME="..."> <TABLE RULES="...">

Given below is the html code for the table represented in Figure 2.1.

```
<html>
	<head> <title>A Sample Table </title></head>
	<body>
		<table border="2">
			<caption>Sample Statistics</caption>
				<tr><th>Name</th><th>Salary</th></tr>
			<tr><td>Andrews</td><td>10000</td></tr>
			<tr><td>John</td><td>40000</td></tr>
			<tr><td>Anthony</td><td>50000</td>
			</tr>
		</table>
	</body>
</html>
```

Attributes of <TABLE> tag

- **BORDER:** This attribute defines the width of the border around the table in pixels. By default a table has no border defined.

- **ALIGN:** This attribute defines the alignment of the table and is deprecated in HTML 4.0. Possible values are left, right and center.

- **CELLSPACING:** This attribute defines the amount of space between the cells in the table.

- **CELLPADDING:** This attribute defines the amount of space between the edges of the cell and its contents.

- **WIDTH:** Specifies the width of the entire table in exact pixel value or percentage of the browser window width.

- **HEIGHT:** Specifies the height of the entire table in pixels or as a percentage of the browser window height.

- **BACKGROUND:** This attribute specifies a background image to be used as the backdrop for the table. All cell contents will be displayed over this image. If the referenced image is smaller than the table size, it will be tiled to fit all of the table area.

- **BGCOLOR:** Specifies the background color of all the table cells. This value can also be overridden at the cell level.

- **BORDERCOLOR:** This attribute sets the external border color to be used for the entire table. Display of this attribute is dependent on the presence of the BORDER attribute in the TABLE element. Internet Explorer version 2.0 and above supports this attribute. Netscape Navigator does not support this attribute.

- **BORDERCOLORDARK:** This attribute allows independent, 3-D color control over the lower and right hand borders of the external border color for the current table. To change the upper and left hand borders of the external cell border color for the current table use the BorderColorLight attribute (see below). Display of this attribute is dependent on the presence of the BORDER attribute in the TABLE element. Internet Explorer version 2.0 and above supports this attribute. Netscape Navigator does not support this attribute.

- **BORDERCOLORLIGHT:** This attribute allows independent, 3-D color control over the upper and left hand borders of the external border color for the current table. To change the lower and right hand borders of the external cell border color for the current table use the BorderColorDark attribute (see above.) Display of this attribute is dependent on the presence of the BORDER attribute in the TABLE element. Internet Explorer version 2.0 and above supports this attribute. Netscape Navigator does not support this attribute.

```
<html>
      <head>
            <center>Table using the <b>BORDERCOLORLIGHT</b> and
            <b>BORDERCOLORDARK</b>attributes</center><br><br><br>

      </head>
<!—Displayed only in Internet Explorer —>

<body>

<TABLE BORDER=2 BORDERCOLORDARK=Red BORDERCOLORLIGHT=Yellow align="center">

<TR>

<TD>Data cell</TD>
<TD>Data cell</TD>

</TR>

</TABLE></body>
</html>
```

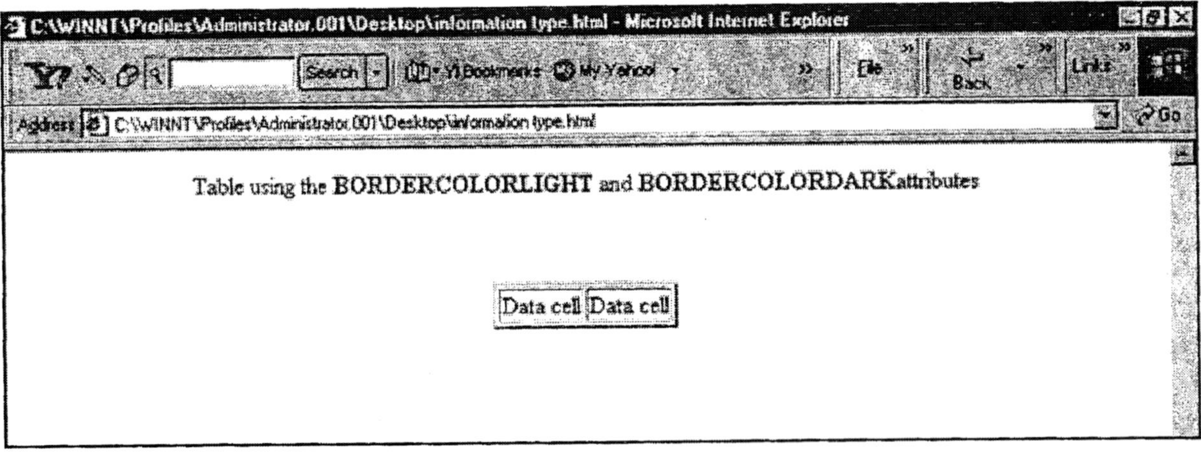

Figure 2.2: Bordercolor

- **SUMMARY:** This attribute provides a summary of the table's purpose and structure in non-visual browsers.
- **FRAME:** Only *Internet Explorer* supports the use of this attribute. It requires the BORDER attribute to be set and affects the display of the table borders. It can accept any of the following values:

- **Void:** This removes all the external borders.
- **Above:** This displays external borders at the top of the table only.
- **Below:** This displays external borders at the bottom of the table only.
- **Hsides**: This displays external borders at the horizontal sides of the table i.e., at the top and bottom of the table.
- **Lhs:** This displays external borders at the left hand edges of the table only.
- **Rhs:** This displays external borders at the right hand edges of the table only.
- **Vsides:** This displays external borders at both left and right hand edges of the table.
- **Box:** This displays a box around the table (i.e. top, bottom, left and right hand sides).

- **RULES:** Internet Explorer supports this new attribute. It requires the BORDER value to be set and may only be used in tables where the <THEAD>, <TBODY> and <TFOOT> sections have been set. It affects the display of the internal table borders ("rules"). It can accept the following values:
    - **None:** This removes all the internal rules.
    - **Basic:** This displays horizontal borders between the <THEAD>, <TBODY> and <TFOOT> sections.
    - **Rows:** This displays horizontal borders between all rows.
    - **Cols:** This displays horizontal borders between all columns.
    - **All:** This displays all the internal rules.

Attributes of < TR > tag

- **ALIGN:** This attribute indicates the horizontal alignment of the cells within a row overriding the default alignment of heading and table cells. The possible values are LEFT, RIGHT and CENTER.

- **VALIGN:** This attribute specifies the vertical alignment of the cells within a row overriding the default alignment of heading and table cells. The possible values are TOP, MIDDLE and BOTTOM.

- **BGCOLOR:** Microsoft Internet Explorer (version 2.0 and above) has also included use of the BGCOLOR attribute in the TR element. It allows the background colour of the row to be specified using either the specified color names or a rrggbb hex triplet.

- **BORDERCOLOR, BORDERCOLORDARK, BORDERCOLORLIGHT:** Same as stated in the TABLE element. But for border coloring to work it is necessary that the BORDER attribute is specified in the main <TABLE> element.

Attributes of <TD> tag

- **ALIGN:** This attribute specifies whether text inside the table cell(s) is aligned to the left side of the cell, the right side of the cell or centered within the cell. Values are left, right and center.

- **VALIGN:** The VALIGN attribute controls whether text inside the table cell(s) is aligned to the top of the cell, the bottom of the cell or vertically centered within the cell. It can also specify that all the cells in the row should be vertically aligned to the same baseline. Values are top, middle, bottom and baseline.

- **WIDTH:** This attribute is used to describe the desired width of the cell, either as an absolute width in pixels or a percentage of table width. Ordinarily complex heuristics are applied to tables and their cells to attempt to present a pleasing looking table. Setting the WIDTH attribute overrides those heuristics and instead effort is put into fitting the table into the desired width as specified.

- **HEIGHT:** This attribute describes the height of the cell either as a particular pixel value or as a percentage of the table width. As for the WIDTH attribute above setting this attribute will override the browsers internal display mechanism and it will render the table according to the values given.

- **NOWRAP:** If this attribute appears in any table cell (<TH> or <TD>) it means the lines within this cell cannot be broken to fit the width of the cell.

- **COLSPAN:** This attribute can be specified in a table cell (<TH> or <TD>) to specify how many columns of the table this cell should span. The default COLSPAN for any cell is 1.

- **ROWSPAN:** This attribute can appear in any table cell (<TH> or <TD>) and it specifies how many rows of the table this cell should span. The default ROWSPAN for any cell is 1. A span that extends into rows that were never specified with a <TR> will be truncated.

- **BORDERCOLORDARK, BORDERCOLORLIGHT, BORDERCOLOR, BGCOLOR:** These attributes behave in a similar manner as stated in the TABLE element. But for border colors to work it is necessary that the BORDER attribute is specified in the main <TABLE> element.

Attributes of <TH> tag

The Header cells are identical to data cells in all respects with the exception that header cells are in a bold FONT and have a default ALIGN=center.

The attributes are:

- <TH ALIGN=LEFT|RIGHT|CENTER|MIDDLE|BOTTOM>

- <TH NOWRAP>

- <TH COLSPAN=?>

- <TH ROWSPAN=?>

- <TH WIDTH=?> (in pixels) <TH WIDTH="%">

- <TH BGCOLOR="#$$$$$$">

Advanced Table Tags

We can group the table rows into three sections namely table head, table foot & table body. By doing this body of the table can be scrolled independently of the table. Additonally, if a table that contains row upon row of data is printed out in hard copy to your printer the head and foot of the table will repeat on the top and bottom of each page in the table printout. The table head, foot and body sections are defined by the <thead>, <tfoot> and <tbody> elements. Each of these elements must contain the same number of columns.

The <thead> ... </thead> element defines the head of the table which should give information about the columns in the body of the table. The <thead> element contains one or more rows used to define a table heading. The starting <thead> tag is always required when you want to include head section in your table but the closing </thead> tag is optional.

The <tfoot>..........</tfoot> element defines the foot of the table. The starting <tfoot> tag is always required when defining the foot of the table but the closing tag </tfoot> is optional. The foot of the table appears immediately after the head of the table (if one is present) or after the <table> element (if a table head is not present). It must contain atleast one row group defined by the <tr> element. <tfoot> must follow the <thead> tag and precede the <tbody> tag because the browser has to render the foot before it receives all the data in the table body.

The <tbody>.........</tbody> element defines one or more table bodies in your table. A table can contain more than one body and each body can contain one or more rows of data.

Example 1: Cell Alignment

```
<HTML>
	<HEAD><TITLE>Cell Alignments</TITLE></HEAD>
	<BODY>
		<TABLE border=1>
				<TBODY>
				<TR>
				<TH></TH>
				<TH>India</TH>
				<TH>England</TH>
				<TH>Australia</TH>
				</TR>
```

```
                    <TR>
                    <TH>Top</TH>
                    <TD align=left vAlign=top> sachin</TD>
                    <TD align=middle vAlign=top> alec  stewart</TD>
                    <TD align=right vAlign=top>border</TD>
                    </TR>

                    <TR>
                    <TH>Centered</TH>
                    <TD align=left vAlign=center> srinath</TD>
                    <TD align=middle vAlign=center>dominic cork</TD>
                    <TD align=right vAlign=center>Fleming</TD>
                    </TR>

                    <TR>
                    <TH>Bottom</TH>
                    <TD align=left vAlign=bottom>ganguly</TD>
                    <TD align=middle vAlign=bottom>atherton</TD>
                    <TD align=right vAlign=bottom>ponting</TD>
                    </TR>

               </TBODY>
          </TABLE>
     </BODY>
</HTML>
```

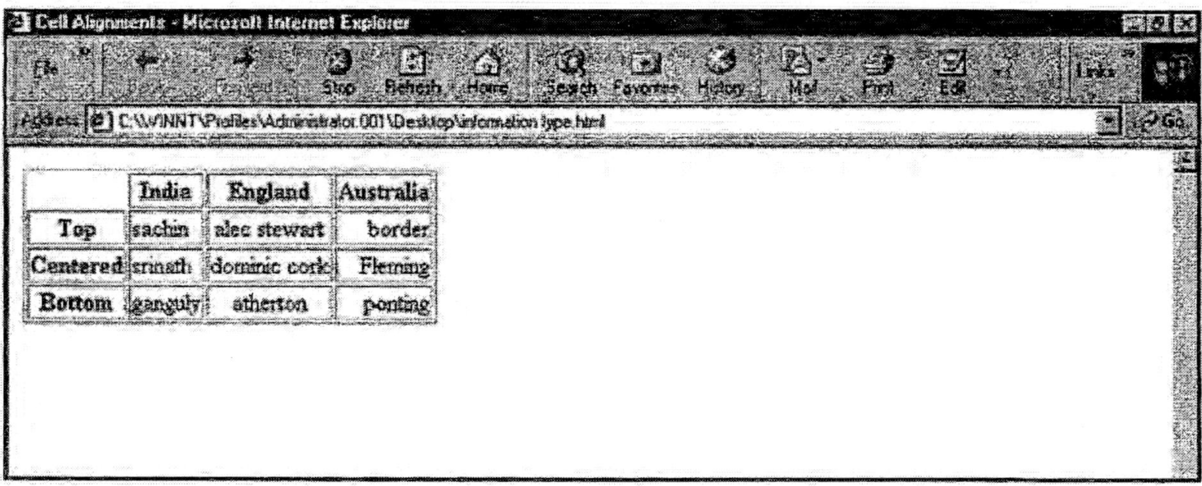

	India	England	Australia
Top	sachin	alec stewart	border
Centered	srinath	dominic cork	Fleming
Bottom	ganguly	atherton	ponting

Figure 2.3: Cell Alignment

Example 2: Row and Column Spans

```
<HTML>
     <HEAD><TITLE>Row and Column Spans</TITLE></HEAD>
     <BODY>
          <TABLE border=1>
               <TBODY>
                    <TR>
                         <TH colSpan=2 rowSpan=2></TH>
                              <TH colSpan=2>Month</TH>
                              </TR>
                         <TR>
                         <TH>Summer</TH>
                              <TH>Winter</TH>
                              </TR>
                         <TR>
                              <TH rowSpan=2>Vegetable</TH>
                              <TH>Tomato</TH>
                              <TD>July</TD>
                                   <TD>January</TD>
                                   </TR>
                         <TR>
                              <TH>Potato</TH>
                              <TD>June</TD>
                              <TD>December</TD>
                         <TR>
                    <TBODY>
               </TABLE>
          </BODY>
</HTML>
```

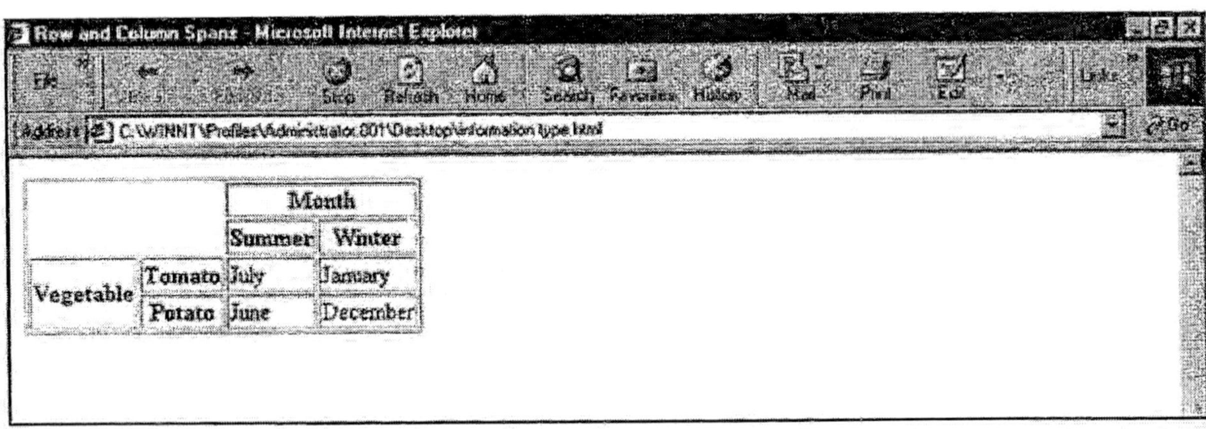

Figure 2.4: Row and Column Spans

Frames

Frames extend the layout flexibility of web pages by allowing the visible client area to be divided into more than one sub-region. Each frame has several properties:

- It can load a URL independently of the other frames.
- It can be given a NAME allowing it to be targeted by other URL's .
- It resizes itself dynamically in response to changes in the size of the visible client area and it can choose to allow or disallow itself to be manually resized by the user.

FRAME enabled web pages can be generated using two basic tags: FRAMESET tags and FRAME tags whereas the <NOFRAME> tag is used to specify a section of a document that will be used by browsers that cannot use frames.

☞ *Note: Netscape supports standard fixed frame documents, while the Internet Explorer also supports the use of floating frames.*

Frame Document

A Frame document has a basic structure very much like your normal HTML document. The BODY container is replaced by a FRAMESET container which describes the sub-HTML documents or Frames that will make up the page.

```
<HTML>
      <HEAD>........</HEAD>
            <FRAMESET>
                  ......................
            </FRAMESET>
</HTML>
```

FRAMESET Element

Frame syntax is similar in scope and complexity to that used by tables and has been designed to be quickly processed by browsers.

<FRAMESET> element is the main container for a Frame. By replacing the BODY element in the document structure the FRAMESET element defines the document layout in terms of areas of the screen containing sub-document URLs (the frame content). A standard frame document has no BODY and no tags that would normally be placed in the BODY can appear before the FRAMESET tag or the FRAMESET will be ignored (unless the frame is a floating frame, supported by Internet Explorer only). The FRAMESET tag has a matching end tag and within the FRAMESET you can *only* have other nested FRAMESET tags, FRAME tags or the NOFRAMES tag.

The attributes of FRAMESET tag are:

- **ROWS ="row_height_value_list":** The ROWS attribute takes its value as a comma separated list of values. These values can be absolute pixel values, percentage values between 1 and 100 or relative scaling values. The number of rows is implicit in the number of elements in the list. Since the total height of all the rows must equal the height of the window row heights might be normalised to achieve this. A missing ROWS attribute is interpreted as a single row arbitrarily sized to fit.

  Syntax of value list are:

  - **value:** A simple numeric value is assumed to be a fixed size in pixels. This is the most dangerous type of value to use since the size of the viewer's window can and does vary substantially. If fixed pixel values are used it will almost certainly be necessary to mix them with one or more of the relative size values described below. Otherwise the client engine will override your specified pixel value to ensure that the total proportions of the frame are 100% of the width and height of the user's window.

  - **value%:** This is a simple percentage value between 1 and 100. If the total is greater than 100 all percentages are scaled down. If the total is less than 100 and relative-sized frames exist extra space will be given to them. If there are no relative-sized frames all percentages will be scaled up to match a total of 100%.

  - **value*:** The value on this field is optional. A single '*' character is a "relative-sized" frame and is interpreted as a request to give the frame all remaining space. If there exist multiple relative-sized frames the remaining space is divided evenly among them. If there is a value in front of the '*', that frame gets that much more relative space. "2*,*" would give 2/3 of the space to the first frame and 1/3 to the second.

Example for 3 rows, the first and the last being smaller than the center row:

<FRAMESET ROWS="20%,60%,20%">

Example for 3 rows, the first and the last being fixed height, with the remaining space assigned to the middle row:

<FRAMESET ROWS="100,*,100">

- **COLS="column_width_list":** The COLS attribute takes as its value a comma separated list of values that has exact syntax as the list described above for the ROWS attribute.

☞ *Note: The FRAMESET tag can be nested inside other FRAMESET tags. In this case the complete subframe is placed in the space that would be used for the corresponding frame if this had been a FRAME tag instead of a nested FRAMESET.*

- **BORDER:** Netscape allows the global setting of frame border thicknesses by using this attribute within the <FRAMESET> element. It accepts a pixel value which determines the thickness of any borders used within the frame set.

- **BORDERCOLOR:** This Netscape specific attribute sets the color for the border of the specified frameset. It can also be used in the <FRAME> element (see below) for setting the border colours of a specific frame. It accepts any #rrggbb hex triplet as a value. Any BORDERCOLOR setting in a <FRAMESET> element is over-ridden by a setting present in the <FRAME> element.

- **FRAMEBORDER:** Netscape allows the use of this attribute (in a similar fashion to that supported by Internet Explorer in the <FRAME> element) to set the borders globally for an entire <FRAMESET>. Values can be either "yes" or "no".

- **FRAMESPACING:** This attribute gives the author the option of whether or not to have borders around all the frames in the FRAMESET. This value can be overridden locally at the FRAME level. It is specified as positive integers representing the pixel space between frames.

The FRAME Tag

This tag defines a single frame in a frameset. It has 6 possible attributes: SRC, NAME, MARGINWIDTH, MARGINHEIGHT, SCROLLING and NORESIZE. The FRAME tag is not a container tag so it has no matching end tag.

- **SRC="url":** The SRC attribute takes as its value the URL of the document to be displayed in this particular frame. FRAMEs without SRC attributes are displayed as a blank space the size the frame would have been.

- **NAME="window_name":** The NAME attribute is used to assign a name to a frame so it can be targeted by links in other documents (These are usually from other frames in the same document). The NAME attribute is optional by default all windows are unnamed.

Names must begin with an alphanumeric character. However, several reserved names have been defined which start with an underscore. These are:

- **_blank:** Always load this link into a new, unnamed window.
- **_self:** Always load this link over yourself.
- **_parent:** Always load this link over your parent (becomes self if you have no parent).
- **_top:** Always load this link at the top level (becomes self if you are at the top).

☞ *Note: Although these are reserved names for the NAME attribute of the <FRAME> element, they should only be referred for using as an Anchor Target. That is, used to target specific windows allowing smoother transition between framed documents and between framed & normal documents.*

- **MARGINWIDTH="value":** The MARGINWIDTH attribute is used when the document author wants some control of the margins for this frame. If specified the value for MARGINWIDTH is in pixels. Margins cannot be less than one so that frame objects will not touch frame edges and cannot be specified resulting in no space for the document contents. The MARGINWIDTH attribute is optional by default. All frames by default let the browser decide on an appropriate margin width.

- **MARGINHEIGHT="value":** The MARGINHEIGHT attribute is just like MARGINWIDTH except it controls the upper and lower margins instead of the left and right margins.

- **SCROLLING="yes|no|auto":** The SCROLLING attribute is used to describe if the frame should have a scrollbar or not. **'Yes'** results in scrollbars always being visible on that frame. **'No'** results in scrollbars never being visible. Auto instructs the browser to decide whether scrollbars are needed and place them where necessary. The SCROLLING attribute is optional and the default value is auto.

- **NORESIZE:** The NORESIZE attribute has no value. It is a flag that indicates that the frame is not resizable by the user. Users typically resize frames by dragging a frame edge to a new position. Note that if any frame adjacent to an edge is not resizable, that entire edge will be restricted from moving. This will effect the resizability of other frames. The NORESIZE attribute is optional and by default all frames are resizable.

- **FRAMEBORDER:** This attribute allows control of the frame border display. With this attribute set to "0" (Internet Explorer) the borders for the specific frame are not drawn. Netscape now also supports use of this attribute (using values of "yes|no") and also supports it in the <FRAMESET> element (see above) for globally setting the borders of a whole frame set.

☞ *Note: In Netscape, frames share borders and for the borders not to be drawn all the frames sharing a common border must have their FRAMEBORDER attribute set to "no".*

- **FRAMESPACING="value":** This attribute is also Internet Explorer specific and allows the setting of extra space around frames to give the appearance of floating frames. The "value" should be the distance required around the frame in pixels.

i.e. <FRAME FRAMESPACING="55" ...>

would present the frame with a spacing of 55 pixels.

- **BORDERCOLOR:** This Netscape specific attribute sets the colors for the border of the specified frame. It can also be used in the <FRAMESET> element (see above) for globally setting the border colors of a whole frameset. It accepts any #rrggbb hex triplet as a value. Setting the BORDERCOLOR attribute in the <FRAME> element over-rides any setting given in the <FRAMESET> element of which the <FRAME> is a part.

Example: Using standard Frame Target values

```
<! - - Save the file as Mainframe.html - - >

<html>
      <frameset cols="25%,*">
      <frame src="f:/html/examples/frame1.html" name="toc" scrolling="no">
      <frame name="content" scrolling="no">
      </frameset>
</html>

<! _ _ Save the file as frame1.html - - >

<html>
      <body>
      <a href="f:/html/example/frame2.html/" target="content"> Target=named frame <br>
      <a href="f:/html/example/frame2.html/" target="_blank"> Target=_blank<br>
      <a href="f:/html/example/frame2.html/" target="__self"> Target=_self<br>
      <a href="f:/html/example/frame2.html/" target="_parent"> Target=_parent<br>
      <a href="f:/html/example/frame2.html/" target="_top">Target=_top<br>
      </body>
</html>

<! _ _ Save the file as frame2.html - - >

<html>
<body>
An example for NAME and TARGET attribute
</body>
</html>
```

The NOFRAMES tag

This tag is for the users who want to create alternative content that is viewable by non-Frame capable clients. A Frame capable Internet client ignores all tags and data between start and end NOFRAMES tags.

Floating Frames

The Internet Explorer (version 3 and above) has introduced the concept of floating frames. These are much like standard frames except they can be anywhere within a standard HTML document. The idea of the floating frame is to create an inline framed region or window that acts similarly to any other embedded object and text can be flowed around it. An inline floating frame is defined within <IFRAME> ... </IFRAME> elements and may occur anywhere within the <BODY> of HTML document. Any HTML between the start and end elements will be displayed by browsers that do not support floating frames while the frame specified in the <IFRAME> elements will be displayed by those browsers that support floating Frames.

Example:

```
<IFRAME NAME="content_displayframe" width="488" height="244" SRC="welcome.html">This
site uses floating frames</IFRAME>
```

The above HTML fragment would display the file "content_displayframe" in Internet Explorer but would display the text also.

The other main difference between floating and normal frames is that floating frames accept WIDTH and HEIGHT and standard <IMG> tag HSPACE, VSPACE and ALIGN attributes to set the display size and alignment of the frame within the document. They can have other files loaded into them exactly as normal frames (by use of the TARGET attribute in the link and the NAME attribute of the frame).

Attributes of <IFRAME> tag:

- **ALIGN [LEFT I RIGHT]:** Floats the floating frame in the left or right margin.
- **FRAMEBORDER [1 I 0]:** Controls the presence of the beveled border around the floating frame.
- **HEIGHT [pixels I percent]:** Specifies the height of the floating frame.
- **LONGDESC = "URL":** Provides the URL of a document that gives a more detailed description of what's in the floating frame. It is useful for non-visual browsers.
- **NAME = "frame_name":** Gives the floating frame a unique name so it can be targeted by hyperlinks .
- **SCROLLING [YES I NO I AUTO]:** Controls the presence of scrollbars on the floating frame.
- **SRC = "url":** Specifies the URL of the document to load into the floating frame.
- **WIDTH [pixels I percent]:** Specifies the width of the floating frame.

Example: Simple Floating Frame

```
<!—Save the file as floatingframe.html  - - >

<html>
        <head>
              <title> Floating Frame Example </title>
        </head>
        <body>

        <h2 align=center> Floating Frame Example</h2>

        <IFRAME NAME="float1" SRC="first.html" width="150" height="150"  align="left"
        frameborder=1 scrolling="yes">

There would be a floating frame here if your browser supported it.
```

```
        </IFRAME>

        <p>
              This is a simple example of how floating frames are used. They act like an
              embedded object on an html page.
        </p>
    </body>
</html>

<!—Save the file as first.html  - - >

<html>
    <head>
        <center><h2><b> welcome <b></h2></center>
    </head>

    <body bgcolor="yellow">
        <font color="blue size="3" face="verdana">
        Hello!!!!!!!!
        </font>
    </body>
</html>
```

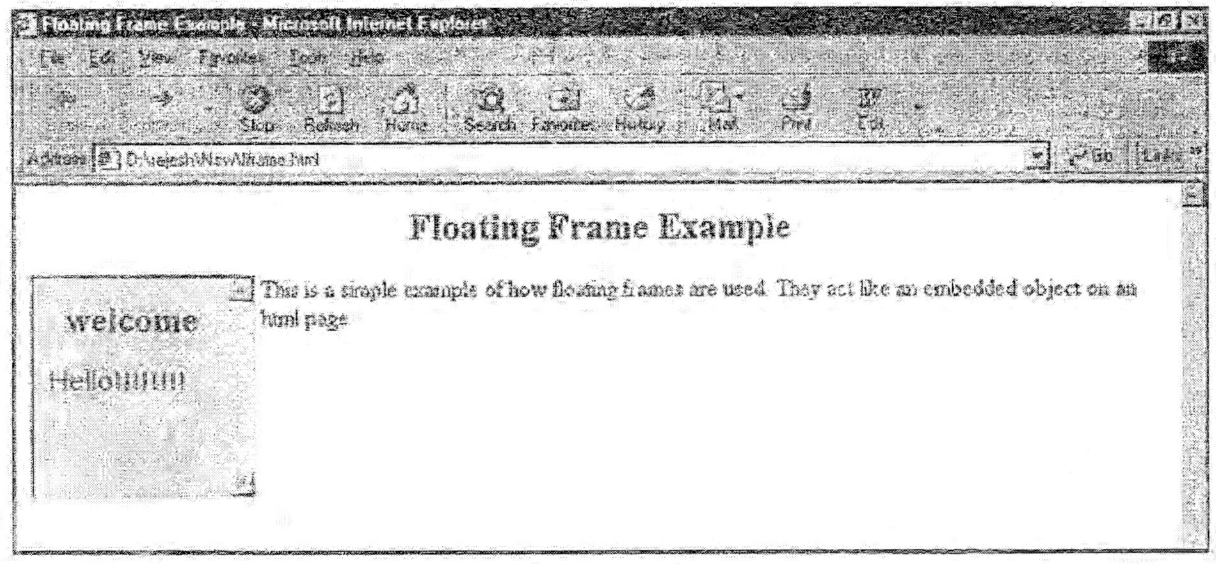

Figure 2.5: Simple Floating Frame

Forms

A form is part of a web page created using HTML element. Each form is made of form elements and controls which provide the most basic means of interactivity on the Web. Fill out forms are handled by various server side tools like Common Gateway Interface (CGI), Active Server Pages (ASP), Cold Fusion, Java Server Pages (JSP) etc. which executes on various Web Servers such as Internet Information Server, Apache Server, Java Web Server, Netscape Enterprise Server.

The most relevant use of forms on the Web are registration forms, subscription forms, order entry form, feedback form, survey form, etc.

Forms and Backend Server Side Communications

Forms and Server Side tools (e.g., Common Gateway Interface) can be considered to be the opposite sides of the same coin. Forms are visible on the front end portion of interactive pages whereas various server side technologies are employed to forward the form data to the back end server for processing and delivering the processed data back to the client browser. The table given below shows few of the client side and server side technologies which can be deployed to add interactivity to a form at the front end and also with the back end servers.

Client Side	Server Side
Helpers	CGI Programs
Plug-ins	NSAPI/ISAPI Programs
Active-X controls	Server-side scripting
Java Applets	Server-side Includes
Scripting Languages	Active Server Pages
JavaScript	Server-side JavaScript (LiveWire)
VBScipt	Database middleware
Dynamic HTML	Cold Fusion

Table 2.1: Web Programming Technology Choices

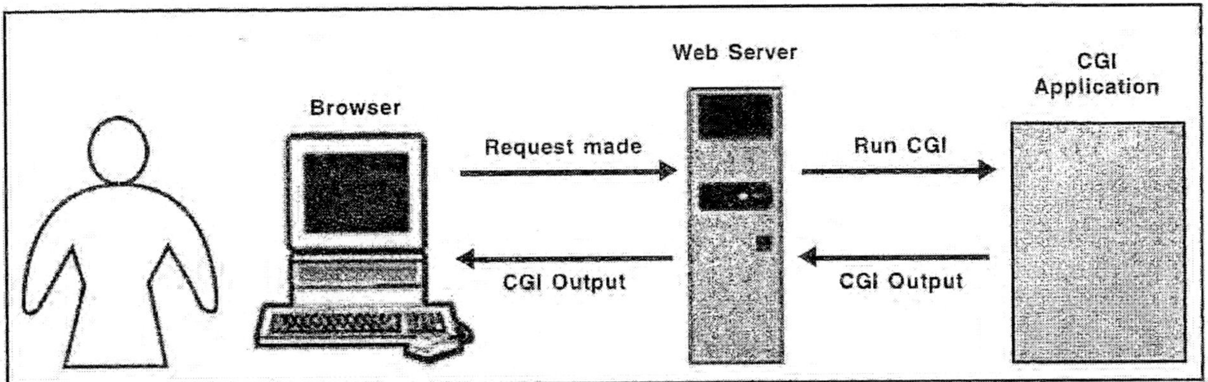

Figure 2.6: Form and Backend Server Interaction

How CGI interacts with a form is summarized by the following steps:

1. The user submits a form.
2. The form is sent to the server and eventually to the CGI program.
3. The CGI program processes the data and responds back to the server.
4. The web server passes the CGI response back to the client.

The Form Element <FORM>......................</FORM>

The Form element is used to delimit a data input form. There can be several forms in a single document but the Form element *cannot* be nested. To make the form functional as stated earlier three things need to be specified:

- The address of the program that will handle the form contents (ACTION).
- The method in which the form data will be passed (METHOD).
- How the form data will be encoded (ENCTYPE).

ACTION Attribute

The ACTION attribute is a URL specifying the location to which the contents of the form are submitted to process a response typically this will be a form handling server side script (e.g., CGI script. ASP, JSP). If the ACTION attribute is missing, the URL of the document itself is assumed. The way data is submitted varies with the access protocol of the URL and with the values of the METHOD and ENCTYPE attributes.

Example:

```
<FORM ACTION ="http://www.itl.com/cgi-bin/post query " METHOD="POST">
```

It is also possible to use a relative URL for the ACTION attribute if the form is delivered by the same server that houses the form handling program.

Example:

```
<FORM ACTION ="../cgi-bin/post query" METHOD="POST">
```

Now, if you do not want to process the user query while exploring your site but instead want him to mail to you and later give the reply e.g., some technical support form or feedback form etc. In such instances you can specify your mail address in the ACTION attribute using *mailto.*

Example:

```
<FORM ACTION="mailto:eacademy@mantraonline.com ?subject=enquiry" METHOD="POST">
```

METHOD Attribute

Now after specifying the URL to process the form the next question arises is how to submit the form to the address specified in the ACTION attribute. METHOD attribute of the form element handles this using two predefined methods GET and POST. The default method if not specified is GET.

GET Method

GET method appends the form data to the end of the URL of the processing script specified in the method attribute itself.It is generally the default method for browsers to submit information. The Get method isn't very secure since the data input appears in the URL. Furthermore, there is a limitation to just how much data can be passed with the GET method. It would be impossible to append a 10,000 word essay to the end of a URL as most browser limit a URL to several thousand characters.

GET is easy to work with even after all these problems. As it comes in the form of an URL it can be set as a link or bookmarked.

POST Method

POST on the other hand sends the form data as a separate section following the HTTP header. This separate section is called the entity body. In situations where a large amount of information must be passed back, the POST method is preferred. The POST method transmits all form input information immediately after the requested URL. In other words, once the server has received the request from a form using POST it knows to continue "listening" for the rest of the information.

ENCTYPE Attribute

The ENCTYPE attribute specifies the format of the submitted data in case the protocol does not impose a format itself.

When data is passed from a Web Server, it is typically encoded just like an URL. In this encoding, spaces are replaced by the "+" symbol and non-alphanumeric characters are placed by *"%nn"* where *nn* is the hexadecimal ASCII code for the character.

The two used encoding types are *multipart/form-data* and *text/plain*. When using a mailto URL in the ACTION attribute, the encoding type text/plain is more desirable.

Other Attributes of FORM element are:

- **NAME:** This attribute is used to give a unique label to a form so that it can be referenced and manipulated with scripting code.

- **ACCEPT:** This attribute specifies the MIME types that the form processing server and script should correctly handle. A browser may use this information to filter out non-conforming files when prompting a user to select files to upload.

- **ACCEPT-CHARSET:** Provides a list of character sets that are acceptable to the server.

- **TARGET:** This attribute specifies the frame names for the browser to display the form results after the user submits information to a processing script. The special frame target values like *_blank, _parent, _self and _top* are applicable. If the value is not specified the form loads over itself.

FORM Controls

A form is made up of fields or controls as well as the markup necessary to structure the form and control its presentation. Form controls include text fields, pull-down menus, scrolled lists, radio buttons, checkboxes, buttons, images etc.

Given below are some basic form controls:

INPUT Element

The input element is a basic form element used to create form controls for user input. The two main attributes of this is TYPE and NAME.

Attributes of the Input element:

- **TYPE:** Defines the type of data the field accepts. Defaults to free text. Several types of fields can be defined with the type attribute:

  - **TEXT:** Text is used for single line text entry fields. Use in conjunction with the SIZE and MAXLENGTH attributes.

  - **CHECKBOX:** Used for simple Boolean attributes or for attributes that can take multiple values at the same time. The latter is represented by a number of checkbox fields each of which have the same name. Each selected checkbox generates a separate name/value pair in the submitted data even if this results in duplicate names. The default value for checkboxes is "on".

- **HIDDEN:** No field is presented to the user but the content of the field is sent with the submitted form. This value may be used to transmit state information about client/server interaction.

- **IMAGE:** Creates a graphical version of the submit button which not only submits the forms but transmits co-ordinate information about where the user clicked in the image. The image is specified by SRC attribute. The example use of this attribute could be to insert a map of India allowing users to click on the regional office where they want to submit their forms.

  ```
  <INPUT TYPE=Image  SRC=India.gif"
  Name="IGNOU" ALT="MBA Forms submission Areas"
  ```

  When clicked the form values would be submitted alongwith two extra values IGNOU.x and IGNOU.y which would be set equal to the x & y co-ordinates of where the image was clicked.

- **PASSWORD:** Password is the same as the TEXT attribute except that text is not displayed as it is entered.

- **RADIO:** Radio is used for attributes that accept a single value from a set of alternatives. Each radio button field in the group should be given the same name. Only the selected radio button in the group generates a name/value pair in the submitted data. Radio buttons require an explicit VALUE attribute.

- **RESET:** Rest is a button that when pressed resets the form's fields to their specified initial values. The label to be displayed on the button may be specified just as for the SUBMIT button.

- **SUBMIT:** Submit is a button that when pressed submits the form. You can use the VALUE attribute to provide a non-editable label to be displayed on the button. The default label is application-specific. If a SUBMIT button is pressed in order to submit the form, and that button has a NAME attribute specified then that button contributes a name/value pair to the submitted data. Otherwise, a SUBMIT button makes no contribution to the submitted data.

- **FILE:** Netscape now supports a FILE option to the TYPE attribute of the INPUT element allowing an ACCEPT attribute for the INPUT element (which is a list of media types or type patterns allowed for the input) and allowing the ENCTYPE of a form to be "multipart/form-data". This allows the inclusion of files with form information which could prove invaluable for example companies providing technical support or service providers requesting data files.

- **VALUE:** Attribute specifies the initial vale of the control. It is optional except when the control type is "radio". This attribute can be used to determine the label of a submit or a reset button, like VALUE="Submit Form" for a submit or VALUE="Clear Form" for a reset.

- **MAXLENGTH:** Indicates the maximum number of characters that can be entered into a text field. This can be greater than specified by the SIZE attribute in which case the field will scroll appropriately. The default number of characters is unlimited.

- **NAME:** Symbolic name used when transferring the form's contents. The NAME attribute is required for most input types and is normally used to provide a unique identifier for a field or for a logically related group of fields.

- **SIZE:** Specifies the size or precision of the field according to its type. For example, to specify a field with a visible width of 24 characters.

  Example:

  ```
  INPUT TYPE=text SIZE="24"
  ```

- **SRC:** A URL specifying an image. For use only with TYPE=IMAGE in HTML Level 2.

- **ALIGN:** Vertical alignment of the image. For use only with TYPE=IMAGE in HTML level 2. The possible values are exactly the same as for the ALIGN attribute of the image element.

- **CHECKED:** Indicates that a checkbox or radio button is selected. Unselected checkboxes and radio buttons do not return name/value pairs when the form is submitted.

The SELECT and OPTION Elements

The SELECT element is used to create a list of choices either as a drop down menu or a list box. Each of the choices in the list is an OPTION element. There are two tags involved in creating select lists, the <SELECT> tag and the <OPTION> tag. The <SELECT> tag offsets the list and has three possible attributes.

- **MULTIPLE:** The MULTIPLE attribute is needed when users are allowed to make several selections, e.g. <SELECT MULTIPLE>.

- **NAME:** Specifies the name that will be submitted as a name/value pair.

- **SIZE:** Specifies the number of visible items. If this is greater than one then the resulting form control will be a list.

By default, the SELECT element displays a drop down menu in which only the first element is displayed. The SIZE attribute is used to make more options visible on the form.

The Option element can only occur within a Select element. The <OPTION> tag is used to list the possible attributes. The two possible attributes are:

- **SELECTED:** Indicates that this option is initially selected.

- **VALUE:** When present indicates the value to be returned if this option is chosen. The value is paired with the "name" attribute of the SELECT element. If this attribute is not set, the submitted value defaults to the contents of the Option element.

The contents of the Option element is presented to the user to represent the option. If no option is initially marked as selected then the first item listed is selected.

Example:

```
<SELECT NAME="flavor">
      <OPTION>Vanilla
      <OPTION>Strawberry
      <OPTION>Rum and Raisin
      <OPTION>Peach and Orange
</SELECT>
```

The TEXTAREA Element

The TEXTAREA element is similar to the INPUT element's text type. The difference is that instead of a single line textbox a multi-line text input control is created. The attributes are: name, rows, cols, disabled, readonly.

- **NAME:** This attribute assigns a name to the element. This name is paired with the content of the element when submitted to the server.
- **ROWS:** Specifies the number of visible text lines.
- **COLS:** Specifies the visible width in average character widths.
- **DISABLED:** To disable the control on the form.
- **READONLY:** Does not allow modification of the text displayed in the textarea control.

Syntax:

```
<TEXTAREA name ="control name" rows = "numRows" cols = "numCols" disabled readonly>
</TEXTAREA>
```

Example:

```
<TEXTAREA NAME="address" ROWS=64 COLS=6 readonly>
      HaL Computer Systems
      1315 Dell Avenue
      Campbell, California 95008
</TEXTAREA>
```

The text up to the end element (</TEXTAREA>) is used to initialize the field's value. This end element is always required even if the field is initially blank.

In a typical rendering the ROWS and COLS attributes determine the *visible* dimension of the field in characters. The field is rendered in a fixed-width font. HTML user agents should allow text to extend beyond these limits by scrolling as needed.

In the initial design for forms, multi-line text fields were supported by the Input element with TYPE=TEXT. Unfortunately, this causes problems for fields with long text values. SGML's default (Reference Quantity Set) limits the length of attribute literals to only 240 characters. The HTML 2.0 SGML declaration increases the limit to 1024 characters.

Recent versions of the Netscape Navigator (from version 2.0) have introduced the WRAP attribute in the TEXTAREA element. Now it is possible to specify how to handle word-wrapping in text input areas in forms.

- **<TEXTAREA WRAP=OFF>:** The default setting - Wrapping doesn't happen. Lines are sent exactly as typed.
- **<TEXTAREA WRAP=VIRTUAL>:** The display word-wraps but long lines are sent as one line without new-lines.
- **<TEXTAREA WRAP=PHYSICAL>:** The display word-wraps and the text is transmitted at all wrap points.

☞ *Note: Word wrapping in a TEXTAREA text box is Netscape specific.*

Example:

```
<html>
      <head><title>Comments about my site</title>
      </head>
            <H3> I value your comments</H3>
            <FORM METHOD="POST" ACTION="mailto:abcdr@yahoo.com">
            <B>Please enter your name: </B><INPUT NAME="name1" size="50"> <BR>
            <B>and your e-mail address: </B><INPUT Name="mail1" size="50">
            <p>
            <CENTER>
```

```
            <B>How do you like my website?</B>
            <P>
            <INPUT TYPE="radio" NAME=name2VALUE="good">Good
            <INPUT TYPE="radio" NAME=name2 VALUE="fine">Fine
            <INPUT TYPE="radio" NAME=name2 VALUE="too heavy">Too Heavy
        </CENTER>
            <H3> Any suggestions you'd like to add</H3>
        <CENTER>
            <TEXTAREA NAME="comment" ROWS=4 COLS=70></TEXTAREA>
            <P>
            <B>Thanks for your comments</B>
            <BR>
            <INPUT TYPE=submit VALUE="submit">
            <INPUT TYPE=reset VALUE="reset">
        </CENTER>
    </FORM>
</html>
```

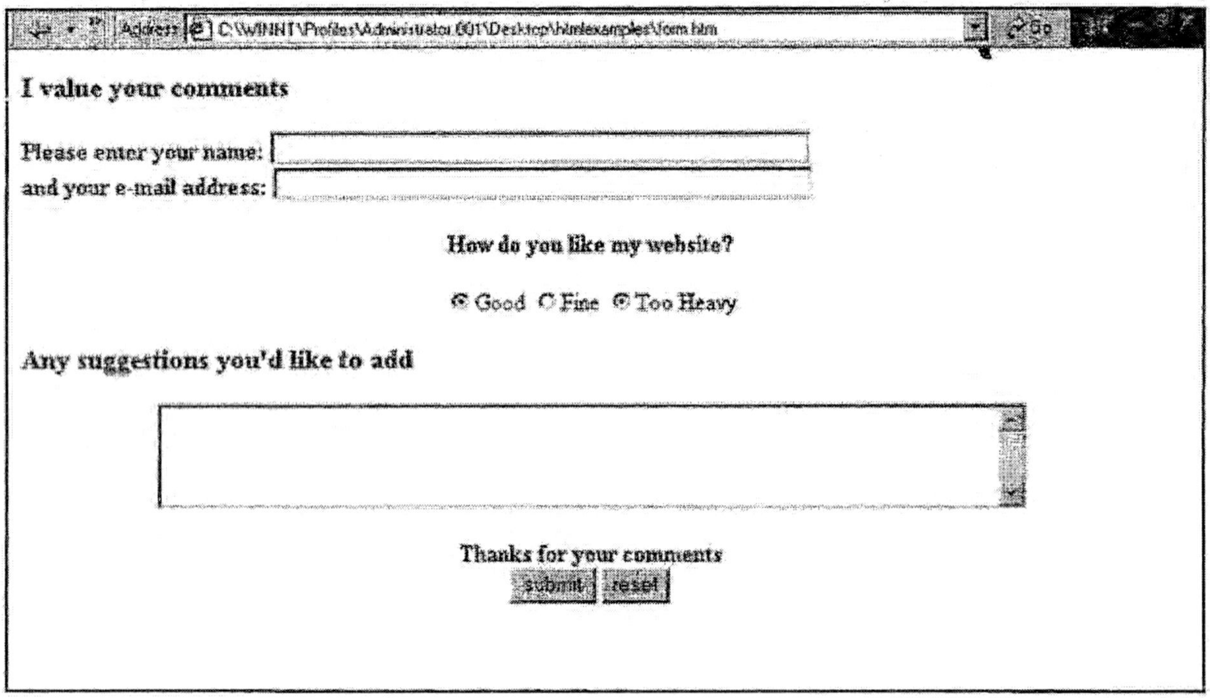

Figure 2.7: Email Form

Some New FORM Elements

The following section discusses some of the new form elements introduced in HTML 4.0.

BUTTON Element

The BUTTON element in an earlier version of HTML was limited to two options- sending or clearing the form. With HTML 4.0, a new option has been added to use the button to trigger the script and also you can include most inline and block level html elements. The basic attributes of BUTTON element are:

- **Name:** Assigns a name to the control
- **Value:** Assigns a value to the button
- **Type:** Declares the type of the button. The three possible values are:
    - **Submit:** Creates a button to submit the form to be processed by the URL specified in the ACTION attribute. This is the default value.
    - **Reset:** Creates a button that resets the form that contains it.
    - **Button:** Creates a simple push button intended to trigger a script.

You can also include images that are displayed as your button. Just enter the <img> element within the contents of the button.

Example:

```
<Button name="mysubmitbutton" type="submit"> <b> Submit</b> Form</button> <br><br>
<Button name="myresetbutton" type="Clear"><u> <b> Clear </b></u> Form Contents </button>
<Button name="mycustbutton" type="button"> <b> Verify</b> Form</button>
<Button name="mysubmitbutton" type="submit"><img src="submit.gif" width="50" height="10"
</button>
```

LABEL Element

The Label element is new to HTML 4. As the name implies it's the text that labels a control. Unlike normal text however the label and its associated control both share the same focus. In other words, if you click on or tab to the label it has the same effect as if you had clicked on the control itself. It's attribute is **For**.

- **For:** This attribute explicitly associates the label being defined with another control. The value of this attribute must be the value of the id attribute of some other control in the same document. In the absence of this attribute, the label being defined is associated with its contents.

The LABEL element may be used to attach information to control elements. Each LABEL element is associated with exactly one form control. Labels are associated with controls in one of two ways either implicitly or explicitly. Explicit attachment is accomplished through the use of a form field ID as the value of the FOR attribute. This method allows attachment of a LABEL to a field elsewhere in the document and has the advantage of allowing multiple labels to be attached to a single form field.

Example:

```
<LABEL FOR="Checkme"> Please, just say No Thank You </LABEL>

<INPUT TYPE="checkbox" name="nobox" id=" Checkme">
```

Form fields are attached implicitly to a LABEL when they are in the contents of the LABEL element. In this case, the LABEL must only contain one form field within the label elements.

Example:

```
<LABEL>Select Your toppings:
      <SELECT name ="flavors" multiple>
      <OPTION> Butterscotch  </OPTION>
      <OPTION> vanilla  </OPTION>
      <OPTION> Choclate  </OPTION>
</SELECT>
</LABEL>
```

☞ *Note: Label element is not supported by Netscape Navigator 4.0 .*

FIELDSET and LEGENDS

The FIELDSET and LEGEND elements are new to HTML 4.0. FIELDSET creates boxes around grouped controls just as panels do in standard programming and LEGENDs are labels that refer to the overall field set. Use of the LEGEND element is optional within a FIELDSET and if used must immediately follow the opening FIELDSET tag.

Syntax:

```
<FIELDSET>................</FIELDSET>
<LEGEND>   Legend Text </LEGEND>
```

Example:

```
<FIELDSET>
    <LEGEND><h2> Build Your Pizza </h2></LEGEND>
        <LABEL><h3> Select your toppings: </h3>
            <SELECT name="toppings" multiple>
                <OPTION> Cheese </OPTION>
                <OPTION> Pepperoni </OPTION>
                <OPTION> Mushroom </OPTION>
                <OPTION> Smoked clams </OPTION>
            </SELECT>
        </LABEL>
    <LABEL><h3> Pick a crust: </h3>
        <INPUT type="radio" name="crust" value="hand tossed">Hand Tossed <br>
        <INPUT type="radio" name="crust" value="whole wheat">Whole Wheat <br>
    </LABEL>
</FIELDSET>
```

There is no provision in the HTML 4 specification for controlling the size of the field sets. They stretch across the entire screen regardless of the space taken up by the controls they contain.

☞ *Note: Netscape Navigator 4.0 does not support <FIELDSET> and <LEGEND>.*

New attributes in HTML 4.0

The following section discusses some of the new attributes added in HTML 4.0.

TABINDEX

Using the keyboard to navigate some computer applications makes filling out forms much easier. Tabbed navigation enables users to press the Tab Key to move from one form control to the next. This attribute allows the tab order between fields to be defined. By default the browser supports tabbing in the sequence the controls are added on the form, but setting the tabindex attribute defines tabbing in ascending order i.e., 0,1,2, ... and so on. Controls with negative tabindex value are left out of the tabbing order. So in the example given below, the last field gets selected first then the first and the second field is completely skipped over.

Example:

```
<input type ="text" name = "first name" tabindex = "2">
<input type ="text" name = "middle name" tabindex = "-1">
<input type ="text" name = "last name" tabindex = "1">
```

ACCESSKEY

Access keys are used to make navigation in the form easier using keyboard shortcuts. They assign a character to an element that moves the focus to the control when user presses a key or combination of keys.

For example to add an accesskey to a text box:

```
<input type="text" name="username" accesskey = "U"></p>

<input type="text" name="userpassword" accesskey = "P"></p>
```

DISABLED and READONLY

To disable or make a readonly control add the disable a readonly attribute to specific form control element.

Example:

```
<input type = "text"  name="text1" value = "Check this out!!!"  readonly>

<textarea name="text2"  height="10" width="20"  disabled>
      Write here if you can.
</textarea
```

The form control element when disabled in the browser appears in light shade of gray or dimmed to indicate that it is not available. Whereas, a readonly control appears normal in a browser but when user wants to access it, denies the access.

ImageMap

An image map also referred to as clickable image, is a single image that represents multiple links. It can also be considered as an extended version of an image hyperlink. Instead of having an image represent only one link, the image can represent several different links depending on where in the image (i.e, the hot spots) you click. Imagemaps are the most popular method for creating menus on World Wide Web.

There are two basic forms of image: *server side* and *client side*. In the server side image map, the user clicks on an image but the server must decode where the user clicked before the destination page (if any) is loaded. With client-side image maps all of the map information - which regions map to which URLs can be specified in the same HTML file that contains the image. Including the map data with the image and letting the browser decode has several advantages including:

- There is no need to visit a server to determine the destination so links are resolved faster.
- Destination URLs can be shown in the status box as the user's pointer moves over the image.

- Image maps can be created and tested locally without requiring a server or system administration support.
- Client-side image maps can be created so that they present an alternate text menu to users of text-only browsers.

Server-side maps are older and are discouraged from use because of higher overhead in response time and bandwidth use. When a user clicks on a server-side imagemap the Web browser sends the co-ordinate information to the server which passes it to a CGI program to retrieve a URL from a .map file. The CGI program then sends the URL back to the Web browser which responds to the server with the URL of the requested page. Two network exchanges plus server and CGI processing time take their toll on performance.

Imagemap is accomplished by determining the pixel co-ordinates of the hot spots boundaries in the graphic. This can be done using a graphics program such as Photoshop or Paint Shop Pro but there are many programs available on World Wide Web that can automate this process such as MapTHIS, Web Image, Mapedit for Windows, etc.

Server-Side Image Maps

The way the server-side maps are stored depends on the software installed on the Web server. The two most common server-side map standards are NCSA and CERN. Both of these standards require maps stored in text files.

To specify a server-side image map, the <A> element is used to enclose a specially marked <IMG> element. The <A> elements HREF attribute should be set to the URL of the program or map file to decode the image map. The <IMG> element must contain the attribute ISMAP so the browser can decode the image appropriately.

Client-Side Image Maps

To specify a client-side map you need to specify the USEMAP attribute in the <IMG> element and have it referenced to a <MAP> element that defines the image map's hot spots. USEMAP tells the browser that the image to be used is a client side imagemap.

Example:

```
<IMG SRC="imagemap.gif" USEMAP="#map1">
```

The <MAP> element has one attribute NAME, which is used to specify the identifier associated with the map. The map name is then referenced within the <IMG> element using the USEMAP attribute. The <MAP> element must have a closing </MAP> element. Within the <MAP> and </MAP> tags are defined "shapes" that are mapped onto an image and defines the hot spots for the imagemap. Shapes are defined by the <AREA> element defined within the <MAP> element.

The attributes of the <AREA> tag are:

Attribute	Purpose
ACCESSKEY	Designates a shortcut key for the region.
ALT	Provides a text based alternative to the hot region.
COORDS	Lists the coordinates of points needed to define the hot region.
HREF	Supplies the URL to be associated with the hot region.
NOHREF	Specifies that no URL is associated with the hot region.
SHAPE	Set equal to the keyword (rect, circle, poly and default) that specifies the shape of the hot spot.
TABINDEX	Specifies the region's position in the page's tabbing order.
TARGET	Identifies the frame where the linked document should be rendered.

Table 2.2: Attributes of the <AREA> tag

The four types of the SHAPE attribute:

- **Rectangle** is the default shape for the AREA element. It requires two sets of coordinate pairs. The first pair gives the coordinates of the upper-left corner and the second pair gives the coordinates of the lower-right corner:

  ```
  Coords = "upper_left_x, upper_left_y, lower_left_x, lower_left_y"
  ```

- **Circles** require one set of coordinate pairs which gives the co-ordinates of the center point and the third number that gives the radius of the circle:

  Coords = "center_x, center_y, radius"

- **Polygons** are more complex shapes than rectangles or circles and thus require a series of coordinate pairs that define points along the outline of the figure:

  Coords="first_point_x, first_point_y,..........last_point_x, last_point_y"

- The **Default** shape establishes a URL that will be activated if a user clicks inside the imagemap but outside any of the other areas.

To set up a circular hot region, the code will be:

Example:

```
<MAP NAME="circle">
<AREA SHAPE="circle" COORDS="123,89,49"
HREF=http://www.server.com/circle.html ALT="CircleLink">
</MAP>
```

The preceding HTML sets up a map named circle that has one hot region. The COORDS list comprises the co-ordinates of the center point followed by a single number that represents the radius of the circle.

☞ *Note: You can have as many <AREA> tags as you like, but if the hot spots defined by two <AREA> tags overlap, the <AREA> tag listed first has precedence.*

The pound sign (#) before the map name indicates that the map data is found in the same html file. But if the map data is in another file called maps.html then the syntax will be:

```
<IMG SRC = "images/mainpage.gif"

USEMAP = "http://www.server.com/maps.html#circle">
```

☞ *Note: It is possible to combine support for both server-side and client-side image maps into one file.*

Example:

```
<html>
	<head> <title>Example of Client-Side Imagemap </title></head>

	<body bgcolor="#FFFFFF">

		<div align="center">
		<h1> Click Me!!!!!!!!!! </h1>
		<img src="f:/html/images/imagemap.gif" usemap="#map1" border="0">

			<map name="map1">
				<area shape="rect" coords="50,50,150,100" href="e:\web\firstmap.htm">
				<area shape="circle" coords="125,175,30" href="e:\web\shooter.gif">
				<area shape="default" nohref>
			</map>
	</body>
</html>
```

Figure 2.8: The Imagemap example as viewed in the Browser

Advanced HTML

This section talks about object embedding using <OBJECT> element, how to include JavaScript, VBScript and Java Applet codes in HTML page.

Object Embedding

The <OBJECT> element is currently only supported by Internet Explorer. The <OBJECT> element provides a way for the ActiveX controls and other media to be embedded directly into HTML documents. It substitutes the role of the <IMG> element providing an insertion mechanism for media other than static images. As far as the Internet Explorer is concerned the <OBJECT> element (at present) is used for the inclusion of ActiveX controls.

JavaScript

JavaScript is currently supported by the Netscape Navigator (version 2 and above) and Internet Explorer (version 3.0 and above). A script is embedded in HTML within <SCRIPT> element.

Syntax:

```
<SCRIPT>...</SCRIPT>
```

The text of a script is inserted between <SCRIPT> and its end element.

Attributes within the <SCRIPT> element can be specified as follows:

```
<SCRIPT LANGUAGE="JavaScript">
................................
</SCRIPT>
```

The LANGUAGE attribute is mandatory unless the SRC attribute is present and specifies the scripting language.

☞ *Note: Use of the LANGUAGE attribute is important now that Internet Explorer supports JavaScript. In order for the Internet Explorer to know it is to process the script as lavaScript, it needs to know that it is JavaScript.*

The SRC attribute is optional and if given specifies a URL that loads the text of a script.

Syntax:

```
<SCRIPT LANGUAGE="language" SRC=url>
```

Both attributes may be present.

VBSCRIPT

A lightweight, yet fully compatible version of Visual Basic, designed for use on the Internet. Visual Basic Script allows full automation, customization and scripting within web pages. Coming into its own when used to control ActiveX controls, Visual Basic is the easiest of the available methods for creating dynamic content to learn (Internet Explorer specific).

To use Visual Basic Script within a HTML document the code needs to be wrapped in <SCRIPT> ... </SCRIPT> elements, just like Netscape's JavaScript. As with JavaScript the LANGUAGE attribute is required, in this case the value is "VBScript". Visual Basic Script comes into its own when used in conjunction with ActiveX OLE controls which allow for full automation with any OLE compliant application, but can be used for almost any purpose on a page allowing for truly interactive web sites to be created easily.

For example, the following code section assumes that a button named 'btnHello' has been created somewhere on the HTML document.

```
<SCRIPT LANGUAGE="VBScript">

<!— These comment delimiters ensure the code is hidden from those browsers that do not support Visual Basic Script

Sub btnHello_OnClick
      MsgBox "Hello, It's a fine day"
End Sub
—>
</SCRIPT>
```

The button called 'btnHello' responds to being clicked by displaying a message box with the text "Hello, It's a fine day".

Java - Adding an Applet

Applet is a Java program which is executed on a web page. Applet are executed on Java enable browsers. Applets can be used to develop fancy web pages using images/drop down menu/media tracker/database front end. Applets exist on a remote machine and have to be downloaded to a local machine. Before execution they need to be interpretated and linked to resource on local machine and then executed. To add an applet to a HTML page, you need to use the <APPLET> HTML element.

Example:

```
<APPLET CODE="MyApplet.class" WIDTH=100 HEIGHT=140></APPLET>
```

This tells the viewer or browser to load the applet whose compiled code is in MyApplet.class (in the same directory as the current HTML document) and to set the initial size of the applet to 100 pixels wide and 140 pixels high.

 Hands On Exercise

Write the following code in notepad or any other JavaScript compliant tool and save it with extension *.htm*. Open the file in browser to view the output.

Exercise 1: Advanced Table Tags

```
<HTML>
	<HEAD><TITLE>advanced table tags</TITLE></HEAD>
	<BODY>
		<TABLE BORDER="1" WIDTH="100%">
			<CAPTION><B>E-academy result</B></CAPTION>
				<COLGROUP WIDTH="20%" ALIGN="CENTER" VALIGN="TOP">
				<COLGROUP SPAN="2" WIDTH="40%" VALIGN="TOP">
				<TR>
					<TH>Mission</TH>
					<TH>Student name</TH>
					<TH>Aggregate</TH>
				</TR>
				<TR>
					<TD>Mission-I</TD>
					<TD>Amit</TD>
					<TD>80%</TD>
				</TR>
				<TR>
					<TD>Mission-II</TD>
					<TD>Gaurav</TD>
					<TD>97%</TD>
				</TR>
				<TR>
					<TD>Mission-III</TD>
					<TD>Deep</TD>
					<TD>76%</TD>
				</TR>
				<TR>
					<TD>Mission-IV</TD>
					<TD>Neeraj</TD>
					<TD>80%</TD>
				</TR>
				<TR>
					<TD>Mission-V</TD>
				      <TD>Hemant</TD>
				       <TD>90%</TD>
				</TR>
```

```
        </TABLE>
    </BODY>
</HTML>
```

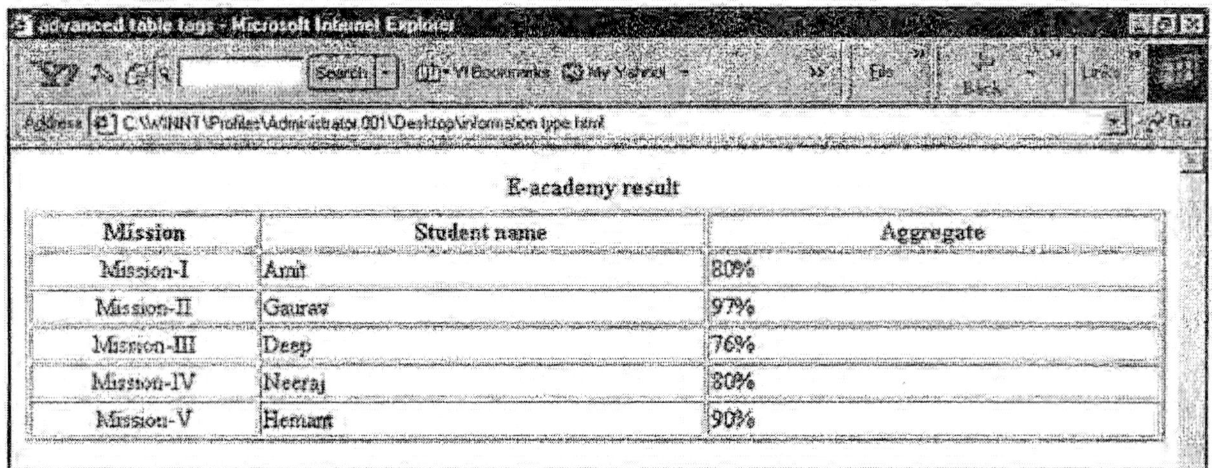

E-academy result

Mission	Student name	Aggregate
Mission-I	Amit	80%
Mission-II	Gaurav	97%
Mission-III	Deep	76%
Mission-IV	Neeraj	80%
Mission-V	Hemant	90%

Figure 2.9: Advanced Table Tags

Exercise 2: New Table Attributes

```
<html>
    <head>Table using new elements and attributes</head>

    <body><TABLE BORDER FRAME=hsides RULES=cols>

        <COL ALIGN=left>
            <COLGROUP SPAN=3 ALIGN=center VALIGN=middle>

            <THEAD>

                <CAPTION ALIGN=center><FONT SIZE=+1><B>A section of the Comparison
                Table</B></FONT>
                </CAPTION>

                <TR>
                    <TD>Element</TD><TD><B>Internet          Explorer</B>
                    </TD><TD><B>Netscape</B></TD><TD><B>Mosaic
                    </B></TD>
                </TR>
            </THEAD>
```

```
        <TBODY>
            <TR><TD>&lt;B&gt;</TD><TD>X</TD><TD>X</TD><TD>X</TD></TR>

            <TR> <TD>&lt;BASE ...&gt;</TD><TD>X</TD><TD>X</TD><TD>X</TD>
            </TR>

            <TR><TD> ...HREF</TD><TD>X</TD><TD>X</TD><TD>X</TD></TR>
            <TR><TD> ...TARGET</TD><TD>X</TD><TD>X</TD><TD></TD></TR>
            <TR><TD>&lt;BASEFONT ...&gt;</TD><TD>X</TD><TD>X</TD><TD>
            </TD></TR>
            <TR><TD VALIGN=top> ...SIZE</TD><TD>X<BR><FONT SIZE=-1>(only
            visible<BR>when FONT<BR>SIZE= used<BR>as well)</FONT></TD>
            <TD VALIGN=top>X</TD><TD></TD></TR>
            <TR><TD> ...FACE</TD><TD>X</TD><TD></TD><TD></TD></TR>
            <TR><TD VALIGN=top>&lt;BGSOUND ...&gt;</TD><TD VALIGN=top>X
            </TD><TD></TD><TD>X<BR><FONT SIZE=-1>(will spawn<BR>player
            for<BR>.mid files)</FONT></TD></TR>
        </TBODY>
        <TFOOT></TFOOT>
    </TABLE>
  </body>
</html>
```

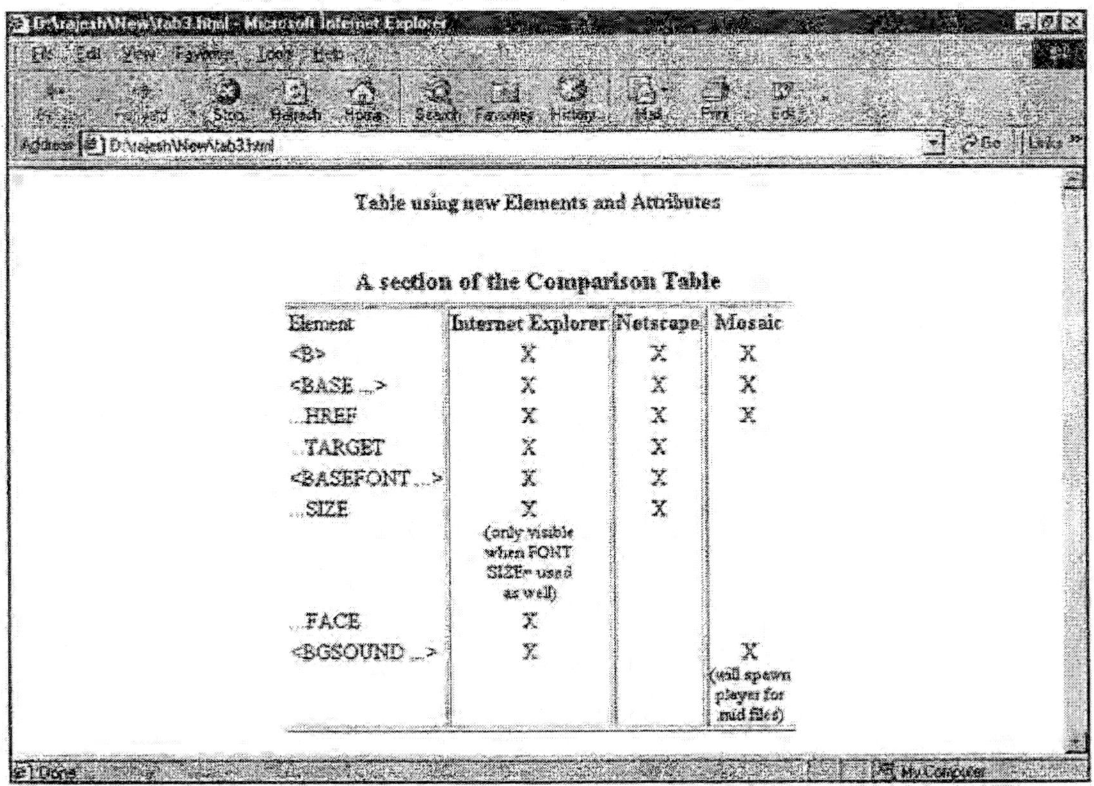

Table using new Elements and Attributes

A section of the Comparison Table

Element	Internet Explorer	Netscape	Mosaic
<B>	X	X	X
<BASE ...>	X	X	X
...HREF	X	X	X
...TARGET	X	X	
<BASEFONT ...>	X	X	
...SIZE	X (only visible when FONT SIZE= used as well)	X	
...FACE	X		
<BGSOUND ...>	X		X (will spawn player for .mid files)

Figure 2.10: New Table Elements

Exercise 3: Newspaper Layout

```
<html>
    <head>
        <title> Table Example </title></head>
            <body link="yellow" vlink="red" alink="blue">
            <table border="0" width="100%" cellspacing="0" cellpadding="0" valign="top">
        <tr>
    <td colspan="5">
    <!— HEADER CELL —>
    <h1 align="center">Discover Himachal Pradesh </h1>
        <hr>
            </td>
            <!— 4 unused <td> cells here —>
        </tr>
            <tr valign="top">
            <td width="30%">
                <p><strong><a href="#intro" alt="history">history</a></strong>
                </p>
                <p><strong><a href="#contact" alt="people">
                The People of Himachal</a></strong><br>
                </p>
                <p><Strong><a href="#custom" alt="art & culture">art & culture
                </a></strong><br>
                <img src="himachalcol.jpg">
            </td>
            <td width="55">
    <!— Gutter —>
        </td>
        <td width="30%">
            <p><a name="intro"><b>HISTORY</B><BR>The Dasa tribals, who entered
            the hills from the Gangetic plains, between the third and second millennium
            B.C, were the earliest known inhabitants of this region. Later around 2000 BC
            the Aryans joined them. Following independence, 30 princely states of the
            area were united and Himachal Pradesh was formed on 15 April 1948. Certain
            areas of Punjab were also included on November 1, 1966 following its
            re-organization. On January 25, 1971, Himachal Pradesh was declared a state
            of the Indian Union with Shimla as the capital.
        </td>
        <td width="5%">
    <!— Gutter —>
        </td>
        <td width="30%" rowspan="5">
            <h2><a name="custom"> ART & CULTURE </a> </h2>
                <p><em>The inaccessibility of the desolate regions of Lahaul and Spiti
                has helped to preserve the Buddhist culture of the people. The monasteries
                are the strongholds of tradition and the lives of the people are closely
```

```
                    connected with them. In Spiti, for instance, in the winter months the
                    Buchan, monks from Pin, move from village to village singing lads,
                    enacting comic farces and performing acts of daredevilry.
                <BR>
            </td>
            </tr>
                <tr valign="top">
                <td width="30%" colspan="3" valign="bottom">
            <hr>
                <h2><a name="contact"> The People of Himachal </a> </h2>
                </td>
        <!— Unused cells <td width="5%"><td width="30%>—>
            <td width="5%">
        <!—Gutter —>
            </td>
        <!—<td width="30%"></td>—>
            </tr>
                <tr valign="top">
                <td width="30%">
                    <p>The beauty of Himachal is enhanced by its inhabitants - mostly
                    farmers and semi-nomadic pastoralists - known for their charm, their
                    tolerance and honesty.
                </p>
            </td>
            <td width="5%">
        <!— Gutter —>
            </td>
            <td width="30%">
                <p>Perhaps the most exotic amongst them are the Kinnauras, known often for
                their extraordinary beauty, their ornate jewellery and their love for music and
                dance.
                </p>
            </td>
            <td width="5%">
        <!— Gutter —>
            </td>
        <!—<td width="30%"></td> —>
            </tr>
            <tr valign="top">
            <td width="30%"></td>
            <td width="5%">
        <!— Gutter —>
            </td>
            <!—<td width="30%"></td> —>
            </tr>
            <tr valign="top">
            <td width="30%"></td>
            <td width="5%">
```

```
        <!— Gutter —>

                </td>
                <td width="30%"></td>
                <td width="5%">

        <!— Gutter —>

                </td>

        <!—<td width="30%"></td> —>
                </tr>
                </table>
        </body>
</html>
```

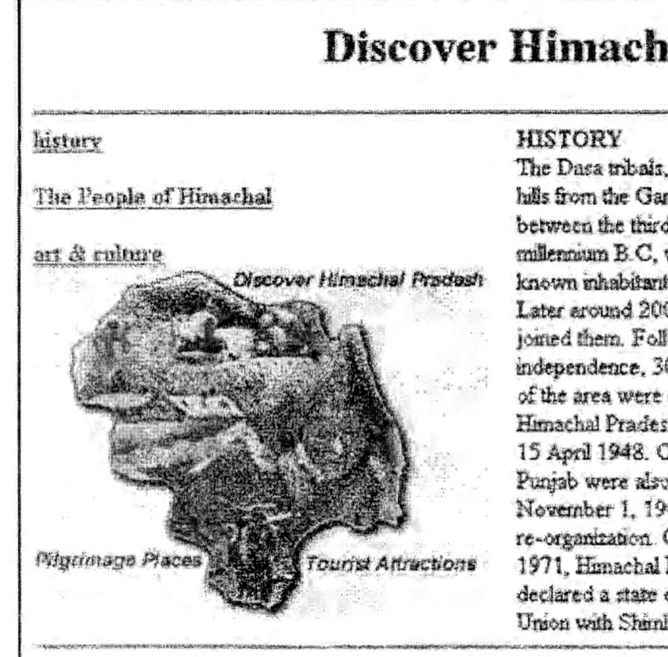

Figure 2.11: Newspaper Layout

Exercise 4: A Simple Order Form

```
<html>
	<head> <Title> Order Form example </title> </head>

	<body bgcolor="f8f7d9">
		<basefont color="#800080">
		<h1 align="center"><b>Order Form</b></h1>
		<form name="orderform" action="mailto:eacademy4u@mantraonline.com ? subject=order">
		<I>Please fill in your name, address and payment information:</i>
		<hr size=4>
		<b>NAME: <input type="text" name="name" size=25 maxlength=25></b>
		<b>PHONE: <input type="text" name="phone" size=25 maxlength=12></b>
		<b>STREET ADDRESS:<input type="text" name="street" size=27 maxlength=20><br>
		</b>
		<b>CITY:<input type="text" name="city" size=20 maxlength=20></b>
		<b>STATE:<input type="text" name="state" size=20 maxlength=20><br></b>
		<b>ZIP CODE:<input type="text" name="zip" size=10 maxlength=8><br><br></b>
		<b>ITEM CODE:<input type="text" name="itemcode" size=10 maxlength=8></b>
		<b>Price:<input type="text" name="price" size=10 maxlength=8><br><br></b>
		<fieldset><br>
		<b>CREDIT CARD#:</b>
			<input type="radio" name="cc"  value="mastercard">MaterCard
			<input type="radio" name="cc" value="visa">VISA
			<input type="radio" name="cc" value="citibank">CitiBank
			<input type="radio" name="cc" value="american express">American Express<br>

		<b>CC# </b><input type="text" name="number" size=37><br>
		<b>Expires </b><input type="text" name="expires" size=37><br>

	</fieldset>

	<hr size=4>
	<textarea name="order" rows=6 cols=54><b>PLEASE DONOT TYPE INTO THIS FIELD
	</b>

	*Chosen items and their calculated prices appear here.
	*5% is added to your total to cover Shipping Costs.
	*8.5% Sales Tax is calculated on every purchase.
	*Click the Submit Order button to send us your order.
	*Click the Clear Form button to clear All form fields.
	</textarea><br>

	<br>
```

```
        <b>Tax $<input type="text" name="tax" size=8 value=0.00></b>
        <b>Courier Charges $<input type="text" name="ship" size=8 value=0.00></b>
        <b>Sub $<input type="text" name="sub" size=8 value=0.00></b><br>
        <b>Total $<input type="text" name="total" size=8 value=0.00></b>
        <br><br><center>

        <input type="submit" value="Submit Order" name="submit">
        <input type="reset" value="Clear Order Form" name="clear">
        </center>

        </form>
    </body>
</html>
```

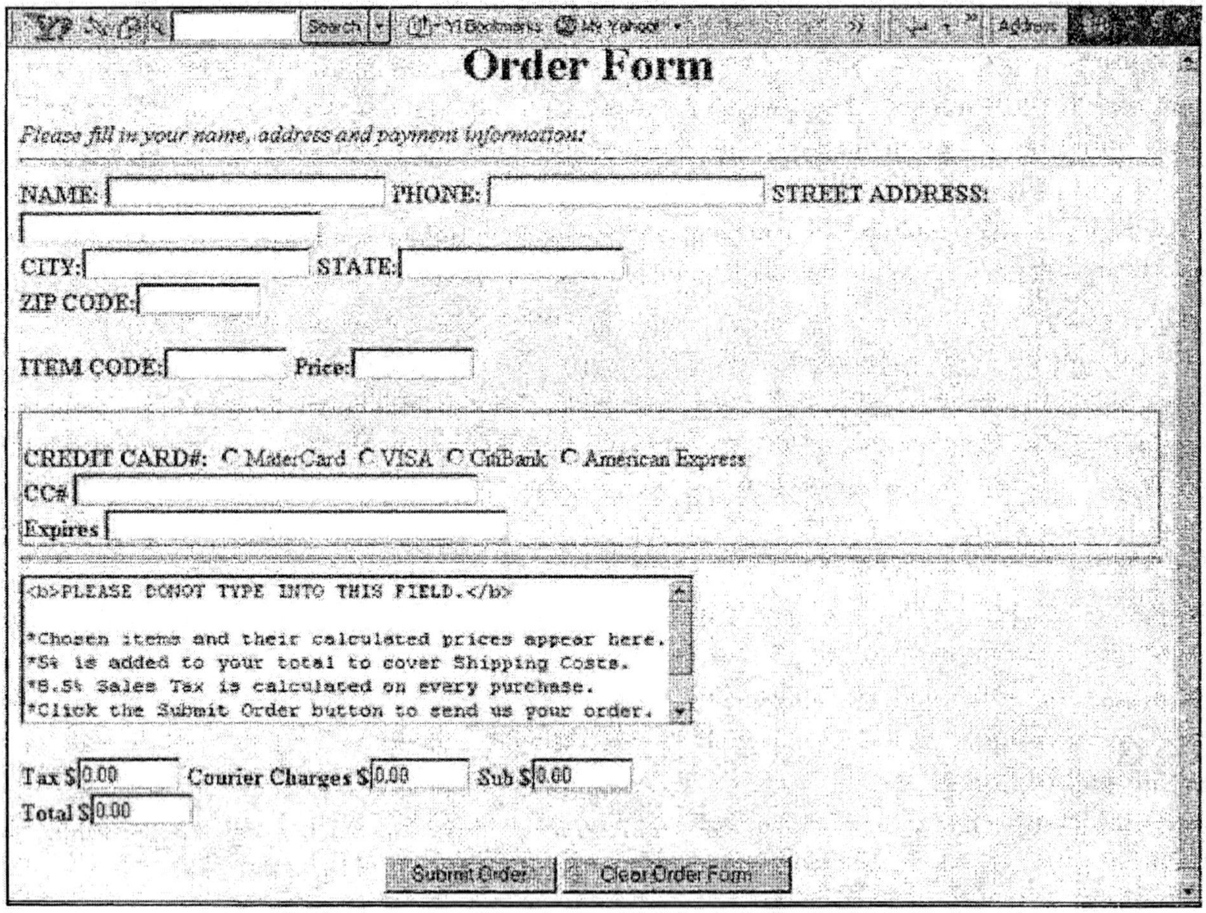

Figure 2.12: Order Form

Exercise 5: Frames

```
<HTML>
	<HEAD><TITLE>Frameset Samples</TITLE></HEAD>

	<FRAMESET
		cols="100, 50%, 2*, *"><FRAME name=third
		src="-maroon.html"><FRAME name=first
		src="yellow.html"><FRAME name=second
		src="blue.html"><FRAME name=fourth
		src="green.html">
	</FRAMESET>
</HTML>
```

<!—save file as yellow.html →

```
<HTML>
	<HEAD><TITLE>Yello Page</TITLE></HEAD>
	<BODY bgColor=#ffff00 text=#000000 >
	<H1>Yellow</H1>
	</BODY>
</HTML>
```

<!—save file as marron.html →

<! - - Write down the code - - >

<!—save file as blue.html →

<! - - Write down the code - - >

<!—save file as green.html →

<! - - Write down the code - - >

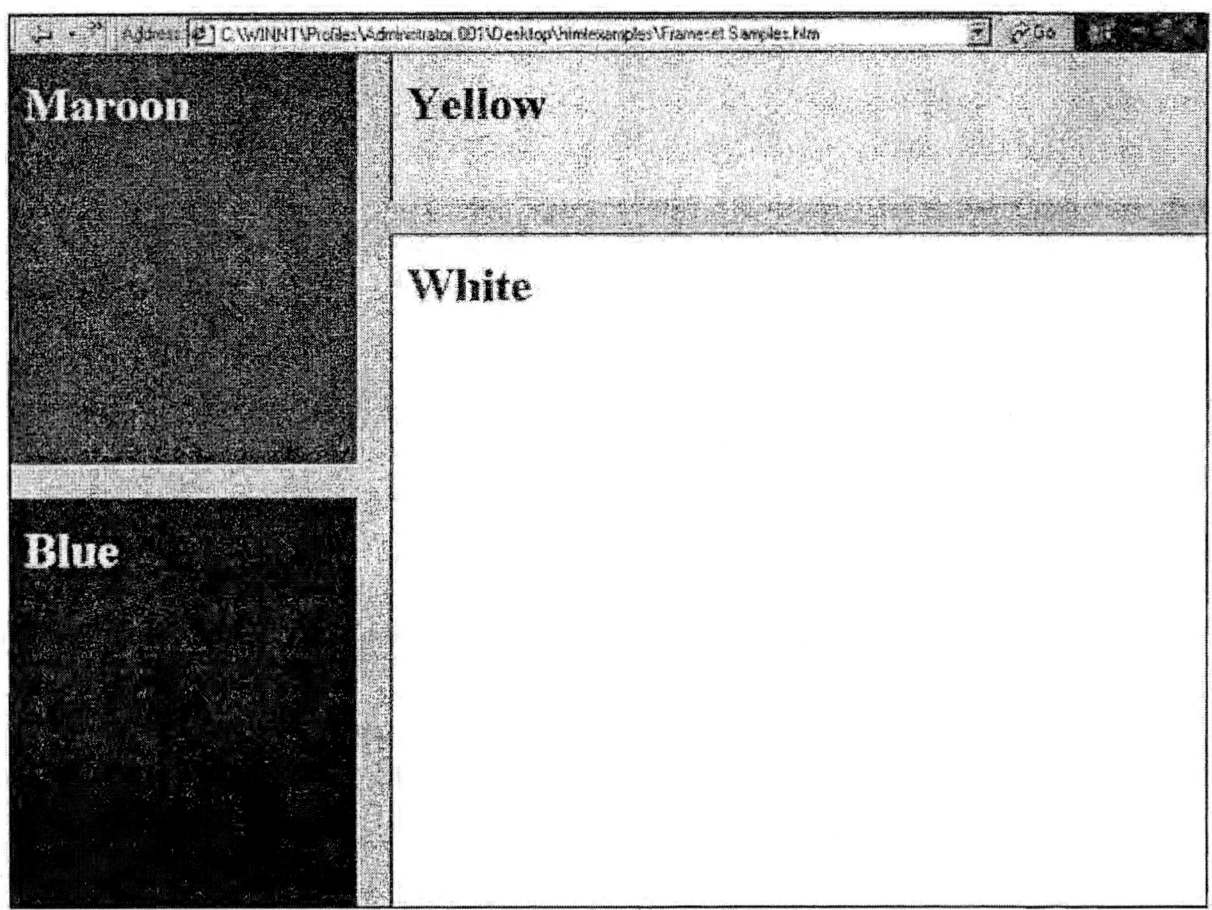

Figure 2.13: Frames

Exercise 6: Form Attributes

```
<html>
      <head><title> e-Academy </title></head>
      <body>
            <center>
                  <h1><u> <font color="blue" face="verdana">Welcome </font></u></h1>
                  </center >
                  <table border="0">
            <tr>
                  <td align="center"> <img src="e:/spazzman.gif" height="146" width="200">
                  </td>
                  <td rowspan="3">
                  <table border="0" bgcolor="#ffcc33">
                  <form action="mailto:itl@mantraonline.com" method="post">
```

```
<tr>
      <td colspan="4"> Today's survey about Mimimg </td>
</tr>
<tr>
      <td colspan="2"> I like miming because: (Check all that apply) </td>
      <td></td>
</tr>
<tr>
      <td> </td>
      <td> It's fun <input type="checkbox" name="whyilikeit" value="fun"> </td>
</tr>
<tr>
      <td> </td>
      <td> I meet interseting people <input type="checkbox" name="whyilikeit" value="people">
      </td>
</tr>
<tr>
      <td> </td>
      <td>It's who I am <input type="checkbox" name="whyilikeit" value="personality">
      </td>
</tr>
<tr><td> </td>
      <td> The money <input type="checkbox" name="whyilikeit" value="money"</td>
</tr>
<tr>
      <td colspan="2">The most difficult thing about being a mime is:</td>
      <td></td>
</tr>
<tr>
      <td> </td>
      <td><input type="radio" name="difficult" value="unitard">
      Wearing a spandex unitard</td>
</tr>
<tr>
      <td> </td>
      <td><input type="radio" name="difficult" value="nottalking">Not Talking </td>
</tr>
<tr>
      <td colspan="2"> Upload a picture of yourself miming! </td>
      <td></td>
</tr>
<tr>
      <td></td>
      <td> <input type="file" name="picture"></td>
</tr>
<tr>
      <td colspan="2" align="center" <input type="submit" value ="submit">
      <input type="reset" value="reset"></td>
      <td></td>
```

```
	</tr>
		<input type="hidden" name="surveynumber" value="091899">
		</form>
		</table>
		</td>
	</tr>
	<tr>
		<td valign="top">
		<table	border="0"	bgcolor="#ffff99"	width="100%"><form
		action="mailto:itl@mantraonline.com" method="post">
	<tr>
		<td align="center" colspan="2"> Enter your detail's here:</td>
		<td></td>
	</tr>
	<tr>
		<td>Username:</td>
		<td> <input type="text" name="username" maxlength="20"></td>
	</tr>
	<tr>
		<td> Password:</td>
		<td><input type="password" name="userpassword" size="10" maxlength="10">
		</td>
	</tr>
		<tr align="center">
		<td colspan=2><input type="submit" value="submit">
		<input type="reset" value="clear"></td>
	</tr>
		</form>
		</table>
		</td>
	</tr>
	<tr>
		<td>
		<table border="0" width="100%" bgcolor="#ffcccc">
		<form action="mailto:itl@mantraonline .com" method="get">
	<tr>
		<td> Serach your system</td>
		<td><input type="file" name="serachstring"></td>
	</tr>
		</form>
		</table>
		</td>
	</tr>
		</table>
	</body>
</html>
```

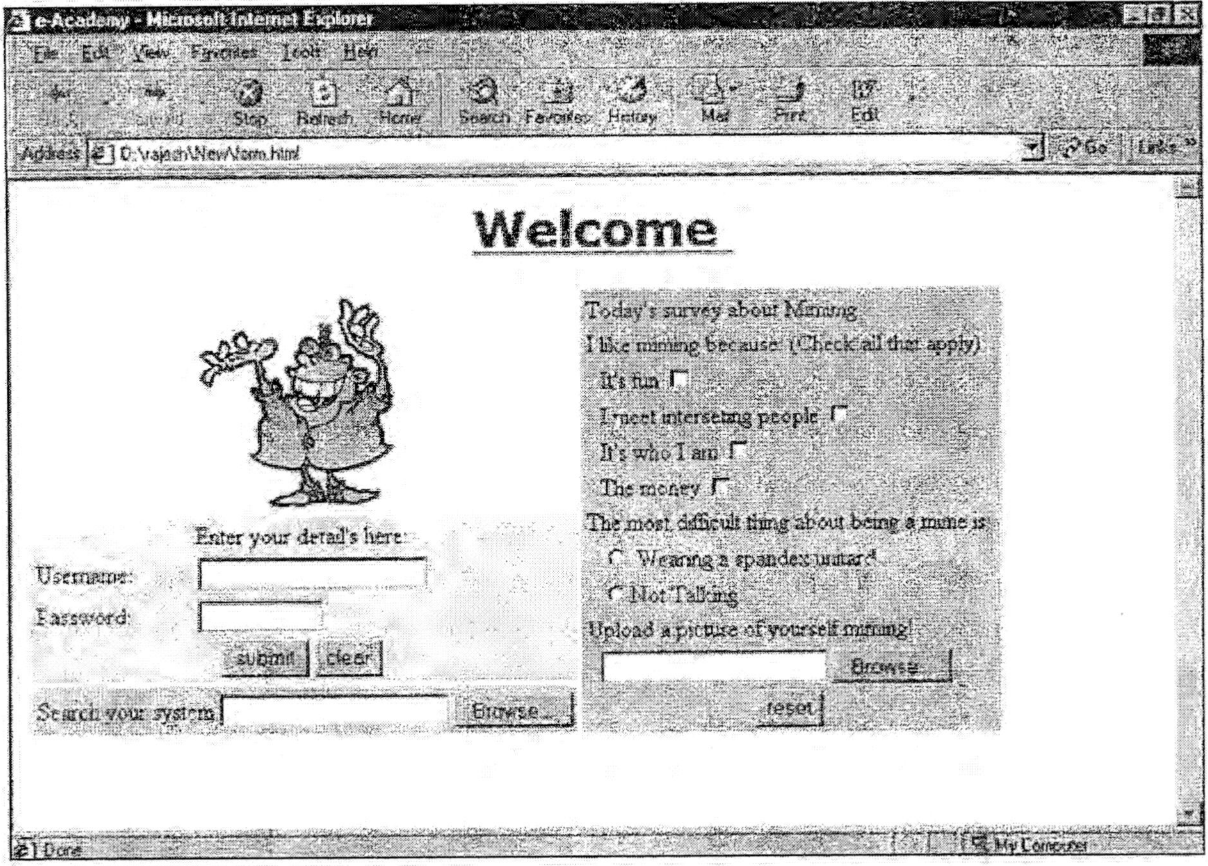

Figure 2.14: Form

 Test Your Knowledge

Students must solve the following assignment and submit to the faculty.

I Multiple Choice Questions:

1. The <TABLE> tag __________ attribute determines the amount of space between cells.
   a. Cellpadding
   b. Cellspacing
   c. Frame
   d. None of the above

2. A blank space in a cell can be accomplished by __________
   a. Putting nothing between <TD> and </TD>
   b. By placing a nonbreaking space between <TD> and </TD> as <TD>   </TD>
   c. Putting nothing between <TR> and </TR>
   d. None of the above

3. __________ tag specifies a section of a document that will be used by frame-capable browsers.
   a. <IFRAME>
   b. <FRAMESET>
   c. <NOFRAME>
   d. None of the above

4. The LABEL element __________ attribute explicitly associates a label with any control element on the form.
   a. TYPE
   b. FOR
   c. ID
   d. None of the above.

5. __________ method appends the form data to the end of the URL of the processing script specified in the METHOD attribute of the <FORM> tag.
   a. GET
   b. POST
   c. REQUEST
   d. None of the above.

6. To remove an element from tab navigation order, without using the disable attribute is __________
   a. Set the tabindex value to 0
   b. Set the tabindex value to -1
   c. Set the tabindex value to null
   d. None of the above

II State whether True or False:

1. The <FRAMESET> tag has to be specified within the <BODY> tag.

2. GET method appends the form data to the end of the URL of the processing script specified in the METHOD attribute of the <FORM> tag.

3. <FRAME> tag and its attributes is used for splitting the browser window into frames, and also for defining the content of each frame.

4. Imagemap in an html page is marked within <MAP> and </MAP> tag.

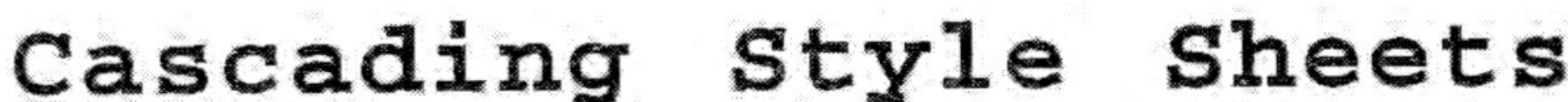

Cascading Style Sheets

Objectives

- Cascading Style Sheets
- Benefits of CSS
- Applying a style sheet to a document
- Grouping Styles
- Inheritance
- Taking Control
- Cascading
- Properties

Cascading Style Sheets

***Cascading Style Sheets* (CSS) is the term used to describe a mechanism that applies a style across one or more Web pages. The style of cascading style sheets refers to a color scheme, layout or other strategy for organizing the visual components of a Web page.**

Style Sheets allow the HTML author to separate presentation definitions from content in HTML documents. Style Sheets allow you to control the rendering, e.g. fonts, colors, leading, margins, typefaces and other aspects of style, of a Web document without compromising its structure. CSS is a simple style sheet mechanism that allows authors and readers to attach style to HTML documents.

Style rules combine HTML tags (such as h1 or p) with properties (such as color: blue) to format each HTML tag. The term "Cascading" Style Sheets is used because more than one Style Sheet can affect the same page.

A CSS style rule consists of two parts: a *selector,* which can be an HTML tag such as h1 or p, and a *declaration,* which defines the property and value of the selector.

Example:

```
H1   {color : blue}
P    {font-family : Arial, Helvetica, verdana; color:red }
```

In the preceding example the style rule renders the heading h1 on the page in blue. The second line defines the font style of the paragraphs displayed on the page and font color.

The first implementation of Cascading Style Sheets known as CSS1, enables the user to specify everything from typefaces for different HTML elements to font colors, background colors and graphics, margins, spacing, type style and much more. Internet Explorer 3.0, Internet Explorer 4.0 and Netscape Navigator 4.0 later supports few aspects of CSS1 specification.

CSS2 includes all the capabilities of CSS1 and adds improved typographic control, including dynamically downloadable fonts. There are new positioning properties to control layout for example, to produce sidebars and navigation areas.

Images and text can be layered and overlapped and can be dynamically moved around the screen with scripts. CSS2 also adds control over table layout, particularly useful for XML documents and allows the automatic numbering of headings and lists.

The next generation of style sheets CSS2, became a formal recommendation in May 1998, Many CSS2 tags are supported in the latest versions of both Internet Explorer and Netscape Navigator. CSS2 specifications enable the users to generate Web pages with more enhanced features such as designing audible style sheets that speak page elements to a user while using audio and surround sound properties. It also allows to split Web pages into multiple pages, control page breaks, etc. The CSS2 Recommendation is supported by the W3C CSS2 Package, consisting of the CSS2 Validation Service, a set of W3C Core Style Sheets and the CSS Test Suite. The CSS2 Package helps document authors use CSS2 and also help developers create CSS2-compliant software.

Furthermore, many industry pundits support a type of sheet known as DSSL (Document Style Semantics and Specification Language), which was developed by the SGML community. The most recent addition to style sheets are XSL (eXentisible Style language). XSL is an industry standard based on DSSL and uses XML (eXtensible Markup Language) syntax.

The fact that W3C has started developing XSL in addition to CSS has caused some confusion. Why develop a second style sheet language when implementors have not even finished the first one? The answer can be found in the table below:

	CSS	XSL
Can be used with HTML?	yes	no
Can be used with XML?	yes	yes
Transformation language?	no	yes
Syntax	CSS	XML

Table 3.11: XSL and CSS

Benefits of Cascading Style Sheets

The unique features are that CSS can be used to style HTML documents. XSL, on the other hand is able to transform documents. For example, XSL can be used to transform XML data into HTML/CSS documents on the Web server. This way, the two languages complement each other and can be used together.

But, the content providers do not have the control they have in print media over screen rendering.

A style sheet language offers a powerful and manageable way for authors, artists and typographers to create the visual effects they want, e.g.

- margins and indents
- line spacing and length
- background images and colors
- fonts, font sizes, and font colors

  ... and much more

You can embed a style sheet inside an HTML document, or insert a link to an external style sheet that can influence any number of documents. CSS is implemented in several browsers, including Microsoft Internet Explorer 3/4 and Netscape Navigator 4.0.

Some of the benefits of using CSS:

- *Style sheets allow you to separate the style and layout of your HTML files from their informational content.*

  You can define the look of a site in one file, and change the whole site by changing just the one file. You can make all of your HTML layout and formatting changes in one location, either in an external file referenced by any number of pages or the style can be applied to a specific section of text within the body of a page.

- Using *relative measurements* in your style sheet, you can present your documents to look good on any monitor at any resolution.

- You have finer and more predictable control over presentation. CSS has been designed to deal with issues which HTML was not.

- Older browsers will simply ignore your style sheets so they will not break existing pages.

- The CSS style sheet mechanism allows readers to influence the presentation of HTML documents. Style sheets allow both document authors and readers to specify rendering rules for HTML documents. Cascading means that if both parties supply style sheets then the browser will apply both, using further rules for resolving conflicts.

- Style sheets will allow companies to easily adopt a house look and feel, and this will help give readers a sense of where they are and what they are reading. Style sheets can be pointed to from Web documents via hyperlinks and this will dramatically simplify the maintenance of Web sites. If the company later changes the house style they only need to make changes in one place.

- Style sheets improve the printing of Web documents. Paper has different properties than a computer screen and the differences can be accounted for in a style sheet. Web authors should be confident that their documents will look as good on paper as they do on computer screens.

- People with disabilities have better access to your pages. Visually impaired Web users may need increased font sizes and will be among the first to benefit from style sheets. CSS provides a framework for speech style sheets. A style sheet can produce rich aural presentations by describing pauses intonation and other components of speech along with non-speech sound cues.

Applying a style sheet to a document:

Style definitions can be applied to documents and their elements in one of the four ways:

- Using the **<LINK>** attribute to point to an *external style sheet*
- Using the **@import mechanism** (similar to the <LINK> method above, this allows the importing of external style sheets).
- Using the **<STYLE>** element within the <HEAD> of a document *embedding style sheets.*
- Using the **STYLE attribute** in an element. This is allowed for any elements allowed within the <BODY> of a HTML document. (*Including style information inline).*

External Style Sheet

External Style Sheet is a template/document/file containing style information which can be linked with any number of HTML documents. This is a very convenient way of formatting the entire site as well as restyling it by editing just one file.

The file is linked with HTML documents via the LINK element inside the HEAD element. Files containing style information must have extension .css, e.g. style.css.

Example:

```
<HEAD>
<LINK REL=STYLESHEET TYPE="text/css" HREF="style.css" >
</HEAD>
```

- The **REL** attribute is used to specify the RELationship of the referenced file to the main document (i.e. it is a style sheet).

- The **TYPE** attribute is used to specify the MIME type of the style sheet.
- The **HREF** attribute provides the reference for the style sheet.

Importing a Style Sheet

Style sheets can be imported in a page using the following syntax:

```
<html>
      <head>
            <STYLE TYPE="text/css">
            @import url(http://www.w3c.org/style2);
            </style>
      </head>
</html>
```

Style information imported in this way is automatically pulled into the document for use and can be overridden only by explicit style rules named within the document itself.

☞ *Note: Of the four style information in a Web page, only linking to external style sheets and importing style sheets allow the style to cascade across multiple pages. Imported style information is automatically included in the document whereas externally linked style information will be selected only if previously referenced style information is unavailable.*

Embedding a Style Sheet

Embedded style is the style attached to one specific document. The style information is specified as a content of the STYLE element inside the HEAD element and will apply to the entire document.

```
<HEAD>
      <STYLE TYPE="text/css">
            <!— P {text-indent: 10pt} —>
      </STYLE>
</HEAD>
```

The <STYLE> tag has one parameter, TYPE, which specifies the Internet Media type as "text/css".

The <STYLE> tag is followed by any number of style definitions and terminated with the </STYLE> tag. Older browsers will ignore the <STYLE> element, but its content will be treated as part of the document body and rendered as such. <STYLE> element content may be hidden using SGML comments:

```
<Style Type   = "text/css">
<!—
      BODY    {     background:    #ffff99;          }
      H1      {     color:         #33ff33;          }
      P       {     color:         #330000;
                    font-family:   Garamond, serif;
              }
—>
</Style>
```

☞ *Note: The styling rules are written as a HTML comment, that is, between <!— and —> to hide the content in browsers without CSS support which would otherwise be displayed.*

<STYLE>

The <STYLE> and </STYLE> tags indicate a style sheet. Inside <STYLE> and </STYLE> you can specify styles for elements, define classes and IDs, and generally establish styles for use within the document. This element should be defined within the <HEAD> element of a document. Style rules within a document's <BODY> element should be set with the STYLE attribute for a particular element. It has six attributes:

♦ **DIR:** This attribute is used to set the text direction of the title for the style sheet either right to left (RTL) or left to right (LTR).

♦ **DISABLED:** The Microsoft defined attribute is used to disable a style sheet.

♦ **LANG:** This attribute is used to define the language of the TITLE attribute rather than the content of the element.

- **MEDIA:** This attribute is used to specify the destination medium for the style information. The possible values of this attribute includes SCREEN, PRINT, PROJECTION, BRAILLE, AURAL and ALL.
- **TITLE:** This attribute associates an informational title with the style sheet.
- **TYPE:** This attribute is used to define the type of style sheet. The value used is - "text/css".

<DIV> Tag

The <DIV> element is generally used (with Style Sheet attributes) to indicate a block of document as being a separate logical unit. Essentially, text surrounded by the <DIV> ... </DIV> elements will be formatted according to the description attached to the ALIGN attribute within the <DIV> elements.

Example:

```
<DIV ALIGN="left">Left justify text by putting it within the DIV tags.</DIV>

<DIV ALIGN="center">Centre some text by putting it within the DIV tags.</DIV>

<DIV ALIGN="right">Right justify some text by putting it within the DIV tags.</DIV>
```

<SPAN> Tag

The <SPAN> tag is a useful markup tag introduced by style sheets. Using this tag, you can apply style definitions to entire sections of your page. Here's how you specify the style for the spanned section in the document header:

Syntax:

```
SPAN { font: Arial; color: white}
```

Then, in the body of the document you simply insert the begin and end <SPAN> tag wherever you want to apply your style definition:

```
<SPAN>
      <H1> A heading using the SPAN style definitions.</H1>
      <P> A paragraph using the SPAN style definitions.</P>
      <P> A paragraph using the SPAN style definitions.</P>
</SPAN>
```

You can specify style definitions for spanned sections directly in the text, as well:

```
<SPAN STYLE="font: Arial; color: white">
      <H1> A heading using the SPAN style definitions.</H1>
      <P> A paragraph using the SPAN style definitions.</P>
      <P> A paragraph using the SPAN style definitions.</P>
</SPAN>
```

Including an Inline Style Sheet

Inline style is the style attached to one specific element. The style is specified directly in the start tag as a value of the STYLE attribute and will apply exclusively to this specific element occurrence.

```
<P STYLE="text-indent: 10pt">Indented paragraph</P>
```

Using a 'STYLE' attribute on an element inside 'BODY'.

Inline style definitions affect individual occurrences of a tag. These are embedded within the tag itself using the STYLE attribute. The following HTML code colors a specific <P> tag:

```
<P STYLE="color: red">This line will be red.<P>
```

The text specified in the style defined in the <p> tag. If the inline style conflicts with an embedded or linked style, the inline style overrides for that particular occurrence. For example, if the line above appears on a Web page that defines <P> to be green through a linked style sheet all paragraphs will be green except for the <P> above, which will be red.

Example:

```
<HTML>
    <HEAD>
        <TITLE>Need New Glasses</TITLE>
        <STYLE TYPE="text/css">
        <!—
            P {font-family: Arial, Helvetica, sans-serif; color: black}
            P.bigger {font-family: Arial, Helvetica, sans-serif; font-size: larger}
        —>
        </STYLE>
        </HEAD>
            <P> Are you having a hard time reading the text on these pages?
            If you haven't had your eyes checked lately, and the following paragraph is still
            hard to read, you might want to have your eyes checked.</P>
        <P CLASS="bigger">You might need new glasses!</P>
    </BODY>
</HTML>
```

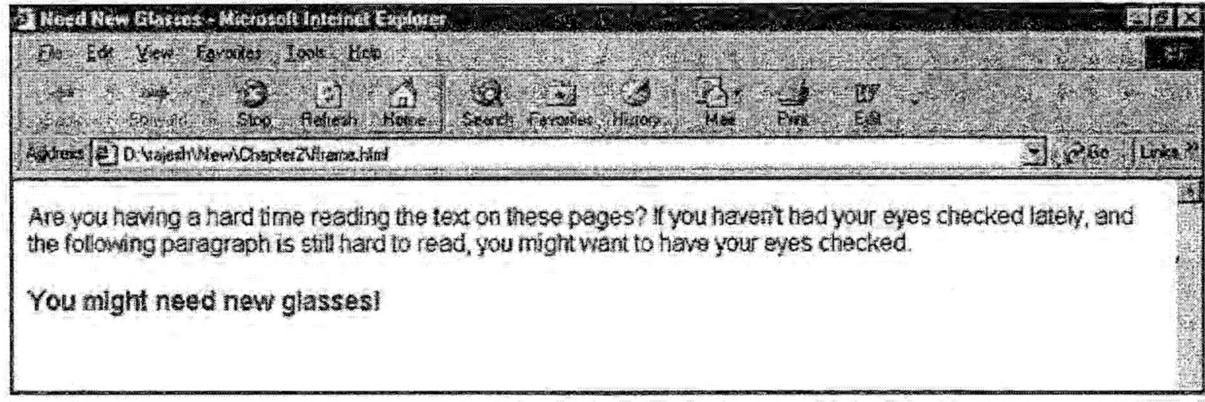

Figure 3.1: Using Style tag

Grouping Styles

To avoid redundancy in code both *selectors* and *declarations* can be grouped together within style sheets.

For example, say if you want in your web page that all headings (H1,..........., H6) to appear in Red, then you have got two options - either create a separate rule for each heading or group all the headings in a single style rule. Given below is an example of both the options:

Example of **Grouping Selectors:**

Creating a separate rule for each heading:

```
<STYLE TYPE="text/css">
< ! - -
      H1 {color: Red};
      H2 {color: Red};
      H3 {color: Red};
      H4 {color: Red};
      H5 {color: Red};
      H6 {color: Red};
- - >
</STYLE>
```

Grouping the selectors into one large rule:

```
<STYLE TYPE="text/css">
<! - -
      H1, H2, H3, H4, H5, H6 {color: blue}
- - >
</STYLE>
```

Example of **Grouping Declarations**:

Now consider that you want your web page body background to be black and fonts style to be displayed in Arial and bold.

Defining each rule separately:

```
<STYLE TYPE="text/css">
<! - -
      H1 {background – color: green };
      H1 {font – style: italic};
      H1 { font-family: arial};
- - >
</STYLE>
```

Grouping the declarations into a single rule:

```
<STYLE TYPE="text/css">
< ! - -
      H1 { background – color: green: font – style: italic; font – family: arial;  }
- - >
</STYLE>
```

Inheritance

A HTML element that contains another element is considered to be the parent element of the element it contains and the element it contains is considered to be its child element.

For example, in the following HTML text, the <BODY> element is the parent of the <H1> element which in turn is the parent of the <EM> element.

```
<BODY>
      <H1>The headline <EM>is</EM> important!</H1>
</BODY>
```

In many cases, child elements acquire or inherit the styles of their parent elements. For example, suppose a style has been assigned to the <H1> element as follows:

```
<STYLE type="text/css">
      H1 {color:blue;}
</STYLE>
<BODY>
<H1>The headline <EM>is</EM> important!</H1>
```

In this case, the child <EM> element takes on the style of its parent, which is the <H1> element, so the word appears in blue. However, suppose you had previously set up a style specifying that <EM> elements should be displayed in red. In that case, the word would be displayed in red, because properties set on the child override properties inherited from the parent.

Inheritance starts at the top-level element. In HTML, this is the <HTML> element, which is followed by the <BODY> element.

To set default style properties for all elements in a document, you can specify a style for the <BODY> element. For example, the following code sets the default text color to green.

Example:

```
<STYLE TYPE="text/css">
      BODY {color: green;}
</STYLE>
```

Taking Control

To exploit the powers of CSS in the best possible ways, few new selectors have been added to HTML, i.e., CLASS and ID as well as the capability to determine the context in which selectors occur.

Class Selector

Another method of defining which tags get a style sheet definition is by using classes. Classes give authors ability to apply styles to specific parts of a document while not applying them to others. Any element that occurs inside the <BODY> of a HTML document may have a class associated with it. Style sheet classes are defined by placing a period (a dot) before a unique name. This can be defined after the tag or independently. It can be used to define many different styles for the same tag.For example:

```
H1.firstclass { color: blue }
.myclass {color: red}
```

In the above example an <H1> tag set to CLASS attribute firstclass would be blue and any tag with the CLASS attribute set to myclass would be red as specified below:

```
<H1 CLASS="firstclass" > This text would be in blue. </H1>
<P CLASS="myclass"> The text would be red. </P>
```

You can specify several classes or tags at once, defining as

```
H1. * {color: blue}
```

This will make the text for all defined classes of the H1 tag blue.

```
* {color: yellow }
```

defines the text color of all the tags as yellow.

Example:

```
<HTML>
	<HEAD>
	<TITLE>The HTML Reference Library</TITLE>
	<STYLE>
	P.main {font-family : Arial;
	font-size : 12pt}
	p.info { font-family : Arial;
	font-style : italic}
	</STYLE>
	</HEAD>
	<BODY>
	<P CLASS="main">The HTML Reference Library is a Windows HLP file, detailing all
	currently useable HTML syntax. It is available in the following formats:
	<UL>
	<LI>Windows 3.x
	<LI>Windows 95/NT
	</UL>
	<P CLASS="info">For more information about the HTMLib, contact <A
	HREF="mailto:itl@mantraonline.com">itleducations</A>
	</BODY>
</HTML>
```

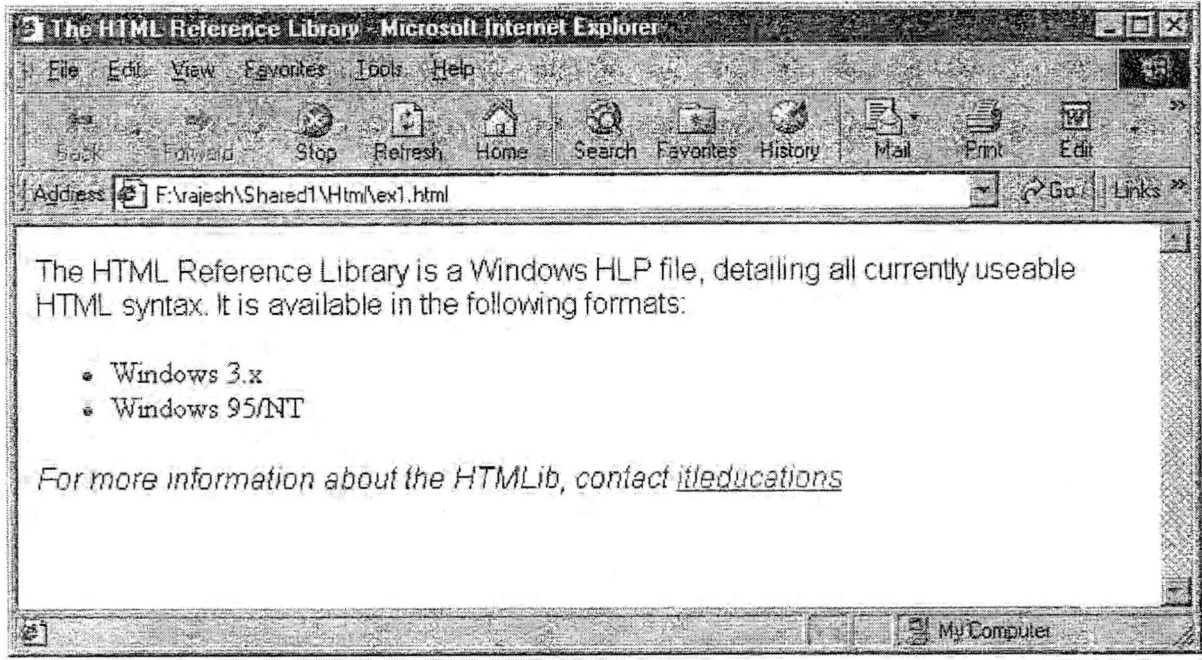

Figure 3.2: Class Selector

ID as a Selector

The new ID selector can be used in a way similar to the class element, except that the ID attribute has a unique value over the document. In the <STYLE> declaration the ID name should be preceded by a #, like this:

```
<html>
      <head>
            <title> ID Style Sheet Example </title>
                  <style type="text/css">
                        # firstid {color : yellow }
                  </style>
            </head>
      <body>
            <P ID= firstid > This text will be displayed in yellow. </P>
      </body>
</html>
```

Like CLASS, ID can be set to apply to all selectors, as in the previous example or they can be bound to a specific one, like this:

```
<STYLE TYPE="text/css">
      <! - - A below is referring to anchor tag - ->
      A#secondid {background – color : black }
</STYLE>
```

```
<A Id=secondid href= "http://somewhere.com/" > This link has an black background. </A>
```

Contextual Selector

Inheritance saves CSS designers typing. Instead of setting all style properties, one can create defaults and then list the exceptions. To give 'EM' elements within 'H1' a different color, one may specify:

```
H1 { color: blue }
EM { color: red }
```

When this style sheet is in effect all emphasized sections within or outside 'H1' will turn red. Probably, one wanted only 'EM' elements within 'H1' to turn red and this can be specified with:

```
H1 EM { color: red }
```

The selector is now a search pattern on the stack of open elements and this type of selector is referred to as a *contextual selector.* Contextual selectors consist of several simple selectors separated by whitespace (all selectors described up to now have been simple selectors). Only elements that match the last simple selector (in this case the 'EM' element) are addressed and only if the search pattern matches. Contextual selectors in CSS1 look for ancestor relationships but other relationships (e.g. parent-child) may be introduced in later revisions. In the example above the search pattern matches if 'EM' is a descendant of 'H1', i.e. if 'EM' is inside an 'H1' element.

```
UL LI    { font-size: small }
UL UL LI { font-size: x-small }
```

Here, the first selector matches 'LI' elements with at least one 'UL' ancestor. The second selector matches a subset of the first, i.e. 'LI' elements with at least two 'UL' ancestors. The conflict is resolved by the second selector being more specific because of the longer search pattern.

Suppose you wanted to make all text that was defined as strong within a paragraph be rendered using a lime green color. You could use:

```
STRONG { color : #00FF00}
```

In the style sheet definition. However, this would cause all text that was enclosed in <STRONG> ... </STRONG> elements to be rendered lime green. This is where context sensitive selectors are useful. If you use:

```
P STRONG { color : #00FF00}
```

In the style sheet definition then only text enclosed in <STRONG> ... </STRONG> elements enclosed in <P> ... </P> elements would be lime green.

For instance:

<P><STRONG>This will be lime green</STRONG></P> This <STRONG>other bit</STRONG> won't be.

As with the two methods of style definition above this can be used for all elements normally contained within the body of a document.

Pseudo Classes

Pseudo classes allow style sheets to recognize different selector types. Like classes they are specified with the element in the style sheet. Pseudo classes use as the separator character. Classes and pseudo classes may be mixed:

```
A : visited {properties}
P.initial : first-letter
{properties}
```

The first example here changes the properties of visited HTML links, the second changes the properties of the first letter of paragraphs with the CLASS "initial".

```
<html>
<head>

    <style>
    a:active {color: #0000FF}
    a:visited {color: #00FF00}
    a:link {color: #FF0000}
    a:hover {color: #FF00FF}
    </style>

    </head>

    <body>

    <p><b><a href="a.html" target="_blank"><blink>Click Me</blink></a></b></p>

    </body>
</html>
```

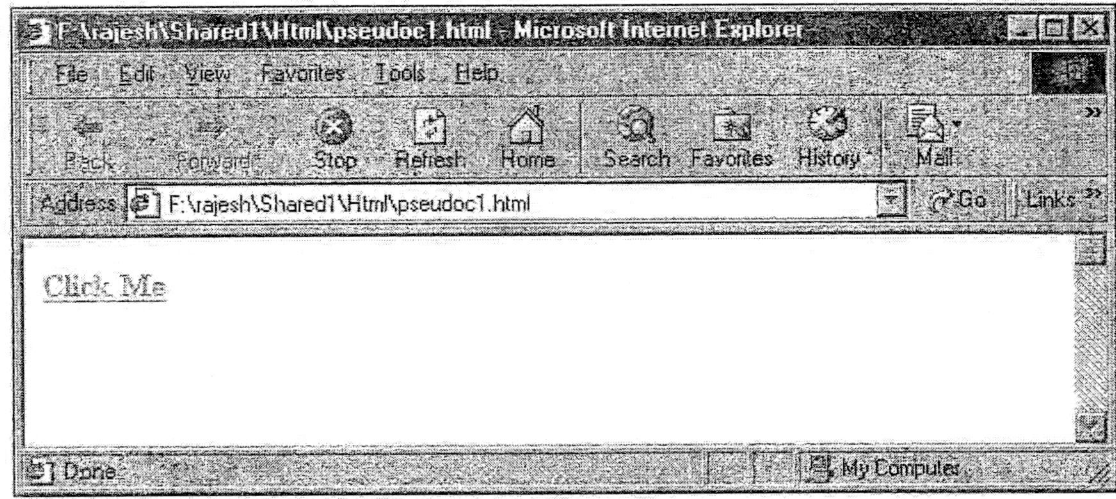

Figure 3.3: Pseudo class

Pseudo Elements

Pseudo elements allow style sheets to access different subparts of elements. There are no HTML tags that represent these element subparts. The two pseudo elements currently supported by style sheets are first-line and first-letter.

The first line pseudo elements applies whatever styles you specify to text on the first line as displayed by the browser.

Syntax:

```
<HTML>
      <HEAD>
            <STYLE TYPE="text/css">
            <! - -
            P.first-line {font-style: italic };
            - - >
            </STYLE>
      </HEAD>
            <BODY BGCOLOR="blue">
            <P> This text will be rendered in italic.
            From this line the text displayed will be normal </P>
      </body>
</html>
```

Example:

```
<html>
<head>

	<style>

	div:first-line
	{
	color: #ff0000;
	font-variant: small-caps
	}
	</style>

	</head>

	<body>

	<p><b>Note:</b> Netscape 4 does not support the "first-line" property.</p>
	<p><b>Note:</b> Internet Explorer 5.5 supports the "first-line" property.</p>

	<div>
	You can use the first-line pseudo-element to add special style to the first line of a text.
	<br><br>

	This is second line of the paragraph.
	</div>

</body>
</html>
```

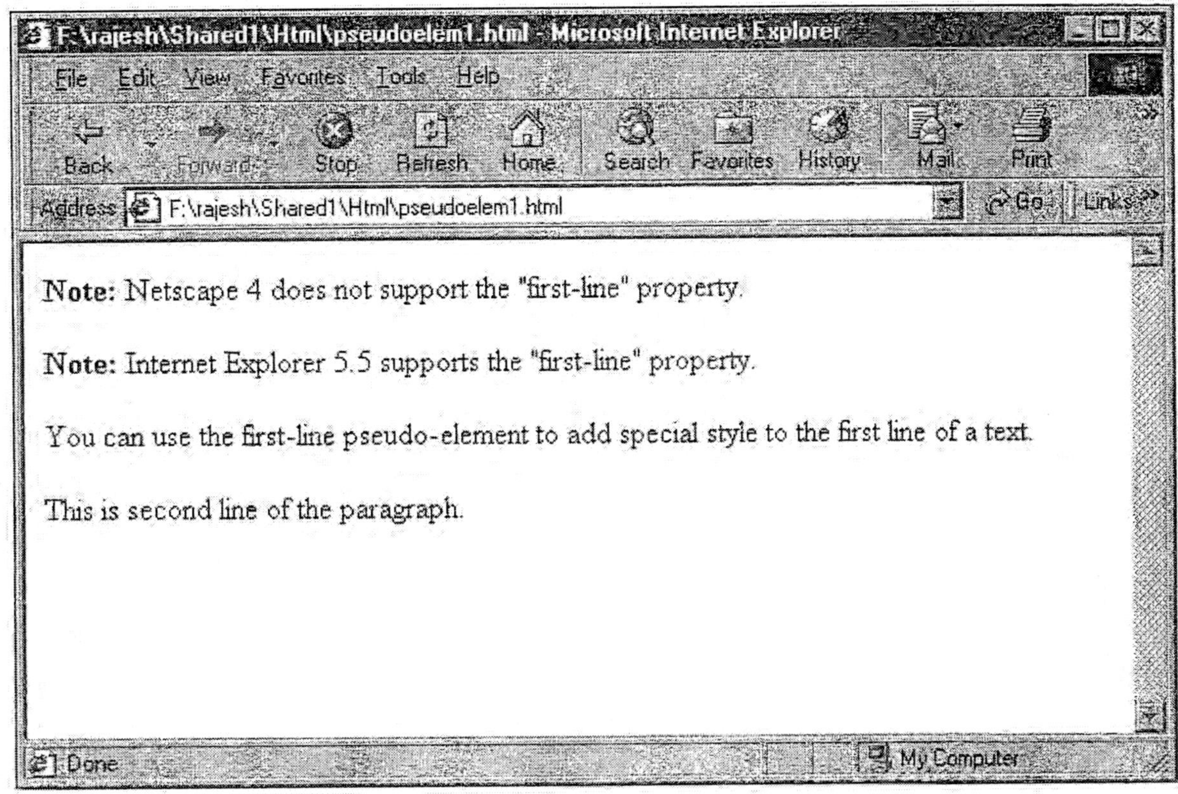

Figure 3.4: Pseudo Element

There are some restrictions on the use of the first-line pseudo element. It can be used only with block-level elements and can access only the following properties: font properties, color and background properties, word spacing, letter spacing, text-decoration, vertical-align, text-transform, line-height and clear.

The first-letter pseudo element is used to create drop caps in a document. The first-letter pseudo elements are also applied only to block level elements and has restrictions on the properties it can access. They are font properties, color and background properties, text-decoration, vertical align, text-transform, line height.

Cascading

This is the capability provided by some style sheet languages such as CSS to allow style information from several sources to be blended together. These could be for instance corporate style guidelines styles common to a group of documents and styles specific to a single document. By storing these separately, style sheets can be reused. The cascade defines an ordered sequence of style sheets where rules in later sheets have greater precedence than earlier ones. Not all style sheet languages support cascading.

In CSS, more than one style sheet can influence the presentation simultaneously. But, sometimes conflicts may arise between the style sheets that influence the presentation.

When style sheets cascade, they follow a specific precedence order for style definitions which is based on three key factors listed in lowest to highest precedence order:

- **The weight of the definition**
- **The origin of the definition**
- **The specificity of the definition**

When resolving a style conflict and determining which style to display when the first factor a client examines is the *weight* of the definition. By default, all definitions have a weight of normal. You can change the weight of a definition by declaring it as **important.**

Example:

```
<STYLE>
H1, H2, H3, H4, H5, H6 {color: brown !important}
P, BLOCKQUOTE {color: blue !important} </STYLE>
```

The second factor examined is the *origin* of the definition. The current specification allows both Web publishers and Web users to create style sheets. The publishers' definitions have higher precedence than users' definitions.

The final factor examined is the *specificity* of the definition. A definition that applies to a general element on the page such as a page division has a lower precedence than a specific element, such as a listed item in an unordered list. Similarly a definition imported from an external style sheet has a lower precedence than a definition defined inline.

The imported style sheets also cascade with each other, in the order they are imported. Any rules specified in the style sheet itself override rules in imported style sheets. That is imported style sheets are lower in the cascading order than rules in the style sheet itself. Imported style sheets can themselves import and override other style sheets, recursively.

In CSS1 all '@import' statements must occur at the start of a style sheet before any declarations. This makes it easy to see that rules in the style sheet itself override rules in the imported style sheets.

Properties of Cascading Style Sheet (CSS)

Cascading Style Sheet contains four basic types of presentational information, called properties. They are:

- **Foreground and background colors and background images**
- **Font properties**
- **Text properties (word spacing, letter spacing, etc.)**
- **Boxes**

Foreground and Background Colors and Images

CSS1 supports a variety of properties that can be used to control the colors and backgrounds in a document. With style sheets you can create arbitrary regions with different background colors and images. CSS1 Style sheets support three basic forms of color specifications: color names, hexa values in three or six digit format and RGB values. There are two properties for specifying colors: **color** and **background**.

The COLOR property controls the foreground color of an element. Usually this is the color of the text of an element.

Syntax:

```
selector {color : value }
```

Example:

```
H2 {color : red }
H2 {color : #ff0000}
```

Some of the defined color names are as: Aqua, Navy, Black, Olive, Blue, Purple, Fuchsia, Red, Gray, Silver, Green, Teal, Lime, White, Maroon, Yellow.

The BACKGROUND property describes the background of an element, i.e. the surface onto which the text content is displayed. The background can be transparent, one color, two colors (blended in the direction specified by the <blend-direction> (see below) value or an image, possibly combined with one or two colors.

Syntax:

```
selector {background: transparent/<color> [/<color>]<url>//<repeat>/<scroll>/<position>}
```

Example:

```
P { background: transparent }
BODY { background: red }
H1 { background: blue / red }
BODY { background: url(chess.gif) 50% repeat fixed }
```

This property does not inherit, but the parent element's background will shine through by default due to the initial transparent value. If neither an image or a color is found, a value of 'transparent' is assumed.

Background - image

This property associates a background image with an element. If an image is specified and found through the URL, it will be overlaid on top of any color specified. The color (or color combination) will be used to fill any transparency in the image, or to fill the image space while the image is loading.

Example:

```
B { background-image : url (new.gif); background-color : white }
```

Background - repeat

This determines the extent of repetition of any specified background image. The possible values are - repeat, repeat-x , repeat-y , no-repeat. If no value is set, 'repeat' is assumed, i.e. the image is repeated both horizontally and vertically.

- **repeat:** repeat the image both horizontally and vertically in the background.

  Syntax: BODY { background: url(cool.gif) repeat}

- **repeat-x:** repeat the image along the x axis (horizontally) in the background.

  Syntax: BODY { background: url(cool.gif) repeat-x}

- **repeat-y:** repeat the image along the y axis (vertically) in the background.

  Syntax: BODY { background: url(cool.gif) repeat-y}

- **no-repeat:** do not repeat the image in the background, displays it on the window only once.

  Syntax: BODY { background: url(cool.gif) no-repeat}

Background - scroll

This controls whether any specified background image should be fixed to the background, or allowed to scroll as the document is viewed. Possible values are *fixed* and *scroll*. The default value is *'scroll'*.

Syntax:

```
BODY { background: url(Globe1.gif) fixed}
```

Background - position

This property specifies the initial position of any specified background image. There are three possible ways to specify a position.

- First, the top left corner of the image can be specified as an absolute distance.
- Second, the position can be specified as a percentage along the horizontal and vertical dimensions.
- Third, the position can be specified with keywords to describe the horizontal and vertical dimensions.

The keywords for the horizontal dimension are left, center and right, for vertical dimension are top, center and bottom. If no value is specified, '0% 0%' is assumed i.e., assumed to be center.

- **LEFT:** Start at the x position 0 percent which is the left-hand side of the element's window.
- **CENTER:** Start at the x position 50 percent which is in the middle of the element's window.
- **RIGHT:** Start at the x position 100 percent which is the right-hand side of the element's window.
- **TOP:** Start at the y position 0 percent which is the top of the element's window.
- **MIDDLE:** Start at the y position 50 percent which is the middle of the element's window.
- **BOTTOM:** Start at the y position 100 percent which is the bottom of the element's window.

With a value pair of '0% 0%', the upper left corner of the image is placed in the upper left corner of the element. A value pair of '100% 100%' places the lower right corner of the image in the lower right corner of the element. With a value pair of '14% 84%', the point 14% across and 84% down the image is to be placed at the point 14% across and 84% down the element.

Specifying only one value sets both the horizontal and vertical offset of the background image. If two values are given the first position is used as the horizontal position.

Example:

```
P { background-image: url (picture.gif) ; background-position:10px 10 px}
P { background-image: url (picture.gif) ; background-position: 20% 40% }
```

Font Properties

Setting font properties is among the most common uses of style sheets. Unfortunately, there exists no well-defined and universally accepted taxonomy for classifying fonts and terms that apply to one font family may not be appropriate for others. E.g. 'italic' is commonly used to label slanted text, but slanted text may also be labeled as being *Oblique, Slanted, Incline, Cursive* or *Kursiv.* Therefore it is not a simple problem to map typical font selection properties to a specific font.

CSS1 defines the properties 'font-family', 'font-style', 'font-variant' and 'font-weight', 'font-size' and 'font'.

Cascading Style Sheet defines five font specific properties that can be set:

- **font-family:** The font-family property allows the Web page designer to designate which font family will be used. A series of names may be requested, but the first available font will be used. There are five classes of "generic" fonts that may be specified *serif* (e.g., Times New roman); *sans-serif* (e.g., Helvetica); *monospace* for *fixed width fonts* (e.g.,Courier); *cursive* (e.g., Zapf-Chauncery) and *fantasy* (e.g.,Western).
- **font-style:** Identifies the style of the face, normal italic or oblique.

- **font-variant:** Identifies another variation on face either normal or small caps. Small caps refers to fonts that have lowercase letters replaced by uppercase ones. These letters occur in slightly different proportions than the true uppercase letters.
- **font-weight:** It specifies the boldness of text on a page. The font-weight for normal text is medium.
- **font-size:** It specifies the sizes of the face. Font size may be specified in absolute units or relative to "current" size.

font-family

The value is a prioritized list of font family names and/or generic family names. Values are separated by a comma to indicate that they are alternatives:

```
BODY { font-family: gill, helvetica, sans-serif }
```

There are two types of list values:

- **<font-family>:** The name of a font family of choice. In the last example, "gill" and "helvetica" are font families.
- **<generic-family>:** In the above example, the last value is a generic family name or general font style. If you want to make sure your text has a certain style, you should use a general font style which is universal across platforms. The following generic families are defined:

- **'serif'** (e.g. Times) — **Syntax:** Selector {font-family: serif }
- **'sans-serif'** (e.g. Helvetica) — **Syntax:** Selector {font-family: sans-serif}
- **'cursive'** (e.g. Zapf-Chancery) — **Syntax:** Selector {font-family: cursive}
- **'fantasy'** (e.g. Western) — **Syntax:** Selector {font-family: fantasy}
- **'monospace'** (e.g. Courier) — **Syntax:** Selector {font-family: monospace}

It is useful to offer a generic font family as a last alternative, in case the specified font is not available on the viewers system.

Font names containing white space should be quoted:

```
BODY { font-family: "new century schoolbook", serif}
<BODY STYLE="font-family: 'My own font', fantasy">
```

font-size

Font-size property controls the size of the fonts displayed. Values are of four possible types: absolute size, relative size, percentage and length.

- **absolute-size:** Cascading Style Sheet defines seven keywords as valid absolute size value: xx-small, x-small, small, medium, large, x-large and xx-large. Although they may be of different sizes in different browsers, the following relationship will always exist between the sizes:

  xx-small <= x-small <= small <= medium <= large <= x-large <= xx-large

  Syntax:

  ```
  Selector {font – size: xx-large }
  ```

  Example:

  ```
  H1 {font – size: xx-large }
  ```

- **<relative-size>:** A <relative-size> keyword is interpreted relative to the table of font sizes and the font size of the parent element. Possible values are: [larger I smaller].

  For example, if the parent element has a font size of 'medium', a value of 'larger' will make the font size of the current element be 'large'.

  Syntax:

  ```
  Selector {font – size:medium }
  ```

  Example:

  ```
  H1 {font – size: medium }
  ```

Percentage values work in a very intuitive way. Values such as 50% and 210% are valid. Length values specified in pt, px, em and ex are also valid methods for specifying font size. Negative percentage or point sizes are not allowed.

Syntax:

```
selector {font-size:x pt}
```

Example:

```
H1 {font–size:12pt}
```

Some of the valid measurement types include the following:

- em : font-width
- ex : font height
- px : pixels
- in : inches
- cm : centimeters
- mm : millimeters
- pt : point size
- pc : picas

font-weight

The font-weight property specifies the weight or darkness of the font. The value can either be absolute or relative. Some values used to specify the property are: *bold, bolder, lighter, extra-light, light, demi-light, medium, demi-bold, bold* and *extra-bold.*

Syntax:

```
selector {font-weight: bolder}
```

Example:

```
P { font-weight: medium }
STRONG { font-weight: bolder }
```

font-style

The font-style is used to specify normal, italic or oblique font style for the font being used. The default value is normal.

Syntax:

```
Selector {font-style: normal}
Selector {font-style: italic}
```

Font-variant

The font-variant property is used to select a variation of the specified (or default) font family. The only current variants supported with this property is small-caps, which displays the text as small uppercase letters,

Example:

```
H1 { font-variant : small-caps }
```

font

The font property provides a concise way to specify all the font properties with one style rule. One attribute that is also included within font is line-height which specifies the distance between two lines of text. Each font-attribute can be indicated on the line separated by spaces except for line height that is used with font-size and separated by slash. The general form of the font rule is:

Syntax:

```
selector { font : font-style font-variant font-weight font-size/line-height font-family }
```

Example:

```
P { font : italic small-caps 600 18pt/24pt "Arial, Helvetica" }
```

You need not use to specify all the attributes of the font property.

Example:

```
P { font : italic 18pt/24pt }
```

Text Properties

Text properties are used to affect the spacing and layout of text inline namely the text within block elements such as paragraphs. The eight text properties provided by Cascading Style Sheet are:

- **word-spacing**
- **letter-spacing**
- **text-decoration**
- **vertical- align**
- **text-transform**
- **text-align**
- **text-indent**
- **line-height**

word-spacing

The word-spacing property allows a web page designer to control the amount of space between words on a page. The default value, normal, uses the browser's word-spacing default.

Syntax:

```
Selector {word-spacing: x pt}
```

Example:

```
H1 {word-spacing: 2 pt}
```

letter-spacing

This property specifies the amount of space between letters. The default value normal uses the browser's letter spacing default.

Example:

```
P {  letter-spacing :  0.2 em  }
BODY  { letter-spacing :  2 px  }
# Fun  {letter-spacing :  2 cm }
```

text-decoration

This property is used to define an effect on text. The standard values for this property includes - **blink, line-through, overline, underline** and **none**. The meaning of all the values are self explanatory except overline, which creates a line above text.

This property can be used to decorate text blocks. Any colors required for the decoration are inherited from the any color property value settings.

Example:

```
A:link, A:visited, A:active { text-decoration: underline }
```

Would underline all links within the document.

vertical-align

This property determines the vertical positioning of text and images with respect to the baseline currently in effect. The possible values are baseline, sub, super, top, text-top, middle, bottom, text-bottom and percentage values. The default value of vertical-align is baseline.

The defined keywords set the alignment of the element realtive to the parent element.

- **Baseline:** align the baseline of the element with the baseline of the parent
- **Middle:** align the middle of the element with the baseline plus half the x-height of the parent
- **Sub:** subscript the element
- **Super:** superscript the element
- **Text-top:** align the top of the element with the top of the parent element's font.
- **Text-bottom:** align the bottom of the element with the bottom of the parent element's font.

The remaining values set the vertical alignment of the element relative to the formatted line that the element is a part of:

- **Top:** align the top of the element with the tallest element on the line
- **Bottom:** align the bottom of the element with the lowest element on the line

Percentage values refer to the 'line-height' of the element itself. E.g., a value of '-100%' will lower the element to where the baseline of the next line should have been.

Example:

```
P          {vertical-align: text-top }
.subscript  {vertical-align: sub; font-size : 75% }
```

text-transform

This property determines the capitalization of the text it affects. The possible values are **capitalize, uppercase, lowercase** and **none**. The transformation that actually occurs is browser dependant. Also, it may differ for different languages.

- **Capitalize:** uppercases the first character of each word
- **Uppercase:** uppercases all letters of the element
- **Lowercase:** lowercases all letters of the element
- **None:** neutralizes inherited value

Example:

```
P { text-transform: capitalize }
.upper { text-transform: uppercase }
```

text-align

This property determines how text in a block-level element such as the paragraph element is horizontally aligned. The allowed values are left, right, center and justify. The default value is left. As above, implementation of this property is browser dependant and may differ for different languages.

Example:

```
P { text – align : justify }
```

text-indent

This property sets the indentation for text before the first character in the first line of a block level element. Acceptable values are lengths and percentage.

Example:

```
P {text-indent: 3pt}
P.half {text-indent: 50%}
```

Box Properties

CSS1 assumes a simple box-oriented formatting model where each formatted element results in one or more rectangular boxes (Elements that have a 'display' value of 'none' are not formatted and will therefore not result in a box). All boxes have a core content area with optional surrounding padding, border and margin areas.

The box properties set the size, circumference and position of the boxes that represent elements. The properties that can be controlled include margins, borders, padding, height, width and positioning. The formatting model suggested by Cascading Style Sheet is one of concentric rectangles. Each element has a margin, inside the margin is an optional border, inside the border is optional padding and inside the padding is the actual formatted content of the element.

Margin Properties

The margin properties determine the distance between edges of an element's box and the edges of adjacent elements. There are four margin properties **margin-left, margin-right, margin-top, margin-bottom** used to set each of element's four margins. A fifth margin property **margin** allows all of them to be set together. The values of the margins could be specified in length units i.e., pt, px, in, cm, mm, em or a percentage value of the block elements or **auto** which attempts to figure out the appropriate margins automatically.

For the 'margin' property the four lengths apply to top, right, bottom and left respectively. If there is only one value it applies to all the sides and if there are two or three values the missing values are taken from the opposite side.

Example:

```
BODY {margin-top:20 px; margin-bottom: 20 px, margin left: 30 px; margin-left: 50 px }

BODY { margin: 1em 2em 3em }

BODY     {
               margin-top: 1em;
               margin-right: 2em;
               margin-bottom: 3em;
               margin-left: 2em
         }
```

would produce the same result.

Border Properties

The border properties determine the visual characteristics of a border surrounding an element's edge. It offers another way to add spacing to elements on your page in the order: border-top, border-right, border-bottom, border-left and border. You can set different border width, border color, url and border styles.

The width of the border can be specified as a relative or absolute value. The possible values are thin, medium, thick, <length>. The default value is 'medium'.

- border - width: thin
- border - width: medium
- border - width: thick
- border - width: .25in

The color to the border can be simply specified by a color name or value:

- border: medium red
- border: .25in #FF00FF

To add a unique style to the border, you can use any of the following. The possible values are none, dotted, dashed, solid, double, groove, ridge, inset, outset. The default value is 'none'.

- none: Do not draw a border
  { border - style: none }

- dotted: Draw the border as a dotted line.
  { border - style: dotted medium red }

- dashed: Draw the border as a dashed line.
  { border - style: dashed thin blue }

- solid: Draw the border as a solid line.
  { border - style: solid thick green }

- double: Draw the border as a double line.
  { border - style: double thin white }

- groove: Draw the border as a 3D line.
  { border - style: groove medium red }

- ridge: Draw the border as a raised 3D line.
  { border - style: ridge .5in blue }

- inset: Draw the border as an inset 3D line
  { border - style: insert medium red }

- outset: Draw the border as an outset 3D line
  { border - style: outset 25px white }

When you use a 3D border you can also specify an image to display in the border space that will be repeated throughout the border. Here's how you could create a fancy border with an image:

```
IMG { border: groove .5in url (coolrule.gif) }
```

Example:

```
<HTML>
      <HEAD><TITLE>Border Samples</TITLE></HEAD>

      <STYLE TYPE="text/css">
            H2 {border-width:20pt; border-color:cyan;width:60%;
             padding:10%;}
      </STYLE>

      <BODY>
            <H2 STYLE="border-style:solid;">SOLID BORDER</H2>
            <H2 STYLE="border-style:double;">DOUBLE BORDER  </H2>
            <H2 STYLE="border-style:groove;">GROOVE BORDER  </H2>
            <H2 STYLE="border-style:ridge;">RIDGE BORDER  </H2>
            <H2 STYLE="border-style:inset;">INSET BORDER  </H2>
            <H2 STYLE="border-style:outset;">OUTSET BORDER  </H2>
      </Body>
</html>
```

Padding Properties

This property describes how much space is inserted between the border and the content of an element. Padding regions can be set using the padding-top, padding-right, padding-bottom and padding-left properties. With borders and margins it is also possible to use a shorthand notation property called simply padding to set the padding for all sides at once. The order is top, right, bottom, left.

Example:

```
P { border-style:  solid; padding-left:  20mm;  padding-right : 50mm}
```

A single value applies to all sides, while using two or three values set the respective sides with the missing values being copied from the opposite side. The surface of the padding area is set with the 'background' property.

Width and Height

The width and height property sets the width and height of an element's content region (the width of the area actually filled with content as opposed to its padding, border or margin. It is similar to creating a table cell by specifying it's width and height.

Example:

```
P {width: 300px ; height: 100px; padding: 10px; border: solid 5px; color: black; background:
yellow }
```

Hands On Exercise

Write the following code in notepad or any other JavaScript compliant tool and save it with extension *.htm*. Open the file in browser to view the output.

Exercise 1: Example using Style tag

```
<HTML>
    <HEAD> <TITLE> CSS</TITLE>
        <STYLE>
            BODY { background : #006000}
            P.main { font-family : Arial;
            font-size : 12pt;
            color : white}
            P.info { font-family : Arial;
            font-style : italic;
```

```
                color : #80C000}
                P SPAN { font-style : italic;
                font-size : 14pt}
                A { color : #C0C8FF;
                font-weight : bold}

            </STYLE>
        </HEAD>
<BODY>

        <P CLASS="main">The <SPAN>HTML Reference Library</SPAN> is a Windows HLP file,
        detailing all currently useable HTML syntax. It is available in the following formats:

        <UL>

            <LI>Windows 3.x
            <LI>Windows 95/NT

        </UL>

            <P CLASS="info">For more information about the <SPAN>HTMLib</SPAN>, contact
            <A HREF="mailto:itleducations@mantraonline.com">itleducations</A>

        </BODY>
</HTML>
```

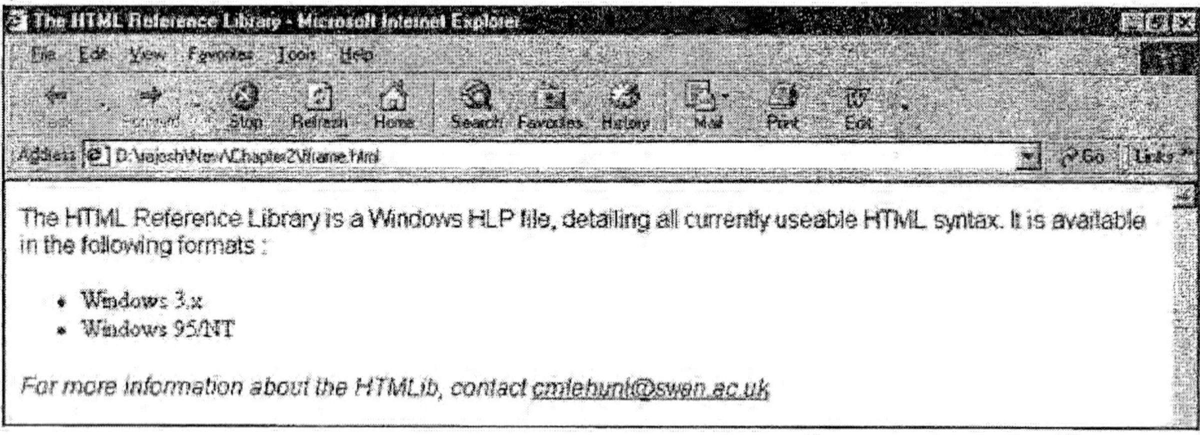

Figure 3.5: Style attribute

Exercise 2: Sample CSS page

```
<html>
      <head><title>Sample CSS page</title>
     <STYLE TYPE="text/css">
          <!—
     P {
          textAlign:center; margin-left:20%; margin-right:20%;}
     H4 {
          text-decoration:underline; color: green};
     H5 {
          text-transform:uppercase; color: red;
          border-width:4pt; border-style:outset;
          background-color:yellow; padding: 4pt;
          border-color:red;}

          BLOCKQUOTE {

               color:blue; font-style:italic;
               line-height:1.5; text-indent:10%;}
          —>
     </STYLE>
</head>

<body bgcolor="cyan">

<H4>Underlined Heading 4</H4>

     <BLOCKQUOTE>

          This is a blockquote. It is usual for blockquotes to be indented, but the first line of
          this blockquote has an extra indent. Also the line height in this blockquote is bigger
          than you usually see in blockquotes.

          <h5>uppercase heading 5 with a border</H5>

     </BLOCKQUOTE>

     <P>This paragraph has a text alignment value of center. It also has large margins, so each
     line is not only centered but is also inset on both sides from the element that contains it,
     which in this case is the document.</P>

     </body>
</html>
```

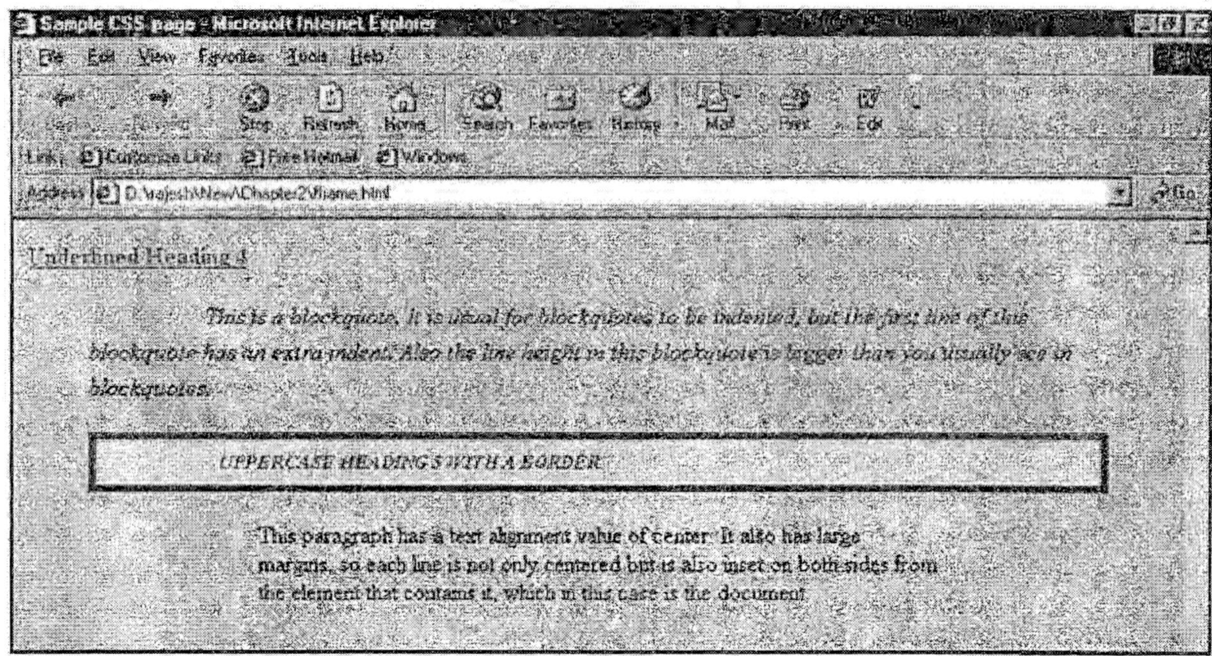

Figure 3.6: Sample CSS page

Exercise 3:

```
<html>
	<head><Title> CSS Example </Title>
	<STYLE TYPE="text/css">
	<!- -
		P {
			background-color:#CCCCFF;
	/* margins */
		margin-left:20%; margin-right:20%;

	/* border widths
		border-top-width: 10pt; border-bottom-width:10pt;
		border-right-width:5pt; border-left-width:5pt;

	/* border style and color
		border-style:outset; border-color:blue;

	/* paddings */
		padding-top:10pt; padding-bottom:10pt;
		padding-right:20pt; padding-left:20pt;

		}
			H3 {
```

```
        /* font size and weight */
               font-size: 14pt;
               font-weight:bold;
               background-image:URL("images/grenlite.gif");

        /* center the heading with a 90% width */
               width:90%;
               float:center;
               border-color:green;
               border-style:solid;

        /* all sides of the border have the same thickness */
               border-width:10pt;

        /* all sides have the same padding */
               padding:20pt;

                - - >}

               </STYLE>
        </head>
    <body>

        <H3>H3 with a Solid Border</H3>

               <P>Borders have their uses in everyday life. For example, borders round a
               paragraph make the paragraph stand out more than it otherwise would.

        </P>

               <P>This is another paragraph with a border. You have to be careful not to make
               the borders too wide, or else they start to take over the page.

        </P>
    </body>
</html>
```

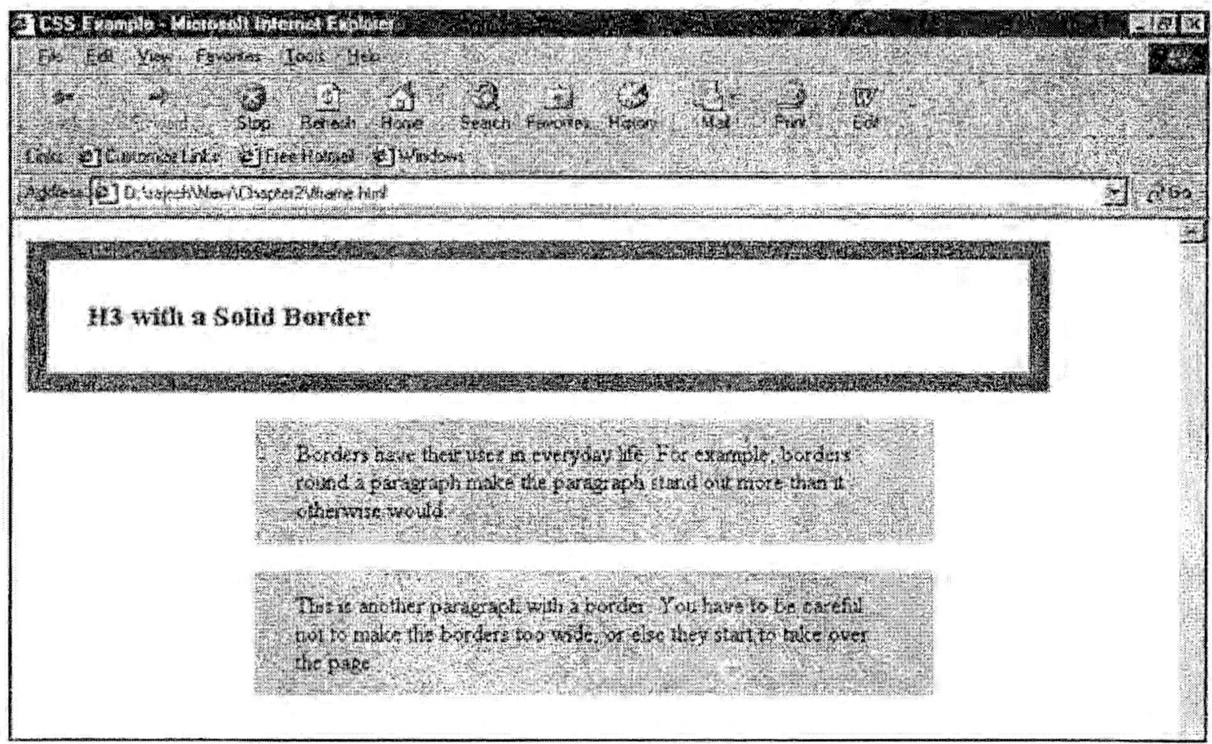

Figure 3.7: CSS code as displayed in IE

Exercise 4: CSS font Attributes

```
<html>
      <head><title>CSS Font Attributes Example </title>
      <style  type="text/css">
            <! - -

            BODY {font-size:14 pt}
                  .serif {font-family: serif}
                  .sans-serif {font-family:sans-serif}
                  .cursive {font-family: cursive}
                  .fantasy {font-family: fantasy}
                  .comic  {font-family: Comic Sans MS}

                  .xx-small {font-size: xx-small}
                  .x-samll {font-size: x-small}
                  .small {font-size: small}
                  .medium {font-size: medium}
                  .large {font-size: large}
                  .x-large {font-size: x-large}
```

```
        .xx-large {font-size: xx-large}
        .smaller {font-size: smaller}
        .larger {font-size: larger}
        .points {font-size: points}
        .percentage {font-size: percentage}

        .italic {font-style: italic}
        .oblique {font-style: oblique}
        .weight {font-style: 900}
        .smallcaps {font-variant: small-caps }

        .uppercase {text-transform: uppercase}
        .lowercase {text-transform: lowercase}
        .capitalize {text-transform: capitalize}

        .underline {text-decoration: underline}
        .blink {text-decoration: blink}
        .line-through {text-decoration:line-through}
        .overline {text-decoration:overline}

        —>
    </style>
    </head>
<body>

<h2> Font Family </h2>

    This text is in <SPAN class="serif"> Serif. </SPAN> <br>
    This text is in <SPAN class="sans-serif"> Sans-Serif. </SPAN> <br>
    This text is in <SPAN class="cursive"> Cursive. </SPAN> <br>
    This text is in <SPAN class="fantasy"> Fantasy. </SPAN> <br>
    Actual fonts can be specified like <SPAN class="comic"> Comic Sans MS.

</SPAN> <br>

<H2> Font Sizing </h2>
    This is <SPAN CLASS="xx-small"> xx-small text. </span> <br>
    This is <SPAN CLASS="x-small"> x-small text. </span> <br>
    This is <SPAN CLASS="small"> small text. </span> <br>
    This is <SPAN CLASS="medium"> medium text. </span> <br>
    This is <SPAN CLASS="large"> large text. </span> <br>
    This is <SPAN CLASS="x-large"> x-large text. </span> <br>
    This is <SPAN CLASS="xx-large"> xx-large text. </span> <br>
    This is <SPAN CLASS="smaller"> smaller text. </span> than the rest<br>
    This is <SPAN CLASS="larger"> larger text. </span>than the rest <br>
    This is <SPAN CLASS="points"> exactly 18 points text. </span> <br>
    This is <SPAN CLASS="percentage"> 200% larger text. </span> <br>
```

```
<H2>  Font Style, Weightand Variant </H2>
        This text is <SPAN CLASS="italic"> italic . </span> <br>
        This text is <SPAN CLASS="oblique"> oblique . </span> <br>
        This text is <SPAN CLASS="weight"> bold . </span> <br>
        This text is <SPAN CLASS="smallcaps"> smallcaps . </span> <br>

<H2> Text Transformation  </h2>

        The next bid of text is tranformed <span class="uppercase"> to all uppercase
        </Span><br>

        The next bid of text is tranformed <span class="lowercase"> to all lowercase
        </Span><br>

        <span class="capitalize">This text is all capitalized. It does not do what you think,
        does it? </Span><br>

<h2> Text Decoration </H2>

        This text should <SPAN clas="blink"> blink under Netscape. </SPAN>
        <br><br>

        This text should be<SPAN clas="underline"> underlined. </SPAN>
        <br><br>

        This text should be <SPAN clas="line-through"> struck. </SPAN>
        <br><br>

        This text should be <SPAN clas="overline"> overline. </SPAN>
        <br><br>

</body>
</html>
```

Exercise 5:

```
<html>
        <head>
        <title>CSS Testing page</title>
        <style>
                BODY {font-family: sans-serif}
                DIV { padding: 0;
                        margin-bottom: 0;
                        margin-top: 0;
                        font-size: 36pt;
```

```
            font-weight: bold;
        }
            .line0 {  color: #99bbbb;}
            .line1 { margin-top: -25; text-indent: 100 ; color: #ff0000;}
            .line2 { margin-top: -25; text-indent: 150 ; color: #0000ff;}
            .e1background { color: "yellow"; font-family: serif; }
            .e1foreground { color: "cyan"; font-size: 14pt; margin-top: -100;
            margin-left: 5%; }
        P { padding: 0;
            margin-bottom: 0;
            margin-top: 6pt;
            margin-left: 5%;
            font-size: 12pt;
            text-align: justify;
        }
            H1 { font-family: serif; font-size: 24pt;}
            H2 { margin-left: 5%; }
        </style>
    </head>
        <body bgcolor="#ffffff">
            <DIV class="line0">Cascading</DIV>
            <DIV class="line1">Style</DIV>
            <DIV class="line2">Sheet</DIV>
            <center>
        <div class="e1background">
            B a c k g r o u n d B a c k g r o u n d
            B a c k g r o u n d
        </div>
            <div class="e1foreground">
            Hi!!!! Is their something at the backgroud
        </div>
        <hr>
    </body>
</html>
```

Figure 3.8: Cascading Style Sheet

Exercise 6:

```
<html>
<head>
        <style>
        a.one:link {color: #ff0000}
        a.one:visited {color: #0000ff}
        a.one:hover {color: #ffcc00}

        a.two:link {color: #ff0000}
        a.two:visited {color: #0000ff}
        a.two:hover {font-size: 150%}

        a.three:link {color: #ff0000}
        a.three:visited {color: #0000ff}
        a.three:hover {background: #66ff66}

        a.four:link {color: #ff0000}
        a.four:visited {color: #0000ff}
        a.four:hover {font-family: fixedsys}

        a.five:link {color: #ff0000; text-decoration: none}
        a.five:visited {color: #0000ff; text-decoration: none}
```

```
    a.five:hover {text-decoration: underline}
    </style>
    </head>

    <body>
    <p>Mouse over the links to see them change layout.</p>

    <p><b><a class="one" href="pseudoc1.html" target="_blank">This link changes color</
    a></b></p>
    <p><b><a class="two" href="pseudoc1.html" target="_blank">This link changes font-size</
    a></b></p>
    <p><b><a class="three" href="pseudoc1.html" target="_blank">This link changes background-
    color</a></b></p>
    <p><b><a class="four" href="pseudoc1.html" target="_blank">This link changes font-family</
    a></b></p>
    <p><b><a class="five" href="pseudoc1.html" target="_blank">This link changes text-decoration</
    a></b></p>
    </body>

</html>
```

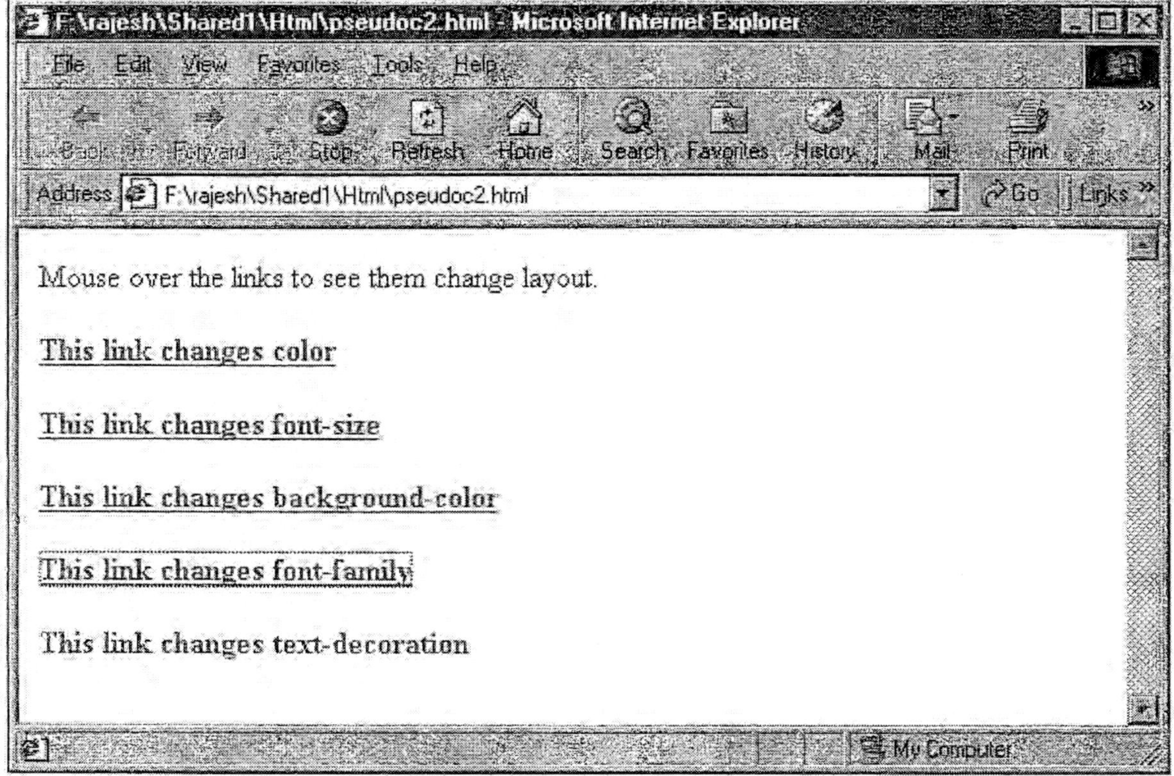

Figure 3.9: Pseudo Class

Exercise 7:

```
<html>
<head>

	<style>

	div:first-letter
	{
	color: #ff0000;
	font-size:xx-large
	}
	</style>

	</head>

	<body>

	<p><b>Note:</b> Netscape 4 does not support the "first-letter" property.</p>
	<p><b>Note:</b> Internet Explorer 5.5 supports the "first-letter" property.</p>

	<div>
	You can use the first-letter pseudo-element to add special style to the first letter of a text.
	</div>

</body>
</html>
```

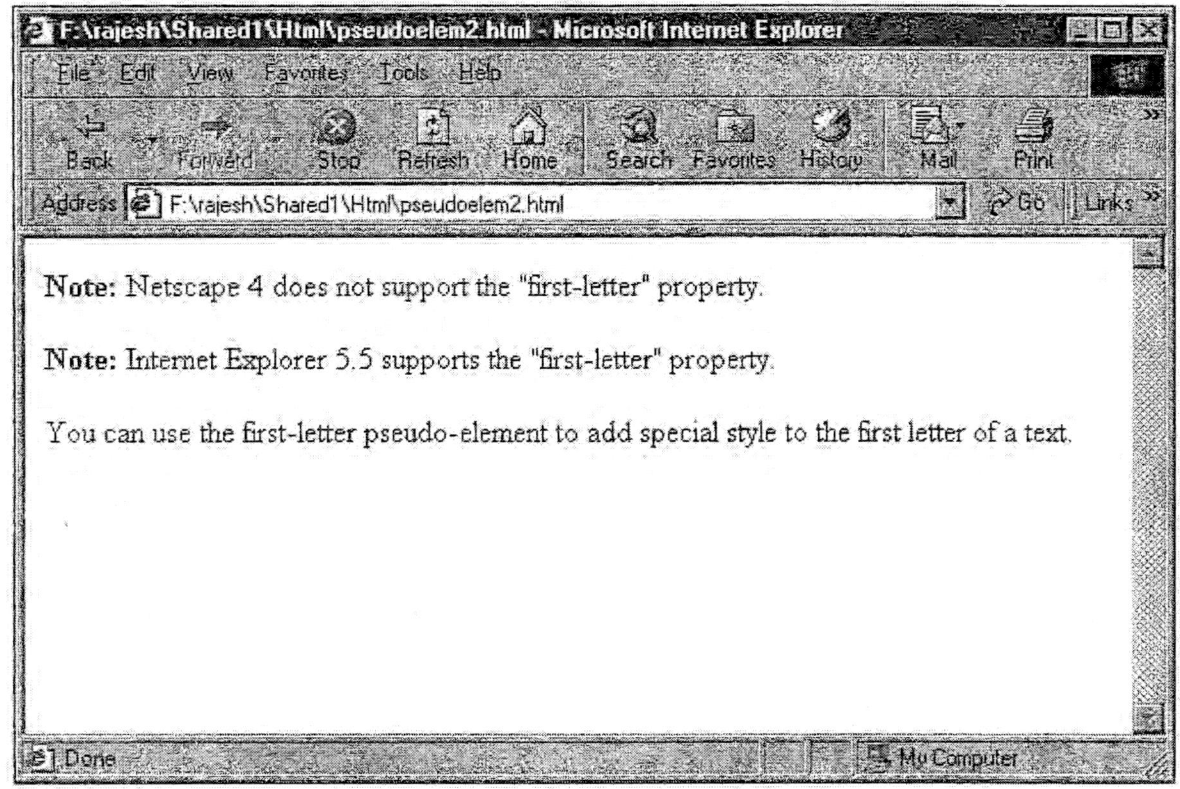

Figure 3.10: Pseudo Element

Exercise 8:

```
<HTML>
    <HEAD> <TITLE>CSS Demonstration Section 2</TITLE>
        <STYLE TYPE="text/css">
        <!—
        BODY      { background: #ff0303;
        color: white }
        P   { color: black;
        text-indent: 20%;
        font-family: Comic Sans MS, Verdana, Arial, Helvetica, helv, sans-serif }

    H1 { color: white;
        margin-left: 5%;
        font-weight: medium;
        font-family: Arial Black, Arial, Helvetica, helv, sans-serif }
```

```
        .contrast { background: darkorange; }

        .opening { font-size: 55%;
              margin-left: 10%;
              margin-right: 50%; }

H2 {  color: white;
      margin-left: 25%;
      font-weight: medium;
      font-family: Arial Black, Arial, Helvetica, helv, sans-serif }

        .section 2 { font-size: 55%;
              margin-left: 30%;
              margin-right: 30%; }

H3 {  color: white;
      margin-left: 45%;
      font-weight: medium;
      font-family: Arial Black, Arial, Helvetica, helv, sans-serif }

        .section 3 { font-size: 55%;
              margin-left: 50%;
              margin-right: 10%; }

        .credit {       margin-top: 5px;
              font-size: 90%;
              font-weight: bold;
              text-indent: 0;
              margin-left: 10%;
              margin-right: 20%; }

        .descript {text-indent: 0;
              color: silver;
              margin-left: 10%;
              margin-right: 20%;
              font-size: 80%;
              font-family: Verdana, Arial, Helvetica, helv, sans-serif }

        A:link { color: cyan;
              font-weight: bold;
              text-decoration: none; }

        A:visited { color: red;
              font-weight: bold;
              text-decoration: none; }
```

```
            .topline {color: silver;
                  text-indent: 0;
                  margin-left: 10%;
                  margin-right: 10%;
                  font-size: 80%;
                  font-family: Verdana, Arial, Helvetica, helv, sans-serif }
                  —>
            </STYLE>
      </HEAD>
<BODY>

<CENTER><P>

<TABLE WIDTH=560
      CELLPADDING=0
      CELLSPACING=0
      BORDER=0>

      <TR><TD WIDTH=30% ALIGN=LEFT VALIGN=TOP HEIGHT=20>
      <A HREF="f:/html/example/css1.html">
      <SPAN STYLE="font-size: 10px;
            text-decoration: none;
            color: #666;
            font-family: Verdana;">previous</SPAN></A></TD>

      <TD WIDTH=40% ALIGN=CENTER VALIGN=TOP>
      <A HREF="f:/html/example/css2.html">
      <SPAN STYLE="font-size: 10px;
            text-decoration: none;
            color: #666;
            font-family: Verdana;">gallery entrance</SPAN></A></TD>

      <TD WIDTH=30% ALIGN=RIGHT VALIGN=TOP>
      <A HREF="f:/html/example/css1.html">
      <SPAN STYLE="font-size: 10px;
            text-decoration: none;
            color: #666;
            font-family: Verdana;">next</SPAN></A></TD></TR>

</TABLE>

      <TABLE WIDTH=95% CELLPADDING=0 CELLSPACING=0 BORDER=0>
<TR>
      <TD COLSPAN=3 VALIGN=TOP CLASS=contrast>
      <P>
<BR>
```

```
<H1>Backcountry Travel!</H1>
        <P CLASS=opening>
                Before You Travel<br>
                <em>How far can you go?<br>
                What should you wear?<br>
                What should you carry?<br>
                What else should you do?</em></p>
                <p><Strong>When Things Go wrong
                </a></strong><br>
                <em><Stay!<br>
                Think!<br>
                Observer!<br>
                Plan!</em>

        <P CLASS=opening>
                Walking in the woods, whether as a hiker, camper, backpacker or hunter,
                provides pplenty of opportunities to practice the skills of a backcontry traveller......</
                p>

                <p><em>This is in no way intended to be a course in backcountry safety or
                survival. It's you against the world, and we're not taking any responsibility for
                the outcome.</em></p>

        <P>
        <BR>

<H2>Phalanstery</H2>
        <P CLASS=section2>

                What should you wear?
                Proper foot gear is one of the most important parts of your journey. Sturdy
                running shows are good for hiking on relatively smooth surfaces, such as
                maintained trails...

        <P CLASS=section2>
                How far can you go?</strong>
                When choosing a location and route, take into account your physical condition,
                the reason for hiking, and the terrain and whether you could possibly encounter...
        <P><BR>

<H3>Experimented on himself</H3>

        <P CLASS=section3>
                When things go wrong </a> </h2>
                <p><em>The worst thing you can do is to get frightened. The truly dangerous
                enemy is not the cold or the hunnger, so much as the fear
```

```
        It robs the wanderer of his judgement and of his limb power; it is fear that turns
        the passing experience into a final tragedy...... Keep cool and all will be well...
        use what you have, where you are, right now.</em><br>

    <CITE> Ernest Thompson Seton, 1906</CITE></p>
        <p> So you've planned, you've prepared, and now you're on the trail. And the
        worst part is, you don't know where you are. There's a four-step process to
        follow, and all you have to do is <em> STOP</em> <strong>S</strong>tay
        <strong>T</strong>hink- <strong>O</strong>bserve
    —
    <P CLASS=credit><BR>

        Excerpts from advertisements in Elbert Hubbard&#146;s <I>Little Journeys to
        the Homes of Eminent Orators: William Pitt</I>. Volume XII, number 6 (1903).
        The Roycrofters. <P><BR><BR> 

    </TD>
    </TR>
    <TR>

        <TD COLSPAN=3 VALIGN=TOP><P CLASS=descript><BR>These pages show
        how the same content can be presented in different ways just by changing the
        style sheet. The BODY of each HTML page is exactly the same, only the
        STYLE section in the HEAD of the HTML file changes for each example.
        <BR><BR>

    </TD></TR></TABLE>

    </CENTER>
  </BODY>
</HTML>
```

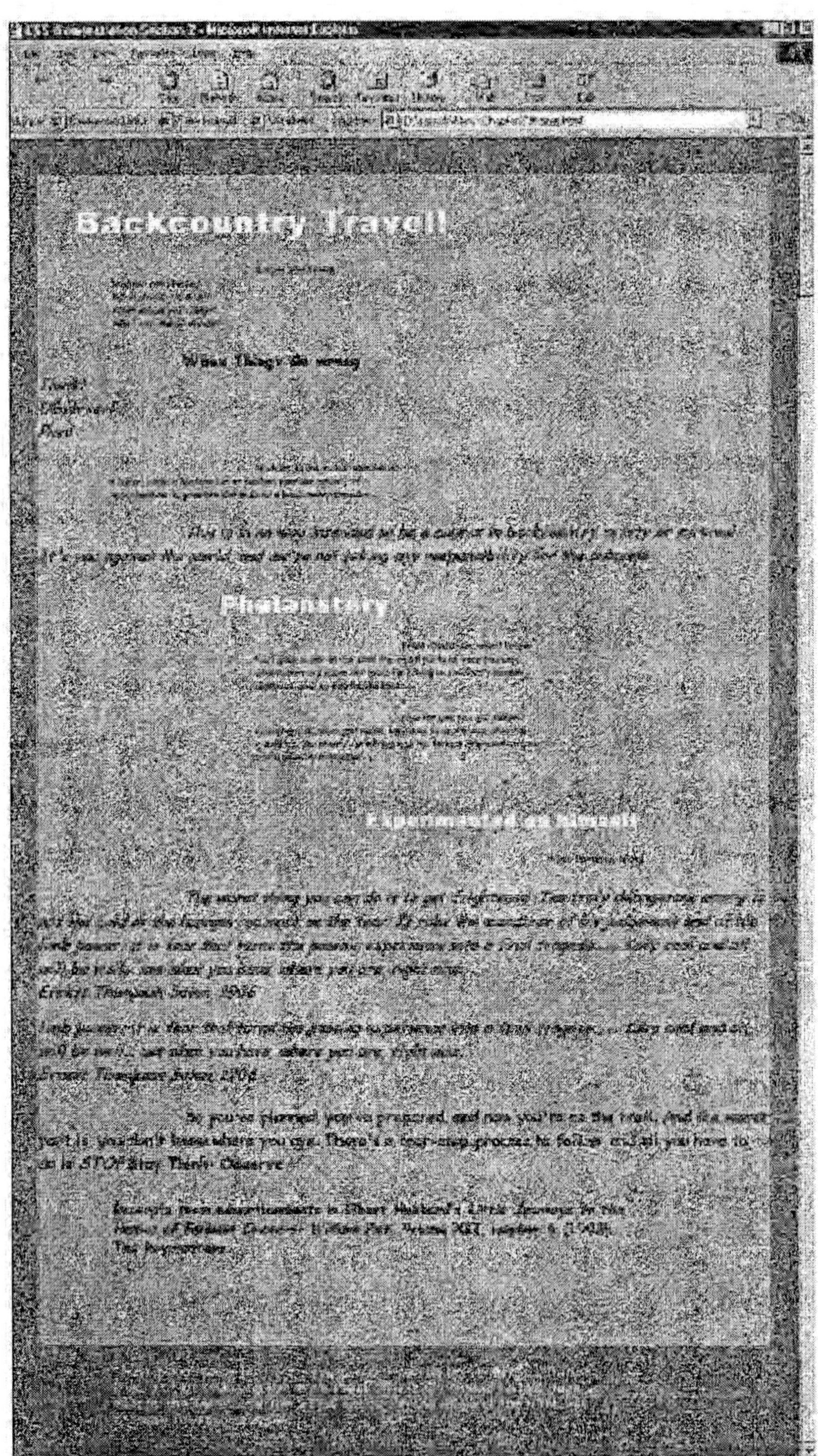

Figure 3.11: CSS page as displayed in IE

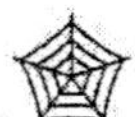 Test Your Knowledge

Students must solve the following assignment and submit to the faculty.

I Fill in the blanks:

1. Pseudo classes use __________ as the separator character.
2. The font-weight for normal text is __________.
3. In Cascading Style Sheet, repeat attribute __________ value, do not repeat the image in the background and display it on the window only once.
4. To increase the spacing between borders and content __________ property can be used.
5. To link an external style sheet, the <LINK> tag __________ attribute is used to specify the browser that the relation of the information being linked to is STYLESHEET.

II State whether True or False:

1. In Cascading style Sheet, an image can be specified in a 3D border defined on a page.
2. Cascading Style Sheet is a formatting as well as transformation language.
3. In Cascading Style Sheet, class types allows to create sets of style rules and then apply them to elements on the page by referring to the class type.
4. The <SPAN> tag applies style definition for a particular section of the page.
5. Style sheet to be imported need to be defined in the <STYLE> container tag.

Dynamic HTML

Objectives

- Introduction to DHTML
- Key Features of DHTML
- DHTML in Netscape Navigator
- DHTML in Internet Explorer
- Cross Browser Dynamic HTML

Introduction to DHTML

Web authors today face significant challenges when making their Web pages interactive. The static nature of HTML pages limits their creative choices and interactive components can be difficult to build and reuse. In addition, using proprietary extensions means authoring browser-specific Web pages.

Dynamic HTML technology helps to remove these barriers for content providers and offers users more engaging and interactive Web pages. Dynamic HTML provides authors with enhanced creative control so they can manipulate any page element at any time.

For a few years DHTML has been a cutting edge technology. The breakthrough represented by DHTML comes from several different capabilities it allows beyond plain HTML. In the old days of web page development you had to make all changes to a displayed web page at the server. For example, if you wanted to change text color the browser had to fetch a new page from the server. With DHTML, you can implement this example without additional server requests.

Although DHTML has been around since 1997, Microsoft and Netscape decided to implement DHTML differently. Thus, when you want to use DHTML you need to understand the differences because you might be forced to check not only which browser you have but also which version. Both Internet Explorer and Netscape Navigator support DHTML but their implementation is different. Both however support the World Wide Web consortium's (W3C) proposed HTML 4.0 and cascading style sheet (CSS) standards.

What is DHTML?

DHTML is the combination of several built-in browser features that enable a web page to be more dynamic. DHTML is NOT a scripting language (like JavaScript), but merely a browser feature or enhancement that gives your browser the ability to be dynamic. The technology of DHTML is currently at its infancy with NS 4 and IE 4 differing quite greatly in their implementation of this great technology.

Making simple updates, such as changing the color of text after a Web page loads traditionally has meant reloading the page. These limitations have slowed the user experience and have impeded interactivity on the Web. Dynamic HTML takes interactivity to the next level. Pages authored with Dynamic HTML come alive, with every element in the page being truly dynamic. Whether the page has loaded already, users can change any element of the page whether text or graphics without a round-trip to the server. This increased control and flexibility result in more compelling sites. For users, the Web experience becomes more responsive.

Dynamic HTML uses standard-based technologies including JavaScript, VBScript, the Document Object Model (DOM) layers & Cascading Style Sheets (CSS) to bring interactivity on the Web. Using DHTML you can develop web pages that have application like behavior not typically found in HTML pages. You can change content and text styles such as color, font face & font size on the fly. You can explicitly position HTML elements and later reposition them. Doing so repetitively can create simple animation. You can apply a variety of visual filters and transitions to create interesting effects. A paragraph could turn blue when the mouse moves over it or a header could slide across the screen. Anything that can be done in HTML can be redone after the page loads.

Technology Components

The major components of Dynamic HTML technology are:

☞ *Note: (NN) stands for Netscape Navigator and (IE) for Microsoft Internet Explorer.*

- **HTML:** The basic building block.
- **Document Object Model (DOM):** The objects that make up the contents of any Web page.
- **JavaScript:** A scripting language that can manipulate the objects.

- **Style Sheets (NN) (IE):** Lets the user to specify the stylistic attributes of the typographic elements of the web page. It allows changing the color, size or style of the text on a page without waiting for the screen to refresh.

- **Content Positioning (NN) (IE):** Lets a web developer animate any element on a web page, moving pictures, text and objects at will or on demand. It ensures that pieces of content are displayed on the page exactly where the user wants them to appear and also that you can modify their appearance and location after the page has been displayed.

- **Dynamic Content (IE):** Actually changes the words, pictures or multimedia on a page without another trip to the web server.

- **Downloadable Fonts (NN):** Allows the user to use the fonts of its choice to enhance the appearance of the text on the web page. The user can also package the fonts with the page so that the text is always displayed with the chosen fonts.

Key Features of Dynamic HTML

- **Document Object Model (DOM):** The Document Object Model is a platform and language-neutral interface that will allow programs and scripts to dynamically access and update the content, structure and style of documents. The Document Object Model (DOM) is a standardized interoperable way of manipulating individual pieces of a web page.

  The Document Object Model provides a standard set of objects for representing HTML and XML documents a standard model of how these objects can be combined and a standard interface for accessing and manipulating them. The DOM treats each element in a web page as an object that can be individually accessed and manipulated by scripts.

General Requirements:

Listed below are the general requirements of the Document Object Model.

1. The Object Model is language neutral and platform independent.
2. There will be a core DOM that is applicable to HTML, CSS and XML documents.
3. The Object Model can be used to construct and deconstruct the document.
4. The Object Model will not preclude use by either agent's external to the document content or scripts embedded within the document.
5. Consistent naming conventions must be used through all levels of the Object Model.
6. A visual UI component will not be required for a conforming implementation of the Object Model.
7. The specific HTML, CSS or XML document object models will be driven by the underlying constructs of those languages.
8. It must be possible to read in a document and write out a structurally identical document to disk (both documents can be represented by the same raw structural model).
9. The Object Model will not expose the user to problems with security, validity or privacy.
10. The Object Model will not preclude other mechanisms for manipulating documents.

- **Dynamic Style:** By using styles you can change the formatting and appearance of HTML elements without reloading the page. DHTML accomplishes these changes through a combination of the exposed object model, styles and cascading style sheets (CSS) and client side scripting.

For styles, <STYLE> tag or the inline STYLE attribute is generally used which assigns a style to an HTML element.

Example 1: Using <STYLE> tag

```
<HTML>
<HEAD>
<TITLE> Dynamic Styles Demo</TITLE>
<STYLE>
      .style1 {color:blue}
      .style2 {color:red;font-size:"48"}
</STYLE>
</HEAD>
<BODY>

<H1 CLASS=style1 onmouseover="this.className='style2'"
onmouseout="this.className='style1'">see how color changes on mouseover! </H1>

</BODY>
</HTML>
```

Example 2: Using <SCRIPT> tag

```
<HTML>
<HEAD>
<TITLE>Dynamic style with script</TITLE>
<SCRIPT LANGUAGE="JavaScript">

function changered() {
      window.event.srcElement.style.color = "red";
}
function changeblue() {
      window.event.srcElement.style.color = "blue";
}
</SCRIPT>
</HEAD>
<BODY>
<H2 STYLE=color:blue onmouseover="changered()"
onmouseout="changeblue()">This program uses javascript</H2>
</BODY>
</HTML>
```

The color of the text would change on mouseover.

Dynamic Content

By using dynamic content you can change the content of a web page after it is located. You can manipulate a set of properties and methods to change the content of many HTML elements. Some of these features operate on the text within an element; others operate on the text and the appearance of the element.

Dynamic Content Properties

Property	Description
InnerHTML	Replaces the content of the existing element and renders any included HTML tags as HTML.
InnerText	Replaces the content of the existing element and renders any included HTML tags as Text.
OuterHTML	Replaces the entire element using HTML.
OuterText	Replaces the entire element using Text.

Table 4.1: Dynamic Content Property

Filters

Filters are extensions to CSS. Filters are implemented by setting style properties within a <STYLE> tag or by using an element's STYLE attribute. Filters and transition effects can be added without using script but if needed to be controlled using script filter collection can be used. Each HTML control has a filter collection that provides script access to the filters. Filters have property, methods and events that control their appearance and behavior.

Filters can be used with HTML elements that are controls. Control elements define a rectangular area in the display.

Filters can be added to following controls:

- <BODY>
- <BUTTON>
- <DIV>
- <IMG>
- <INPUT>
- <MARQUEE>
- <SPAN>
- <TABLE>
- <TD>
- <TEXT AREA>
- <TFOOT>
- <THEAD>
- <TR>

Property	Value	Syntax	Explanation
alpha	opacity finishopacity style startx starty finishx finishy	filter:alpha(opacity=20, finishopacity=100, style=1, startx=0 starty=0,finishx=140 finishy=270)	Allows you to set the opacity of the element
blur	add direction strength	filter:blur(add=true, directions=90, strength=80);	Makes the element blur
chroma	color	filter:chroma(color=#ff0000)	es the specified color transparent
fliph	none	filter:fliph;	Flips the element horizontally
flipv	none	filter:flipv;	Flips the element vertically
glow	color strength	filter:glow(color=#ff0000, strength=5);	Makes the element glow
gray	none	filter:gray;	Renders the element in black and white
invert	none	filter:inver;	Renders the element in its reverse color and brightness values

Property	Value	Syntax	Explanation
mask	color	filter:mask(color=#ff0000);	Renders the element with the specified background color and transparent foreground color
shadow	color direction	filter:shadow(color=#ff0000, direction=90);	Renders the element with a shadow
dropshadow	color offx offy positive	filter:dropshadow(color =#ff0000, offx=5, offy=5, positive=true	Renders the element with a dropshadow
wave	add freq lightstrength phase strength	filter:wave(add=true, freq=1, lightstrength=3, phase=0 strength=5)	Renders the element like a wave
xray	none	filter:xray;	Renders the element in black and white with reverse color and brightness values

Table 4.2: Filters

Example 1:

```
<HTML>
	<HEAD>

		<TITLE> Visual Filters demo</TITLE>
		<SCRIPT LANGUAGE="JavaScript">

		function addGlow() {
		mySpan.style.filter = "glow(red)";

		}

		</SCRIPT>
		</HEAD>
	<BODY>
```

```
        <SPAN ID="mySpan" HEIGHT=20 WIDTH=50
        onmouseover="addGlow()"
        STYLE="position:absolute;top:20;left:10;
        font-size:24;color:blue">
        visual filters demo change of color</SPAN>

    </BODY>
</HTML>
```

Figure 4.1: Visual Filter

Example 2: Glow Filter

```
<html>
<head>
    <title>Example 3</title>
    <script language="JavaScript">
    num=20;

    function glowing() {

    if(num >= 20) {
    num=1;
    }

    if(num < 20) {
    num++;
    }
    Glow.filters[0].strength=num;
    setTimeout("glowing()",10);
    }
    </script>
    </head>
```

```
    <body bgcolor="#000000" text="#ffffff" leftmargin="0" topmargin="0" style="background:#000000;
    font-family:Bank Gothic Light BT, Arial; font-size:10pt" link="#16A5DA" vlink="#16A5DA"
    alink="#16A5DA" onLoad="glowing()"><br><br><br>
    <div style="filter:Glow(Color=#896949, Strength=20); position:absolute; left:50; top:90;
    width:70%; font-size:35pt" id="Glow" align="center">Look at me</div>
    </body>
</html>
```

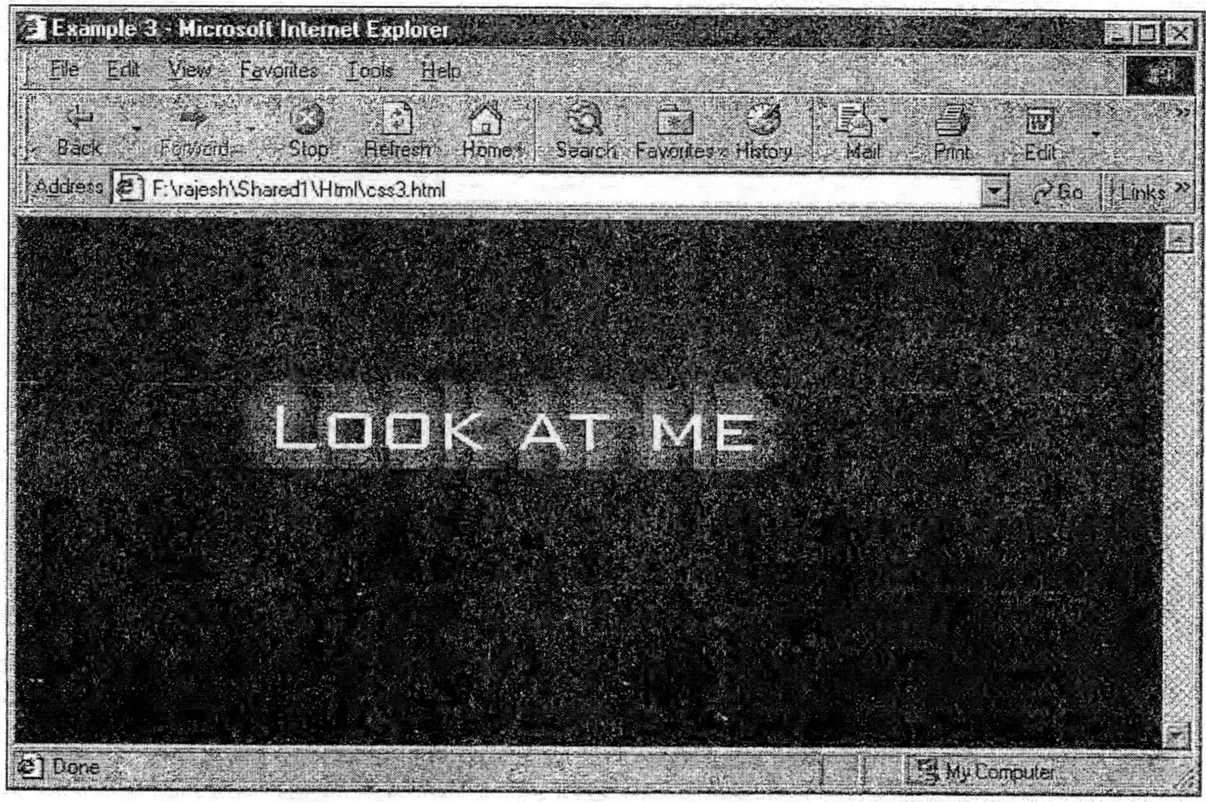

Figure 4.2: Glow Filter

Example 3: Filters

```
<html>

<head>
    <style>
    h2
    {
    width:100%;
    }
    </style>
```

```
    </head>
    <body>
    <h2 style="filter:glow()">Glow</h2>
    <h2 style="filter:blur()">Blur</h2>
    <h2 style="filter:fliph()">Flip H</h2>
    <h2 style="filter:flipv()">Flip V</h2>
    <h2 style="filter:shadow()">Shadow</h2>
    <h2 style="filter:dropshadow()">Drop Shadow</h2>
    <h2 style="filter:wave(Strength=2)">Wave</h2>
    <p>NOTE: Filters don't work if the width property of the element is not set.</p>
    </body>
</html>
```

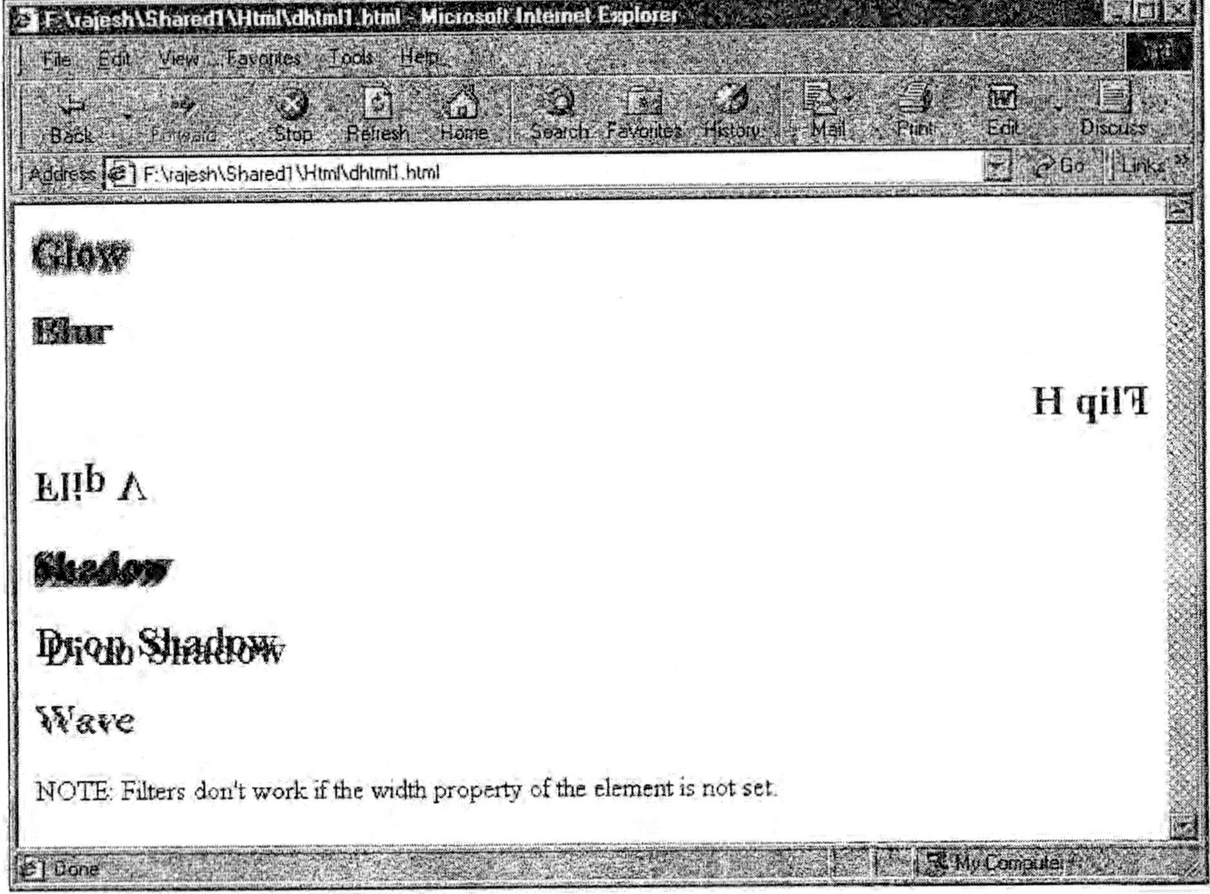

Figure 4.3: Using Filters

Example 4: Using Filters

```
<html>
<head>
	<style>
	div
	{
	width:160;
	height:120;
	}
	</style>
	</head>
	<body>

	Alpha:
	<div style="filter:alpha(Opacity=20)">
	<img src="f:/revision/html/torch.gif" width="100" height="80" />
	</div>

	Gray:
	<div style="filter:gray()">
	<img src="f:/revision/html/torch.gif" width="100" height= 80" />
	</div>

	Invert:
	<div style="filter:invert()">
	<img src="f:/revision/html/torch.gif" width="100" height="80" />
	</div>

	Xray:
	<div style="filter:xray()">
	<img src="f:/revision/html/torch.gif" width="100" height="80" />
	</div>

	Mask:
	<div style="position:absolute;left:10;top:610;">
	<img src="f:/revision/html/torch.gif" width="100" height="80" />
	</div>

	<div style="position: absolute; left: 10; top: 610; filter: mask(color=#ffffff); width: 100;
	height: 180">
	<h2>The mask value makes the text transparent</h2>
	</div>

	</body>
</html>
```

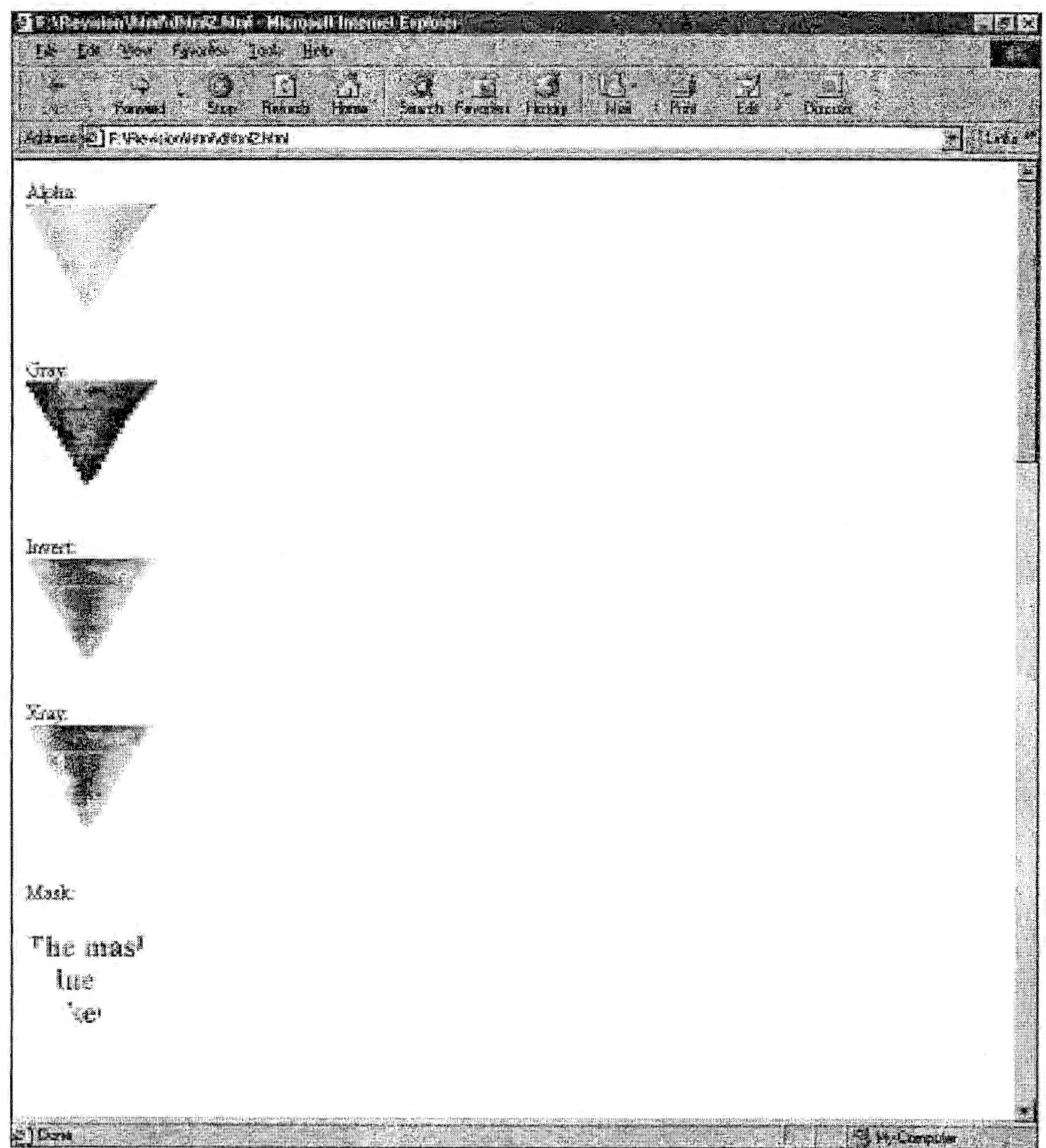

Figure 4.4: Using Filters

Positioning and Animation

You can explicitly place an HTML element at a specific location in a document by using positioning. Positioning is an extension of CSS where you specify an element's position by using the STYLE attribute. You can also specify the position by using the STYLE object which allows you to position elements with scripts and even create animation effects.

Elements are positioned either absolute or relative. When you specify absolute positioning the browser positions the elements with respect to the top-left corner of the container which is the document body by default. When you specify relative positioning the browser places the element relative to its flow within the HTML document.

Elements are also positioned using x and y coordinates as well as a z-index. The z-index specifies how the element "tacks up" with other elements. The element with the largest z-index is on top, and the element with the smallest z-index is on the bottom. Imagine it like a pile of papers on your desk. You can use both positive and negative values for the z-index.

Data Binding

By using data binding you can develop Web pages that display and manipulate data on the client. Without data binding if the user needs to manipulate the data (for example, search or sort) on your Web page doing so would require a trip to the server. Also if your page displays data one record at a time, then each time the user moved forward or backward in the data it would result in a request to the server. With data binding you can cache a record set on the client and allow the user to navigate, search, and sort the data without making repeated requests to the server. Additionally, some elements can update the data if the data source supports updates.

Scriptlets

DHTML is what makes Web pages powerful enough to stand alone as objects. That's the whole idea behind using scriptlets. A scriptlet is a Web page authored with Dynamic HTML which users can use as a component in their Web applications. With scriptlets, users can author content once then easily re-use the content in other Web pages or applications. A scriptlet behaves like an object, exposing properties, methods and events to other Web pages.

DHTML in Netscape Navigator 4.0

Navigator 4 from Netscape which is part of the Communicator product suite, includes three new areas of functionality that taken together give you Dynamic HTML.

Navigator objects are client side JavaScript objects used by the browser.

When you load a document in Navigator it creates a number of JavaScript objects with property values based on the HTML in the document and other pertinent information. These objects exist in a hierarchy that reflects the structure of the HTML page itself. The following figure illustrates this object hierarchy.

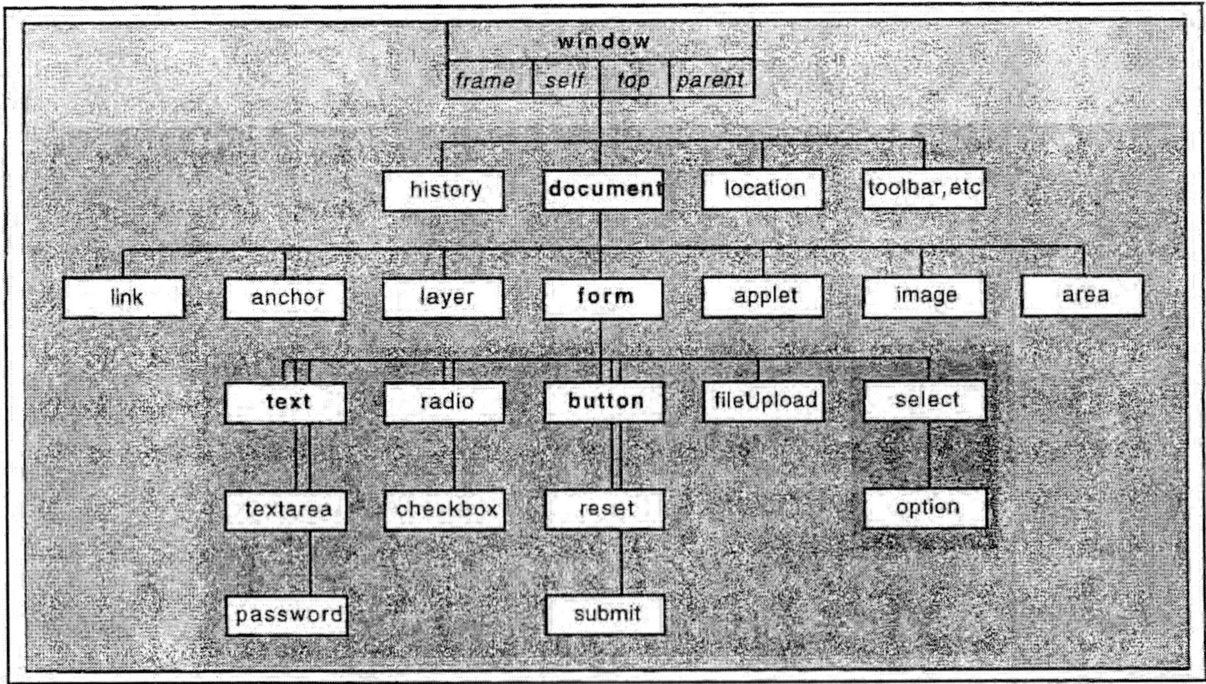

Table 4.5: Navigator Object Model

The three components of Dynamic HTML are style sheets, content positioning, and downloadable fonts. Used together, these three components give you greater control over the appearance, layout and behavior of your web pages.

DHTML in NS comes down to essentially one word LAYER. NS 4 relies completely on a tag, called the <layer> tag, to spin up its DHTML magic. This new tag is dynamic in that it can be positioned anywhere on a web page (without relation to other content) moved around its content inside updated on demand and more.

Basic syntax:

```
<layer>Text inside layer</layer>
```

The <layer> tag is a content tag, which means you can add into it content (like <table>). The text inside the layer floats above other text and overlaps them. Imagine a layer as a sheet of paper that resides on top of the rest of the page and does not take up space within the flow of the document.

Layer Attributes

Id	The name of the layer, used to identify it in your script
Left	The position of the layer in relationship to the x coordinates
Top	The position of the layer in relationship to the y coordinates
Width	The width of the layer, in pix or %
Height	The height of the layer, in pix or %
BgColor	The background color of the layer
Background	The background image of the layer
Src	The external html document contained inside the layer

Table 4.3: Layer Attributes

Example:

```
<html>
	<layer id="layer1" width=100% height=30></layer>
	<script language="JavaScript">

		var thecontents=new Array()
		thecontents[0]="where is e-academy?"
		thecontents[1]="Is it in southex"
		thecontents[2]="yes it is here only"
		var current=0

		function academy(){
		document.layer1.document.write(thecontents[current])
		document.layer1.document.close()
		if (current==2) current=0
		else current++
		setTimeout("academy()",3000)
		}

		window.onload=academy
	</script>
</html>
```

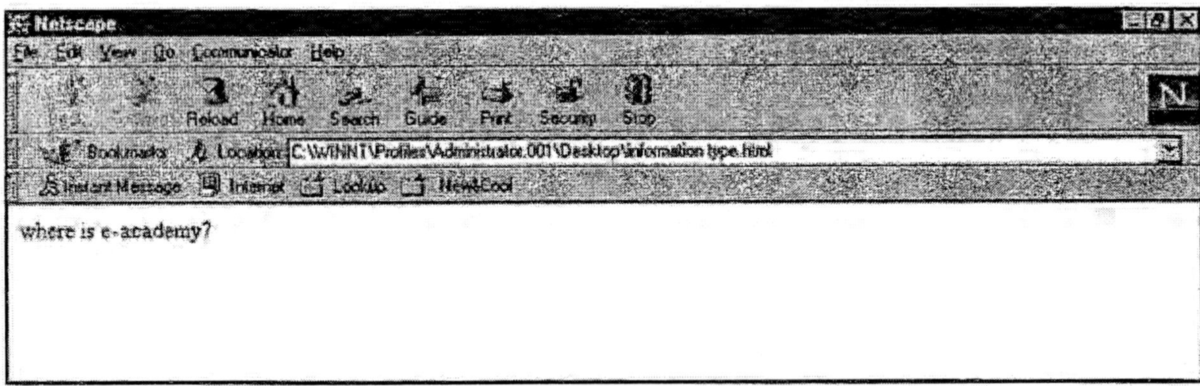

Figure 4.6: Layer Tag

Example:

```
<html>
	<layer name="layer1" left=128>
	<img src="monkey.gif">
	</layer>
	<script>
```

```
        function play(){
        if (document.layer1.left<1000)
        document.layer1.left+=5
        moveid=setTimeout("play()",50)
        }

        function rewind(){
        clearTimeout(moveid)
        document.layer1.left=128
        }

    </script>
    <form>
    <input type="button" value="Move" onClick="play()">
    <input type="button" value="Come back" onClick="rewind()">
    </form>
</html>
```

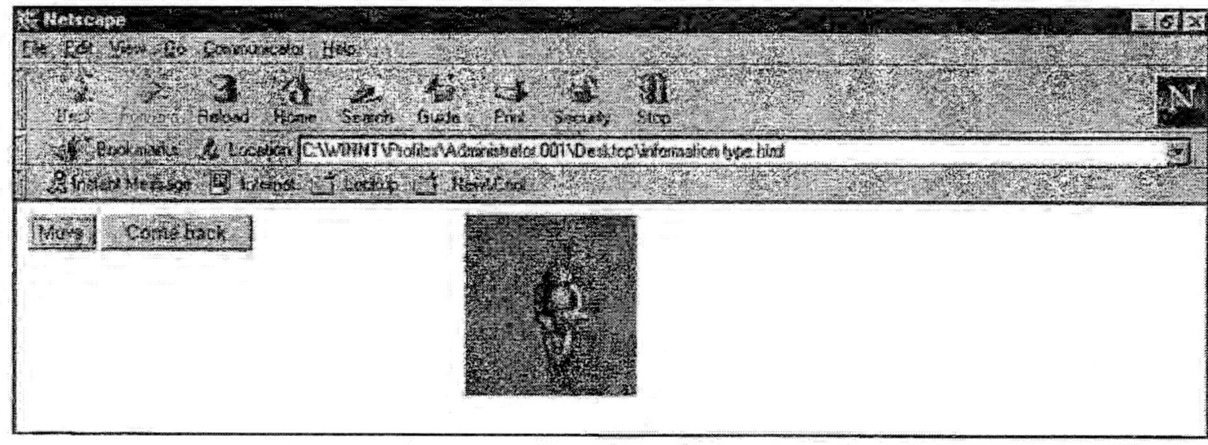

Figure 4.7: Animation using Layer Tag

Dynamic content in Internet Explorer

DHTML in Internet Explorer does not rely on any tag but rather new objects and properties that stem out of the usual HTML tags are used.

Internet Explorer 4.0 exposes virtually every element defined by HTML in a document to the scripting language of choice. DHTML in Internet Explorer does not rely on any tag but rather new objects and properties that stem out of the usual HTML tags that are used such as <div> and <table> tags.

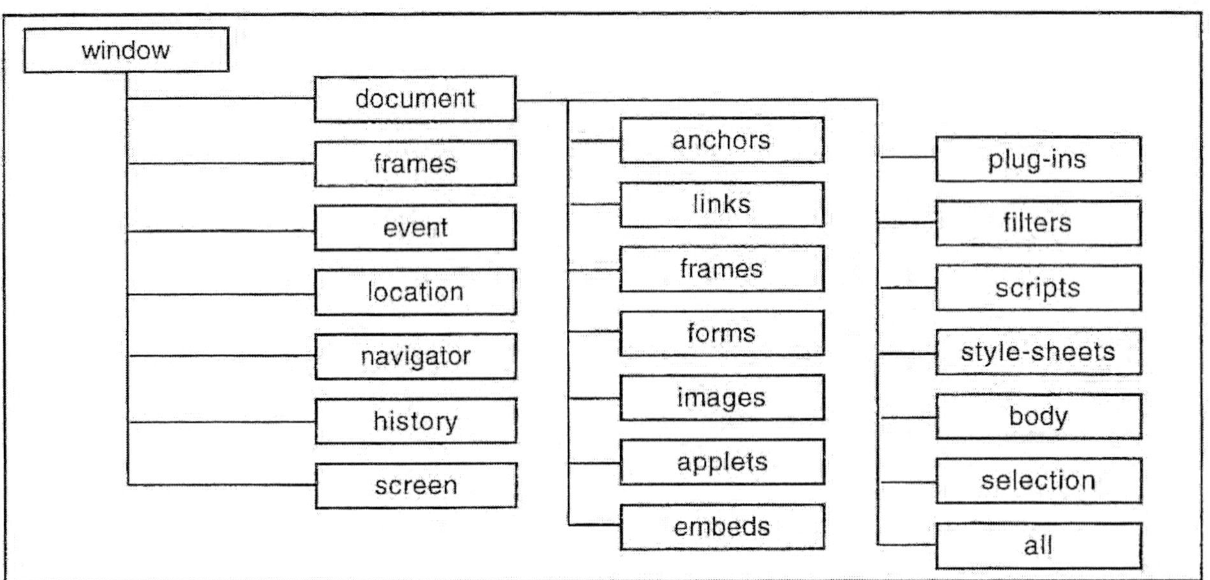

Table 4.8: IE Object Model

Almost every aspect of the World Wide Web Consortium (W3C) recommendation for Cascading Style Sheet (CSS) is implemented in Internet Explorer 4.0 except for some attributes such as word-spacing and white-space.

HTML elements in Internet Explorer 4.0 supports a style object which is essentially the "dynamic" object used to manipulate the look and "feel" of that element. Like the <layer> tag elements can also be assigned an "id" attribute which can then be used to identify it during scripting. For example:

```
<div id= "div1"></div>
```

In the script, the syntax required to access the style object of "div1" would be like:

```
div1.style
```

The style object contains many properties and by manipulating these properties, the look of an element can be altered dynamically.

Some of the important attributes of the style object are:

Attribute	Value
backgroundColor	The background color of the element
BackgroundImage	The background image of the element
color	The color of the element
position	The position type of the element. Accepted values are "absolute" and "relative"
pixelWidth	The width of the element
pixelHeight	The height of the element
pixelLeft	The position of the element in relation to the x coordinates
pixelTop	The pixel of the element in relation to the y coordinates

Table 4.4: Style Object Attributes

Example:

```
<html>
	<div id="div1"></div>
	<script language="JavaScript">

		var thecontents=new Array()
		thecontents[0]="where is e-academy?"
		thecontents[1]="Is it in southex."
		thecontents[2]="yes it is here only"
		var current=0

		function academy(){
		div1.innerHTML=thecontents[current]
		if (current==2) current=0
		else current++
		setTimeout("academy()",3000)
		}
		window.onload=academy
	</script>
</html>
```

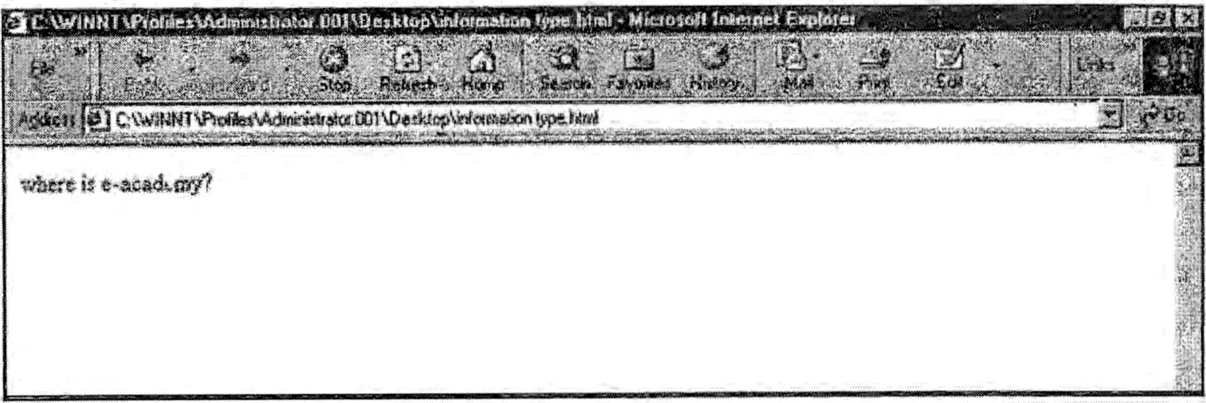

Figure 4.9: div Tag

Example:

```
<html>
        <div id="div1" style="position:relative">
        <img src="save.gif">
        </div>
        <script>
                function play(){
                if (div1.style.pixelLeft<1000)
                div1.style.pixelLeft+=5
                moveid2=setTimeout("play()",50)
                }

                function rewind(){
                clearTimeout(moveid2)
                div1.style.pixelLeft=0
                }
        </script>

        <form>
        <input type="button" value="Move" onClick="play()">
        <input type="button" value="Come back" onClick="rewind()">
        </form>

</html>
```

Figure 4.10: Animation using div Tag

Cross-Browser Dynamic HTML

It's an easy scenario to imagine: you want to make your site dynamic and you want your Dynamic HTML to work in both browsers. But the Document Object Models (DOMs) of Netscape Navigator and Microsoft Internet Explorer are different. The Document Object Model represents the elements of an HTML page as objects with properties. Usually, these elements have been initially positioned with Cascading Style Sheets. To dynamically change these element properties from a scripting language like JavaScript developers access the properties through the DOM.

Since Navigator 4 and Internet Explorer 4 have different DOMs, cross-browser DHTML means that the code has to work on both DOMs. To avoid creating two versions of the page (one for each browser) you can create a custom JavaScript object, which encapsulates the properties and methods of both DOMs and conditionally evaluates the appropriate code for the current browser. This way, when writing applications you'll reference this object's properties or methods and the object will choose the appropriate DOM.

Example:

```
<html><head>
      <title>cross browser</title>
      <script language="JavaScript">
            function version()
            { if ((window.navigator.appName.indexOf("Netscape")==0) &
            (window.navigator.appVersion.substring(0,1)>="4"))
            { location="http://www.yahoo.com" }
            else { if ((window.navigator.appName.indexOf("Microsoft")==0) &
            (window.navigator.appVersion.substring(0,1)>="4"))
            { location="http://www.hotmail.com" }
            else { location="http://www.rediff.com" }
            }
            }
      </script></head>
      <body onload="version()">
      </body></html>
```

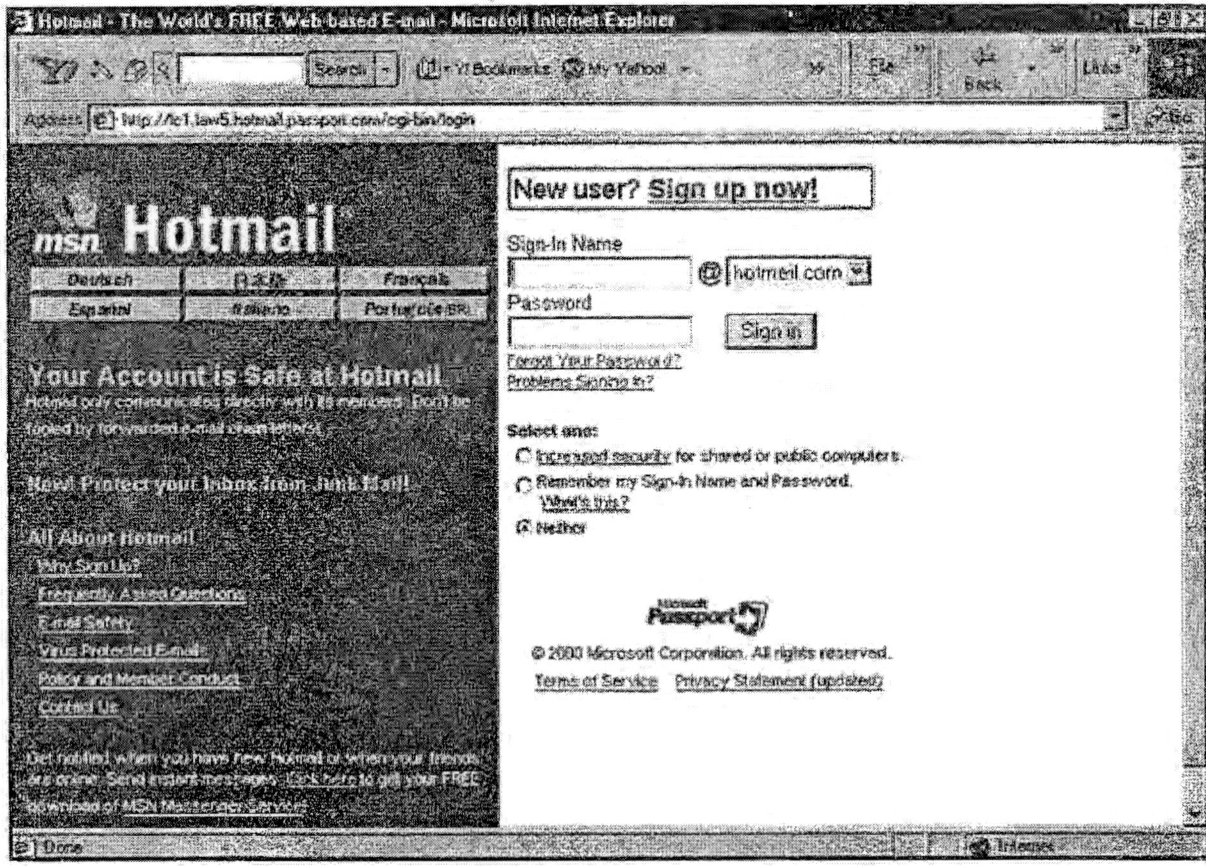

Figure 4.11: IE Specific

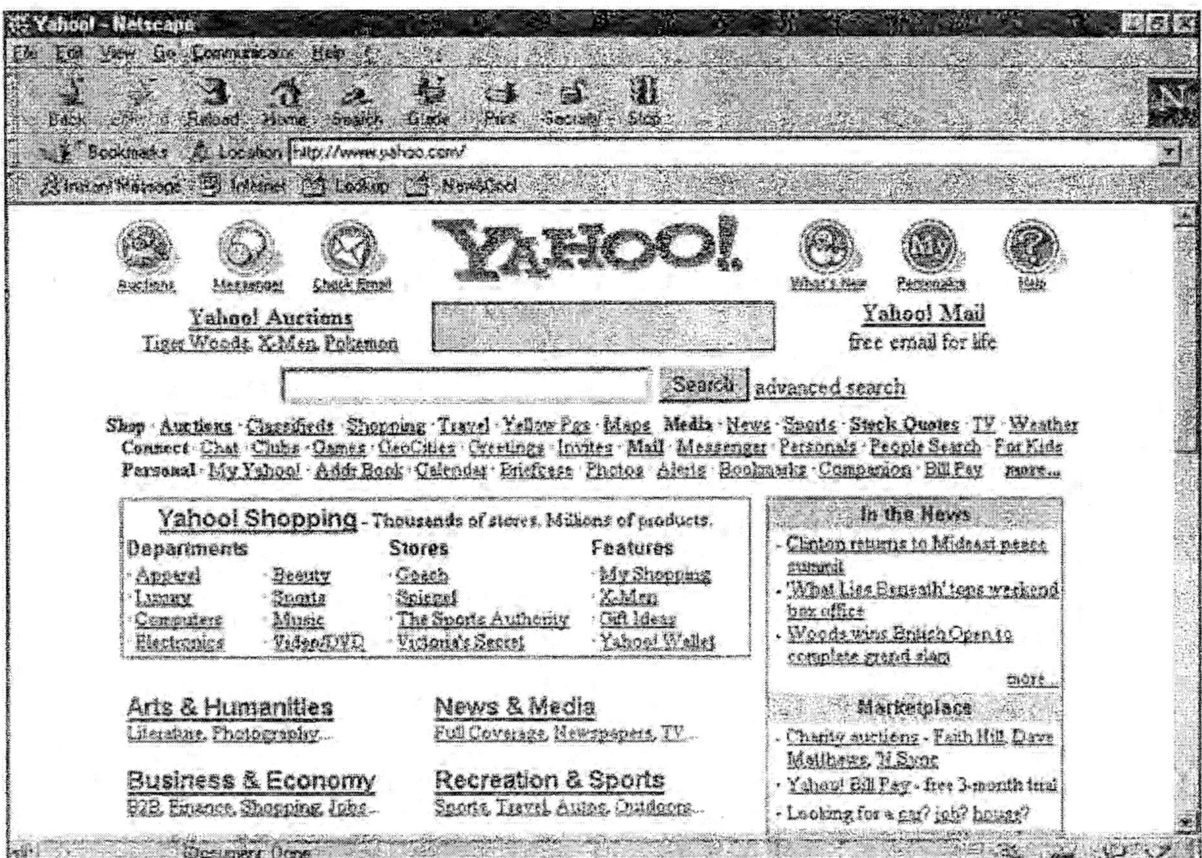

Figure 4.12: Netscape Specific

If the browser is Internet explorer 4.0 or above the hotmail home page would would open and if the browser were Netscape 4.0 or greater yahoo home page would open.

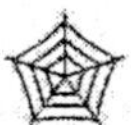 Test Your Knowledge

Students must solve the following assignment and submit to the faculty.

I Multiple Choice Questions

1. Dynamic HTML is a __________
   a. Browser feature
   b. Supported by Netscape Navigator 4.0 and Internet Explorer 4.0
   c. Dynamic HTML is a markup language
   d. None of the above.

2. __________ specific to a browser provides a programming interface between HTML, Cascading Style Sheet and JavaScript.
   a. Window Object Model
   b. Document Object Model
   c. Tree Object Model
   d. None of the above.

3. Dynamic HTML is a __________
   a. Markup language.
   b. Structured Markup language.
   c. Combination of several built in browser features.
   d. None of the above.

II Fill in the blanks:

1. __________ specific to a browser provides a programming interface between HTML, Cascading Style Sheet and JavaScript.

2. DHTML supports two types of filters __________ and __________.

3. In Internet Explorer 4.0, __________ attribute allows to set visual and transitional effect to html elements.

4. Internet Explorer provides two Data Source Objects __________ and __________.

5. The data binding architecture consists of four components ___________, ___________, ___________ and ___________.

6. The three components of Dynamic HTML are ___________, ___________ and ___________.

III State whether True or False:

1. Dynamic HTML is a subset of HTML.
2. Data binding binds database fields to HTML elements.
3. LAYER tags are not supported by Internet Explorer browser.
4. VBScript is supported by both the browsers Netscape Navigator and Internet Explorer.
5. Dynamic web pages are created in advance of the user's request.

Appendix

Objectives

- Version History
- Comparative Chart of HTML Tags

Appendix

Version History

Given below is a brief overview of each of the versions:

Version 2.0 — October 7, 1995.

Lots of changes and corrections in this version.

- Rewrote the introductory material and compatibility table language.
- Added + notation for Netscape extensions that have been adopted by most major browsers. This notation is by nature approximate; it represents my judgment about which tags have are widely supported even though they are not (and may never be) in HTML 3.0.
- Added notation in table of symbols for comma-delimited lists.
- Restructured the hard formatting and soft Formatting sections into Presentation Formatting and Structural Definition. This change makes clear the important distinction between presentation-based and structural markup. A few tags have been moved around as a result of this change, and the <ADDRESS> tag has been moved up from Miscellaneous into Structural Definition.
- Eliminated the Alignment section by shifting the tags listed there into either Structural Definition or Presentation Formatting. Although this results in the Netscape <CENTER> tag being split up from the other alignment tags, it allows the alignment attributes of tags such as <P> and <H? > To be associated with the underlying tags they operate on. This change is consistent with the HTML 3.0 philosophy of handling alignment through attributes to existing tags rather than through dedicated tags.
- Added listing for Netscape client pull animation.

- Support for new Netscape and HTML 3.0 tags implemented in Netscape 2.0:
    - Frames (added a whole new section).
    - Embedded Objects (in Links and Graphics).
    - Divisions (in Structural Definition).
    - Font Color (in Presentation Formatting).
    - Big/Small font size (in Structural Definition).
    - Superscript/Subscript (in Presentation Formatting).
    - File Upload (in Forms).
    - Text wrap (in Forms).
    - Target Windows (in Links and Graphics) and Base Target (in Miscellaneous).
    - Client-side image maps (in Links and Graphics).
- Removed <XMP> tag.
- Moved prologue tags to miscellaneous section, to indicate that they are not required and reduce confusion.
- Fixed listing for <NOBR> container by adding a closing tag.
- Changed "outline type" to "numbering type" for Netscape extension to ordered lists, in order to avoid confusion about what this attribute does.
- Changed wording of <P> tag description to indicate that it is "usually" rendered as a double return.
- Changed notation for hex triplet from $$$ to $$$$$$ to indicate that six characters are required to reference the three hex values.
- Improved consistency of column alignment in the text version.

Version 3.0 — July 21, 1996

- Updated everything to conform to the HTML 3.2 specification.
- Added a new section for Java tags supported by HTML 3.2.
- Revised the introductory material and annotations.
- Redesigned the layout of the "tables" version in order to make it easier to read.
- All major browsers now support tables, so to save time I have decided to eliminate the separate non-table "HTML" version of the Guide and to rename the "tables" version as the "formatted" version. Users who cannot view this version can still use the "plain text" version.
- Added the new tags implemented by beta versions of Netscape Navigator 3.0 up to 3.0b5, including:
    - Table cell colors
    - Multi-column text
    - Spacers
    - Frame border control
    - Strikeout via the <S> tag and underlining via the <U> tag. These were in HTML 3.0 but not HTML 3.2, so I list them as Netscape extensions.
    - The FACE attribute for the <FONT> tag (originally a Microsoft extension)

Version 4.0 — January 1999

In order to keep up with the rapidly changing world of HTML, a new versions HTML 4.0 was introduced. HTML 4.0 introduces eight new elements, deprecates ten (more about deprecation in a bit) and makes obsolete three more.

Tables provide better tabular presentation; forms more readily respond to the needs of the disabled; style sheets provide for better formatting and presentation; and multimedia, scripting and printing are improved. And as if that weren't enough, HTML 4.0 uses a different character-encoding format that expands the number of alphabets and languages able to implement Web documents.

Comparison Table

Element/Attribute

☞ *Note: All elements that can be used within the **<BODY>** of a HTML document can also take the **CLASS, ID** and **STYLE** attributes as well as those listed below. They have not been added for reasons of brevity and clarity. See the **Style Sheets** topic for more information. The browsers used for this comparison table (and all the HTMLib information) are:*

Netscape Navigator version 3.0 beta 6 (32-bit version)
Internet Explorer version 3.0 beta 2 (4.70.1117 Windows 95 / Windows NT 4 version)

Element/Attribute	Internet Explorer	Netscape Navigator
<!— ...	✓	✓
<!DOCTYPE ...>		
<A ...>	✓	✓
...HREF	✓	✓
Mailto : ...TITLE		
...NAME	✓	✓
...TITLE	✓	✓
...REL	✓	✓
...REV	✓	✓
...URN	✓	✓
...METHODS	✓	✓
...TARGET		✓

Element/Attribute	Internet Explorer	Netscape Navigator
<ADDRESS>	✓	✓
<APPLET ...>	✓	✓
...CODEBASE	✓	✓
...CODE	✓	✓
...ALT	✓	✓
...NAME	✓	✓
...WIDTH/HEIGHT	✓	✓
...ALIGN	✓	✓
...VSPACE/HSPACE	✓	✓
...PARAM NAME/VALUE	✓	✓
<AREA>	✓	✓
...SHAPE	✓	✓
...COORDS	✓	✓
<B>	✓	✓
<BASE ...>	✓	✓
...HREF	✓	✓
...TARGET		✓
<BASEFONT ...>	✓	✓
...SIZE	✓ (only visible when FONT SIZE = used as well)	✓
...FACE	✓	
...COLOR	✓	
<BGSOUND ...>	✓	
...LOOP	✓	
...DELAY		
<BIG>	✓	✓
<BLINK>		✓
<BLOCKQUOTE>	✓	✓
<BODY ...>	✓	✓
...BACKGROUND	✓	✓
...TEXT	✓	✓
...LINK	✓	✓
...VLINK	✓	✓
...ALINK		✓

Element/Attribute	Internet Explorer	Netscape Navigator
...BGCOLOR	✓	✓
...BGPROPERTIES	✓	
...LEFTMARGIN	✓	
...TOPMARGIN	✓	
 	✓	✓
...CLEAR	✓	✓
<CAPTION>	✓	✓
...ALIGN	✓ (top, bottom left, right center)	✓ (top, bottom)
...VALIGN	✓ (top, bottom)	
<CENTER>	✓	✓
<CITE>	✓	✓
<CODE>	✓	✓
<COL>	✓	
...SPAN	✓	
...ALIGN	✓	
<COLGROUP>	✓	
...SPAN	✓	
...ALIGN	✓	
...VALIGN	✓	
<COMMENT>	✓	
<DFN>	✓	
<DIR>	✓ (no bullet)	✓
<DIV>	✓	✓
...ALIGN	✓	✓ (left, right, center)
<DL>	✓	✓
<DT>	✓	✓
<DD>	✓	✓
...COMPACT		✓
<DT>	✓	✓

Element/Attribute	Internet Explorer	Netscape Navigator
<EM>	✓	✓
<EMBED ...>		✓
<FONT ...>	✓	✓
...SIZE	✓	✓
...COLOR	✓	✓
...FACE	✓	✓
<FORM>	✓	✓
<FRAME ...>	✓	✓
...SRC	✓	✓
...NAME	✓	✓
...MARGINWIDTH	✓	✓
...MARGINHEIGHT	✓	✓
...SCROLLING	✓	✓
...NORESIZE	✓	✓
...BORDERCOLOR		✓
...FRAMEBORDER	✓ ("0" only for no borders)	✓ ("yes|no")
...FRAMESPACING	✓	
...WIDTH	✓	
...HEIGHT	✓	
...HSPACE	✓	
...VSPACE	✓	
...ALIGN	✓	
<FRAMESET ...>	✓	✓
...ROWS	✓	✓
...COLS	✓	✓
...BORDER		✓
...FRAMEBORDER		✓
...BORDERCOLOR		✓
<H ALIGN= ...>	✓	✓
<H1>	✓	✓
<H2>	✓	✓
<H3>	✓	✓
<H4>	✓	✓
<H5>	✓	✓

Element/Attribute	Internet Explorer	Netscape Navigator
<H6>	✓	✓
<HEAD>	✓	✓
<HR...>	✓	✓
...SIZE	✓	✓
...WIDTH	✓	✓
...ALIGN	✓	✓
...NOSHADE	✓	✓
...COLOR	✓	
<HTML>	✓	✓
<I>	✓	✓
<IFRAME>	✓	
<IMG ...>	✓	✓
...ALIGN	✓	✓
...ALT	✓	✓
...ISMAP	✓	✓
...SRC	✓	✓
...WIDTH	✓	✓
...HEIGHT	✓	✓
...BORDER	✓ (only when image is a link)	✓
...VSPACE	✓	✓
...HSPACE	✓	✓
...LOWSRC		✓
...USEMAP	✓	✓
...VRML	✓	
<INPUT ...>	✓	✓
...ALIGN	✓	✓
...CHECKED	✓	✓
...MAXLENGTH	✓	✓
...NAME	✓	✓
...SIZE	✓	✓
...SRC	✓	✓
...TYPE	✓	✓
...VALUE	✓	✓

Element/Attribute	Internet Explorer	Netscape Navigator
<ISINDEX ...>	✓	✓
...PROMPT	✓	✓
<KBD>	✓	✓
<LI>	✓	✓
<LINK ...>	✓	✓
<LISTING>	✓ (will translate special characters)	✓ (renders 132 characters to the line and translates special characters)
<MAP ...>	✓	✓
...NAME	✓	✓
<MARQUEE ...>	✓	
...ALIGN	✓	
...BEHAVIOR	✓	
...BGCOLOR	✓	
...DIRECTION	✓	
...HEIGHT	✓	
...WIDTH	✓	
...HSPACE	✓	
...LOOP	✓	
...SCROLLAMOUNT	✓	
...SCROLLDELAY	✓	
...VSPACE	✓	
<MENU>	✓ (no bullet)	✓
<META ...>	✓	✓
...HTTP-EQUIV	✓	✓
...NAME	✓	✓
...CONTENT	✓	✓
<MULTICOL>		✓
...COLS		✓
...GUTTER		✓
...WIDTH		✓

Element/Attribute	Internet Explorer	Netscape Navigator
<NEXTID ...>	✓	✓
<NOBR>	✓	✓
<NOFRAMES>	✓	✓
<NOSCRIPT>		✓
<OBJECT>	✓	
<PARAM>	✓	
<OL ...>	✓	✓
...TYPE	✓	✓
...START	✓	✓
...VALUE	✓	✓
<OPTION>	✓	✓
<P>	✓	✓
...ALIGN	✓ (center only)	✓ (left, right, center)
<PLAINTEXT>	✓ (allows closing element)	✓
<PRE>	✓	✓
<S>	✓	✓
<SAMP>	✓	✓
<SCRIPT ...>	✓	✓
...LANGUAGE	✓	✓
...SRC	✓	✓
<SELECT>	✓	✓
<SMALL>	✓	✓
<SOUND ...>		
...SRC		
...DELAY		
<SPACER>		✓
...ALIGN		✓
...SIZE		✓
...WIDTH		✓
...TYPE		✓

Element/Attribute	Internet Explorer	Netscape Navigator
<SPAN>	✓	
<STRIKE>	✓	✓
<STRONG>	✓	✓
<STYLE>	✓	
<SUB>	✓	✓
<SUP>	✓	✓
<TABLE ...>	✓	✓
...BORDER	✓	✓
...CELLSPACING	✓	✓
...CELLPADDING	✓	✓
...WIDTH	✓	✓
...HEIGHT	✓	✓
...ALIGN	✓	✓
...VALIGN	✓	
...BGCOLOR	✓	✓
...BORDERCOLOR	✓	
...BORDERCOLORLIGHT	✓	
...BORDERCOLORDARK	✓	
...BACKGROUND	✓	
...FRAME	✓	
...RULES	✓	
<TBODY>	✓	
<TD ...>	✓	✓
...ROWSPAN	✓	✓
...COLSPAN	✓	✓
...ALIGN	✓	✓
...VALIGN	✓	✓
...WIDTH	✓ (absolute pixel values only)	✓
...HEIGHT	✓	
...NOWRAP	✓	✓
...BGCOLOR	✓	✓
...BORDERCOLOR	✓	
...BORDERCOLORLIGHT	✓	

Element/Attribute	Internet Explorer	Netscape Navigator
...BORDERCOLORDARK	✓	
...BACKGROUND	✓	
<TEXTAREA ...>	✓	✓
...NAME	✓	✓
...ROWS	✓	✓
...COLS	✓	✓
...WRAP		✓
<TFOOT>	✓	
<TH ...>	✓	✓
...ROWSPAN	✓	✓
...COLSPAN	✓	✓
...ALIGN	✓	✓
...VALIGN	✓	✓
...WIDTH	✓ (absolute pixel values only)	✓
...HEIGHT	✓	
...NOWRAP	✓	✓
...BGCOLOR	✓	✓
...BORDERCOLOR	✓	
...BORDERCOLORLIGHT	✓	
...BORDERCOLORDARK	✓	
...BACKGROUND	✓	
<THEAD>	✓	
<TITLE>	✓	✓
<TR ...>	✓	✓
...ALIGN	✓	✓
...VALIGN	✓	✓
...BGCOLOR	✓	✓
...BORDERCOLOR	✓	
...BORDERCOLORLIGHT	✓	
...BORDERCOLORDARK	✓	
<TT>	✓	✓

Element/Attribute	Internet Explorer	Netscape Navigator
<U>	✓	
<UL>	✓	✓
<VAR>		
<WBR>	✓	✓
<XMP>	✓ (will translate special characters)	✓